500
LITTLE-KNOWN FACTS
about NAUVOO

500
LITTLE-KNOWN FACTS
about NAUVOO

GEORGE W. GIVENS
SYLVIA GIVENS

Bonneville Books
Springville, Utah

ISBN 13: 987-1-59955-365-8

Published by Bonneville Books, an imprint of Cedar Fort, Inc., 2373 W. 700 S., Springville, UT 84663
Distributed by Cedar Fort, Inc., www.cedarfort.com

LIBRARY OF CONGRESS CATALOGING-IN-PUBLICATION DATA

Givens, George W., 1932-2004.
  500 little-known facts about Nauvoo / George and Sylvia Givens.
    p. cm.
  ISBN 978-1-59955-365-8
  1. Nauvoo (Ill.)--History--19th century. 2.
Mormons--Illinois--Nauvoo--History--19th century. I. Givens, Sylvia. II.
Title. III. Title: Five hundred little-known facts about Nauvoo.

  F549.N37G57 2010
  977.3'43--dc22

2009043231

Cover design by Megan Whittier
Cover design © 2010 by Lyle Mortimer
Edited and typeset by Megan E. Welton

Printed in the United States of America

10 9 8 7 6 5 4 3 2 1

Printed on acid-free paper

Contents

Foreword.................................... ix

Bakery 1

Blacksmith 4

Brickyard 7

Brigham Young 9

Gun Shop.................................... 14

Carriage Ride 17

Carthage 20

Clothing.................................... 31

Coolidge Home.............................. 33

Entertainment.............................. 36

Emma Smith................................. 41

Exodus 47

The *Nauvoo Expositor* 58

Farming 61

Food and Drink 65

The Groves 68

Homes and Construction 71

Kimball Home............................... 83

King Follett Discourse 87

Law and Order 91

Lucy Mack Smith 96

Lyon Drug Store 99

Maid of Iowa.............................. 102

Medicine and Death......................... 104

Miscellaneous 114

Contents

Money and Mercantilism 135

Native Americans 140

Nauvoo Legion 143

Nauvoo Restoration, Inc. 149

Outdoors and Nature 152

Pastimes and Youth 155

Education 160

Pineries 164

Print Shop 167

Post Office 170

Relief Society 175

Religious Practices 180

Riser Boot Shop 186

The River 190

The Red Brick Store and Others 198

Seventies Hall 203

Streets and Roads 206

Taylor Home 210

Temple 212

Tin Shop 232

Visitors' Center 235

Woodruff Home 237

Conclusion 239

Appendices

   A Nauvoo Chronology 243

   Recommended Sources 255

   Index of Names 265

* *

Foreword

During the summers of 1998–2000, my parents spent time as volunteer historians at Nauvoo Restoration, Inc. Although they led the occasional tour, they primarily focused on answering—after extensively researching, of course—questions Nauvoo visitors had asked but that the guides' scripts did not usually answer. Aware such questions might be asked again and again, and that missionary guides might wish to have a ready source, they compiled those questions and answers here.

Ten years after its first printing, my father would be thrilled to see this Nauvoo fact book printed again. In fact, the only thing that would thrill him more would be to spend another summer with my mother in Old Nauvoo, the city he loved so much, giving more talks, taking more questions, and enjoying not just the answers but the search for those answers.

-Bobbie Givens Goettler

Bakery

Scovil advertised wedding cakes in the Nauvoo Neighbor for $25. Wasn't that a rather exorbitant price for that period of time? Would it have sold any?

Yes, it was exorbitant—comparable to over $1,000 today. He was unlikely to have sold any, but anything that attracts attention to a business is good advertising—and this advertising would certainly have attracted attention.

What might have been some more realistic prices for baked goods?

Robert Gardner traveled from Canada in 1845—a distance of 500 miles—just to see the Prophet. He recorded that he didn't have money to pay for boarding, but by being offered a place to sleep and buying a loaf of bread from the bakery for only **three cents** each day, he got along first rate.

Is the Scovil Bakery an authentic reconstruction? It seems rather small for a business.

The bakery has been restored on the original foundation with as much accuracy as possible. One thing the foundation does not tell us, however, is whether the building had more than one story. Since Lorenzo Snow (a cousin of Sister Scovil and later President of the Church) lived for a time in Nauvoo with the Scovils, there is a distinct possibility there might

* *

have been a second story to this building.

The script also refers to Lucius joining his family in Utah after his brief mission in England. The script does not mention his assignment as an immigration agent for the Church in New Orleans in 1848–49 upon his return from England. According to the Scovil's family history, he was living in Garden Grove at the time of his call. Shouldn't this information be corrected?

The family history is a little confusing, because it has him receiving this last calling while living in Garden Grove on February 10, 1848. Afterward, he left for Winter Quarters to make final arrangements. From there, he left for New Orleans, via St. Louis, *also* on February 10, 1848. Whatever the case, he returned to Winter Quarters in 1850 and left for Utah in June, and yes, this information should be added. Where he joined his family is also a little confusing, since his wife accompanied him to New Orleans, according to family history, but it then says he "joined" his family back in Winter Quarters after New Orleans. At least one daughter, Lucy Loretta, was already in Utah, so he certainly joined that part of his family when he arrived there.

Did Lucius serve in the Staffordshire Pottery area of England when he commissioned the making of the Nauvoo Temple plates?

Lucius appears to have served in the Liverpool area. From there, he made a number of trips to outlying areas on Church business. Apparently, one of those trips was to the Staffordshire Potteries where, in 1846, he commissioned the making of the plates. Records indicate that Scovil sold about 150 dozen plates.

In 1857, Truman Angell, returning from an architectural study mission in England, needed to raise some money to get home to Utah. He visited John Taylor in Brooklyn and sold him one hundred temple plates for $50. He did not record why he had those plates with him. Perhaps he had picked up more of the plates from the original pottery while in England.

The plates in the bakery and Kimball home are original, with the J. Twigg hallmark, but the plate in the Visitors' Center is a replica. The July

* *

* *

1949 issue of *The New York Historical Society Quarterly* states in reference to the Nauvoo Temple plate: "Of all the American churches pictured on old blue china and listed as Staffordshire ware, the rarest is the Mormon Temple. Potter Joseph Twigg Kilnhurst, Old Pottery, England, 1836–1866."

The bakery was also called a "confectionery" shop. Exactly what kinds of sweets did it sell?

The most common confects, as they were called, were dry confects (made of fruit boiled in a syrup and dried in the oven), jellies (fruit juices mixed with sugar and boiled to a thin transparent edible consistency), pastes (fruit pulp and sugar formed in molds and dried in the oven), and conserves (dry confects compounded of sugar and flowers, such as roses, violets, jessamine, and so on).

Did they make and sell candy?

The 1828 Webster's Dictionary defined candy as "to form into crystals, or become congealed; to take on the form of candied sugar." The nearest thing to what we would consider candy was made of clarified sugar mixed with a flavor essence and then evaporated back to an edible consistency. Some families merely served pieces of sugar loaf in a dish with a pair of "sugar scissors" or a "candy hammer," but few families in Nauvoo could likely afford such luxury.

It is of interest to note that the famous Whitman Chocolates were started in a confectionery shop in Philadelphia during the Nauvoo era. The chocolates were not called "candy" however.

Flour would have been a major requirement for a shop like the Scovil Bakery. Was it ground in Nauvoo or shipped in?

Grain was grown in abundance on the prairies east of Nauvoo, and there were several gristmills—both steam and water powered—in the area. These mills were located primarily along the river and would have provided all the flour necessary for such a shop.

* *

Blacksmith

Did blacksmiths shoe horses and oxen as well as make the shoes, or were the two separate occupations?

Most blacksmiths, because they made the shoes, were also adept at shoeing the horses and oxen. Farriers, however, were those whose occupation consisted of shoeing animals. In the 1840s, farriers also treated horses and oxen for diseases. Farriers often traveled the countryside, taking with them a variety of different sized shoes they had purchased from the blacksmith.

What is the difference between a "blacksmith" and a "whitesmith"?

Each term is derived from the color of the metal the smith works with. A whitesmith was an early name for what was known in Nauvoo as a tinsmith. The name was derived as a description of the contrast between the lightly colored tinware and the darker ironware.

What is the origin of the word *smith*?

It is derived from the Gothic, an antecedent of Old English *schmied*, which means "to smite." Thus, a "smith" is a striker or beater of metal.

* *

What did it mean for blacksmiths to do "bespoke" work?

In the 1840s, to "bespeak" something was to order or engage something ahead of time. Today's equivalent of "bespeaking" would be placing a special order.

Where did the smithy acquire all the metal necessary for his work?

Because of the cost and uncertainty of shipping, blacksmiths were always in the market for old iron. However, much of that would have been already tempered, and working soft bar iron—shipped primarily from Pittsburgh—would have been easier. From such iron, Nauvoo blacksmiths made horseshoes, wagon tires, chains, reaping hooks, yoke rings, axles, hoes, augers, bells, files, adzes, plowshares, hackle teeth, and so on.

Is there more than one kind of iron? When was steel invented?

Although basically derived from the same element, processing produces different kinds of iron, from ingot to wrought to cast. Nauvoo blacksmiths used both cast iron and wrought iron, although some kinds of cast iron were not malleable enough for blacksmiths to use. The heating and cooling processes, as well as the percentage of added elements such as carbon, silicon, sulfur, and so forth, determine the different kinds of iron rendered. Malleable cast iron, which the blacksmiths commonly used, is soft, ductile, and has a high tensile strength.

William Kelly developed the process of making steel from iron in 1851. The process involved the oxidation of impurities in iron by blowing air through molten iron. Henry Bessemer perfected the technique in England five years later. Whatever the case, steel was not available in any form until after the Saints left Nauvoo.

How many blacksmiths did Nauvoo have?

Research indicates that the Webb brothers, Martin Peck, Jacob Shoemaker, Jonathan Browning, Warren Smith, and the Lytle Brothers each owned

* *

a blacksmith shop. Keep in mind that each of these shops would have employed a number of workmen, so the number of total blacksmiths in Nauvoo would have been much greater.

Were entire wagons constructed at the Nauvoo wheelwrights?

No. Nauvoo had the Coach and Carriage Manufacturing Company, but building a wagon or carriage is much like building an automobile today. Various parts are made by specialists and then assembled. Wheels would have been purchased from the wheelwright and various iron parts from one of the local blacksmiths. After acquiring these parts, anyone competent with woodworking tools could have put together a wagon. This fact was demonstrated in the final months of preparation leading up to the exodus, when almost every public building in Nauvoo was put to use assembling wagons.

Where did the coal or coke used in the forge come from?

There were a number of coal mines in Illinois, so it was not difficult to acquire. However, the Church, wishing to be self-sufficient, decided to open its own coal mine on Rock River about 100 miles north of Nauvoo in June 1844. The *Maid of Iowa* (the Church-owned steamboat) was used to transport the coal from the mine to the city.

Coke requires the burning off of sulfur or other extraneous or volatile matter by charring coal. This process was difficult, so blacksmiths often resorted to the use of charcoal—which was easier to make—if coal was unavailable. Charcoal was made in what was referred to as "coal pits." Wagon trains moving west even used such miniature charcoal "kilns," consisting of little more than dug holes filled with wood, set afire, and covered over to turn the wood into charcoal. People in the nineteenth century commonly referred to charcoal as "coal." Parley Pratt, on an exploring expedition in southern Utah in 1849, enthused about the thousands of acres of cedar that would contribute "an almost inexhaustible supply of fuel which makes excellent coal."

Brickyard

Was the brickyard rebuilt in its original location?

First of all, Nauvoo had several brickyards, and most were located east of the temple on the hill, placing them closer to the clay pits, which were located northeast of the temple. As for whether the brickyard's current site is the same as the original, brickyards required few permanent structures and thus left little evidence of their locations. Although there were a couple of brickyards on the flats, this location was probably not one of them.

What does the term "brickbat " mean?

In brick-making, half a brick is called a "bat." From this word, we get the term "brickbat," which in common usage refers to any piece of a brick that may be thrown during a riot or demonstration.

Can bricks be made with any kind of clay?

The term "clay" has many meanings. Clay is found throughout the earth's surface with many other minerals. Various applications, including brick-making, depend on the associated minerals that define its plasticity. In general, three kinds of clay are used to make structural brick: surface or alluvial clay, clay shale, and fire clay. Both clay shale (obtained by blasting) and fire clay (obtained by mining) must be ground before mixing with

* *

water. Alluvial clays, which collects in valleys and hollows, can be obtained by mere digging, and it was this latter type that was used back then and is still used in Old Nauvoo today.

How long were bricks made by hand?

Brick-making machinery was not introduced into the industry until around 1885, long after the Saints had left Nauvoo. With the introduction of such machinery, the number of types of clay that could be made into brick greatly increased.

How many men were employed in brick-making in Nauvoo?

An article in the *Nauvoo Neighbor* indicates that the six or seven brickyards were able to turn out 4 million bricks in one season. This meant more than 500,000 bricks were produced per yard for a six- or seven-month season. If a gang of three or four men could mold 2,000 bricks per day, each yard would need no fewer than eight to ten men and two or three boys to turn out 500,000 bricks per season. The work required more than just molding. It required turning bricks, building and firing the kilns, acquiring the clay from the pits, and so forth. Selling the bricks for half a cent apiece, a yard could take in $2,500 per season, which was sufficient to pay the workers and make a profit for the owner. For six or seven brickyards, therefore, we can estimate the total number of brick makers was around seventy.

* *

Brigham Young

Where was the meeting held in which Brigham Young was transfigured and sustained by the people to succeed Joseph?

Helen Mar Kimball was one of the few witnesses who specifically mentioned the location of the "Grove" in which Rigdon spoke, followed by Brigham Young. She referred to it as "a grove some little distance east of the temple, where a great multitude gathered." The hollow where this grove was located can still be seen today near Young and Robinson Streets.

Other witnesses described what occurred on that day, August 8, 1844. At 10 a.m., with several thousand Saints gathered for a meeting William Marks had proposed and Sidney Rigdon had called, a strong wind was blowing from the direction of the audience. Rigdon had gone behind the audience so they could hear him better, at which point the people turned to listen to him speak from his wagon for an hour and a half. When Brigham arose after Rigdon concluded and he spoke from the stand behind them, the people heard the voice of Joseph and turned and saw Brigham transfigured.

How many wives did Brigham Young take west?

At the time of the exodus, Brigham's family unit consisted of fifty people who traveled in fifteen wagons. In addition to his wife Mary Ann, he had taken in four other wives and had four more sealed to him. He also offered to take in Joseph's widowed wives, eight of whom were sealed to the Prophet for this life only. Five of those eight had the status of "name only" marriages, including Eliza Snow.

Brigham, Joseph, and others had plural wives in Nauvoo. Where did they live?

A few of the wives moved into the homes of their husbands, but most of them continued living in their own homes or with their parents. The doctrine of plural marriage was still not a "public" doctrine, and efforts were made to keep it non-public as long as possible, which meant, for the most part, these marriages did not involve conjugal relations or intimate living.

When Brigham led the people out of Nauvoo, did he know his destination?

At the time of the exodus from Nauvoo, Brigham knew the destination would be in the midst of the Rocky Mountains as Joseph had prophesied. Before he left Winter Quarters, he knew the main settlement would be in the Great Basin. As early as August 1846, Brigham told Colonel Kane the settlement would be "in the Great Basin or Bear River valley," which is north of Salt Lake along the Wasatch Front. In September, President Young wrote to President Polk specifically of their intended settlement in "the Great Salt Lake or Bear River Valley."

Oratory was a fine art in the nineteenth century and was taught in most schools. Brigham, however, had very little schooling. What kind of public speaker was he?

John A. Widtsoe, who edited a compilation called *Discourses of Brigham Young*, stated in the preface that Brigham's "simple eloquence rises to great heights." Those who heard him speak have declared that they were held in tense attention, however long the address might be. His vivid imagination, dramatic power and unquestioned sincerity made him a natural orator.

He seldom confined himself to one subject in his discourses. The needs of the day were the themes about which he wound his teachings.

Brigham's wife Mary Ann, saved his life during the winter of 1842–43 in a most unusual way for that period of time. What did she do?

During a severe illness, Brigham stopped breathing. Mary Ann held his nostrils and blew air into his lungs, which started him breathing again. It was one of the first cases of artificial resuscitation ever recorded.

Aside from typical illnesses of the time and place, such as the mountain fever he had on the journey to the Salt Lake Valley, did Brigham have any particular health problems?

Soon after leaving Nauvoo, Brigham recorded in his journal on February 28th, 1846: "I was so afflicted with the rheumatism it was with difficulty I could walk." He was reported to have been occasionally "tortured . . . from his youth" with this particular affliction, which is a painful stiffness and inflammation of the joints.

Toward the end of his life, news reports constantly emphasized Brigham's seemingly good health and his youthful appearance. Nevertheless, he was often sick, usually as a result of a heavy work schedule. During his final years, in addition to his rheumatism, he was troubled with urologic problems. On August 29, 1877, Brigham finally succumbed to an illness listed by his doctors as "cholera morbus." Now it's believed that Brigham died of appendicitis, a malady not officially known of until 1886.

Why did Brigham continue as President of the Twelve for three years instead of immediately forming a First Presidency and becoming the President of the Church?

Brigham Young was publicly sustained as "President" of the Church at the April 1845 General Conference. The Church membership thereafter referred to him as "President Young." The question should be why there

* *

was no First Presidency until 1847. Although President Young later said he was waiting for the Spirit of the Lord to direct him, he was also waiting for the Spirit to direct the Twelve to accept a Presidency that would inevitably diminish their administrative roles. Orson Pratt was opposed to this shift, and so were other members, such as Wilford Woodruff, John Taylor, and Parley P. Pratt. Joseph had called a First Presidency by fiat, but Brigham wanted to the First Presidency to be called by the Quorum of the Twelve.

Were Brigham Young's parents and siblings members of the Church?

Brigham's mother died when he was only fourteen. Father Young and Brigham's brother Joseph encountered Mormonism in 1831 and were baptized in April 1832. Brigham; his wife; his two sisters, Fanny and Rhoda; his brother-in-law, John P. Greene; his other brothers, Lorenzo Dow and Phineas; and his niece, Vilate Kimball, and her husband Heber C. all joined the Church. It is interesting to note that three of Brigham's brothers and a brother-in-law were all ordained Methodist ministers before their conversion. Many of Brigham Young's cousins, uncles, and aunts also joined the Church. Brigham's family, like so many others of that era, understood the need for a restoration of the primitive Church and were obviously receptive when they heard the message.

Brigham was a carpenter, joiner, painter, and glazier in New York before he joined the Church. Did he work at those trades in Nauvoo?

He did not have the time. He spent almost his entire adult life on Church assignments. The story goes that at the time of Brigham's conversion, he was making furniture for a Captain George Hickox. He immediately told the captain, "I can't finish my work for you here, for from now on I have much more important work to do—preaching the gospel."

While on a mission in England, he wrote to his wife in Nauvoo that he did not expect to ever have a home life again. He did, but it was only

* *

* *

through brief interludes between Church assignments, until he was settled in Utah. Even then, because of his rigorous Church schedule, his home life was anything but normal.

* *

Gun Shop

What were the prices of the various guns Browning might have made?

Browning did not advertise in the *Nauvoo Neighbor*, so determining what he charged for guns is rather difficult. We do have a record in the *Missouri Petitions*, however, of one Saint who valued a stolen gun and sword at $25. Also from the *Missouri Petitions*, Sylvester Stoddard claimed the loss of a rifle he valued at $10. Gun prices varied considerably, however, depending on whether it was a pistol, a shotgun, a single-shot or a repeating gun, a pepperbox, and so forth, and the workmanship involved. We also have a record of John D. Lee exchanging "a new Rifle Gun Made expressly for the Mountains" at Winter Quarters for $15 in goods and implying it was worth more. In 1850, when Emma's second husband, Lewis Bidamon, left for California, he listed among his supplies one "rifle gun" at $12.

Before Lucy Mack Smith moved into the Smith-Noble home, she is reportedly lived in the Browning home. Did she move in with the Brownings?

No. Jonathan Browning had closed his gun shop and returned to Quincy in the fall of 1845 to dispose of some property he still owned before moving west. Lucy moved into his home that fall and lived there until she moved into the Noble home the following year. It was in the Browning home that Lucy reportedly finished dictating the book on the history of her son Joseph.

Did Jonathan make flintlock or cap-and-ball (percussion) guns?

He undoubtedly could make either, but percussion guns were becoming fairly common in the 1840s. Joshua Shaw, a Philadelphian, had perfected the simpler and more dependable cap lock gun in 1816.

We don't know how often flintlocks were still used during the Nauvoo era, but Browning might have done special orders for some of his older customers. Many flintlocks were also being altered at this time for percussion caps, so Jonathan was probably doing that also.

How long did it take Browning to make a rifle or handgun?

This question is comparable to asking how long it would take to paint a picture. First of all, making a gun was an art, and the time would vary considerably, depending on the gun being crafted and the detail in the carved stock or the engraving on the metal parts. There was a big time difference between building a single shot and a repeater. Sometimes new barrels were needed before the stocks were made or the lock or cap mechanisms were assembled. Thus, there would not have been a single time frame for any one gun.

An average gun sold for no less than $10 to $15; an average wage at that time was $1 per day. Assuming the average time spent on one gun was a little more than a week, gun-makers were well paid.

Did Jonathan Browning actually invent the first repeating firearm?

No. The first repeating firearm was the Colt revolver, which Samuel Colt invented in 1833 and patented in 1836. Winchester and his New Haven Arms Company produced the first widely accepted repeating rifle in 1860. However, a good case could be made for the slide gun as a repeater, which Jonathan did produce in Nauvoo, long before the Winchester rifle in New Haven.

* *

* *

The most famous gunman in Nauvoo was Porter Rockwell. Do we know if Browning made any guns for him?

Browning supposedly made one of his famous slide (repeating) rifles for Porter. With scant verification, some say it was one of these guns that Porter used to kill Frank Worrell (a leading character in the assassinations of Joseph and Hyrum) on the River Road south of Montebello when Porter went to the aid of Sheriff Backenstos in September 1845.

Why would a family bury a child in their backyard rather than the traditional cemetery, as we see at the Browning home?

Families would have done this for a number of reasons. First of all, the laws permitted it, and in many families, the custom was to have family graves close by. Undoubtedly, many "lost" graves of this type exist around Nauvoo.

There was also the problem of "lost" graves in a large cemetery. In his diary, Hosea Stout mentions looking for the grave of his daughter in the Nauvoo Pioneer Cemetery and being unable to find it. He either didn't get around to marking it after the burial or the marker was lost. Burials were occurring so frequently that unless they were marked immediately, remembering the exact location might have been difficult.

In other cases, family cemeteries filled an emotional need to have the grave nearby. This was the case when Willard Richards, because of the pleading of his daughter, had his beloved wife Jenetta buried in the yard where his daughter could visit and play around the grave site. This marker may be seen today near the sidewalk just north of the Woodruff home on Durphy Street.

* *

Carriage Ride

Who was Lane Newberry?

Newberry was a descendant of Nauvoo pioneers. His father was Captain Charles Newberry of the *Eleanor Hope*, a lighter (or barge) used to cross the Des Moines Rapids south of Nauvoo. His mother was Jennie Bellemay, a native of Salt Lake City. Little evidence exists to suggest Lane was an active member of the Church—if a member at all. As a commercial artist, he started coming to Nauvoo in 1931 to paint the landscapes and buildings of Old Nauvoo. He and his wife, the former Helene Haden, moved to Nauvoo in 1957 and became active members of the community. Lane died in 1961 and is buried in Fort Madison.

Lane Newberry's admirers claim he began the revitalization of Old Nauvoo. Is this true?

As a well-known artist who exhibited at the New York World's Fair in 1939 and as a respected recorder of landmarks along the Mormon Trail, Lane Newberry often receives much credit for the revitalization of Nauvoo. His admirers claim he extracted a promise from the First Presidency of the Church to erect a memorial on the temple block, thereby beginning the rebuilding of Old Nauvoo. Such claims, however, should not detract from the work of Dr. Leroy Kimball, who deserves most of the credit for what we see in Nauvoo today.

How did Inspiration Point get its name?

There is *no* evidence the Prophet visited this spot to gain inspiration! It was named for its picturesque setting. Without any trees to block the view, Fort Madison, Iowa, may be seen to the right and Zarahemla, once a Mormon settlement, can be seen a short distance inland to the left. Also across the river and inland is Sugar Creek, that cold and desolate campground where the Saints began their trek westward. It was also the end of the trail for many who had just started. From this inspiring vantage point, one can also imagine the numerous river craft that plied this river and perhaps even the natives who camped at this point before the coming of the Mormons.

Carriage drivers mention David Moore as having erected a home with wattle construction. Can you tell us more about this kind of home?

This is one of the fastest and easiest ways of constructing a crude home when either large trees or extra help are not available. Poles are placed upright in the ground and branches are woven basket style about these uprights. The "basket" walls are then plastered with mud, making a secure and fairly warm but not very permanent home. These are similar to some of the first homes the English colonists constructed in Jamestown, Virginia, in 1607. Because of the wet climate both there and in Nauvoo, such homes had to be replaced rather quickly with more substantial building material.

Why was the well King Follett petitioned to keep open dug in the center of an intersection?

According to Section 8 of the Nauvoo City Charter, the Council had the power "to provide the city with water, to dig wells, and erect pumps in the streets for the extinguishment of fires, and convenience of the inhabitants." The city constructed this well for the use of nearby inhabitants, without

* *

intruding on anyone's private property.

King Follett was killed while rock-walling a well. How could one dig a well so deep without the sides caving in as the digging went deeper?

The diggers would first start a hole much bigger than the well would be—perhaps as much as 10 to 12 feet in diameter. When the hole became so deep that it was too far to throw the dirt, they would start a second, smaller hole in the center of the first. They would then throw the dirt onto the first shelf where another worker would throw it to the ground above. Depending on the depth, usually not over 20 to 30 feet, a second or third shelf might be needed. Once the diggers reached water, they would lower rocks in buckets to start the walling from the bottom. (The falling of such a bucket killed King Follett.) Walling would then proceed with some of the workers above shoveling dirt behind the wall, filling the outside of the larger hole, and packing it as the wall moved upward. The walls were so well keystoned together that one seldom sees such wells with collapsed walls today.

The carriage ride passes through a great deal of farmland with cattle. Who farms the land and owns the cattle?

The Church owns the land but rents it on an annual basis to local farmers who raise the crops and cattle.

* *

Carthage Jail

Where were the jailer Stigall and his family when the mob attacked the jail?

In his book *24 Hours to Martyrdom*, Reed Blake claims that the entire Stigall family was at home in the lower portion of the jail. When the first shots were fired—some of them into the walls of the ground floor—Mrs. Stigall dropped to the floor of the kitchen, terrified. Although the account sounds very dramatic, we have little evidence of the presence of the entire family. It does appear as though Stigall's daughters were home, however. Fortunately, none of the Stigalls were injured, but the presence of any of the family indicates the jailer had no knowledge of the impending attack.

Who was Dr. Southwick, who went with Joseph on his final trip to Carthage?

Dr. Southwick was a non-Mormon landowner from Texas and Louisiana who was visiting Nauvoo to persuade the Prophet to buy land in the new Republic of Texas. He had been staying some days at the Mansion House before Joseph left for Carthage. He joined Joseph, Hyrum, and the others in jail but left around noon on July 27 to acquire a pass that would allow him entrance to and exit from the jail. For some reason, he did not return. A brief mention in the July 2, 1994, issue of the *Church News* mentions

* *

Southwick was later discovered to have been an enemy, but there is no reference for this revealing statement.

The anti-Mormons of Hancock County called Jacob Backenstos, the non-Mormon sheriff in Carthage, a "Jack Mormon." Explain.

Today, a Jack Mormon is an inactive member of the Church. In the 1830s, however, it was a non-Mormon who sympathized with the Latter-day Saints. As a nickname or diminutive of John, it was used as a general term of contempt for any unlikable person, and people like Jacob Backenstos were certainly not well liked among the anti-Mormons of Hancock County. The *Warsaw Signal* editor, Thomas Sharp, is credited with coining the term.

Where was the Hamilton House where the bodies of Joseph and Hyrum and the wounded John Taylor were taken?

The hotel sat one block east of the Hancock County Court House on the corner of Main and Washington Streets in Carthage. Artois Hamilton, who had planned to flee Carthage as most of the inhabitants did after the assassination, owned the hotel. However, Willard Richards persuaded the Hamiltons to allow John Taylor to be taken in and cared for and the bodies of Joseph and Hyrum to be temporarily laid out there. John Taylor later stated he felt himself a hostage for the safety of the Hamiltons. Artois and his son William aided in returning the bodies of the slain brothers to Nauvoo the following day.

Only two days before his assassination, Joseph told several militia officers in Carthage who sought his blood that they would witness scenes of blood and sorrow to their entire satisfaction and that many then present would have an opportunity to face the cannon's mouth and scenes of desolation and distress. Was that prophecy fulfilled?

Part of his exact prophecy was "inasmuch as you and the people thirst for blood, I prophesy, in the name of the Lord, that you shall witness

* *

scenes of blood and sorrow to your entire satisfaction. Your souls shall be perfectly satiated with blood, and many of you who are now present shall have an opportunity to face the cannon's mouth from sources you think not of; and those people that desire this great evil upon me and my brethren shall be filled with regret and sorrow because of the scenes of desolation and distress that await them." Two years later, as the Saints were being driven from Nauvoo, Hancock County was sending its men off to die in the Mexican War.

Seventeen years later, the Civil War began and Illinois sent far more than her proportional quota of troops to that war, including many of those involved in the Carthage killings. More than 29,000 Illinois troops did not return home.

What eventually happened to Justice of the Peace and Captain of the Carthage Greys, Robert F. Smith, who carried so much responsibility for the deaths of the Smith brothers?

During the Civil War, he was a colonel of the Illinois militia. He took part in the siege of Atlanta and General Sherman's March to the Sea. At the occupation of Savannah, he was made a brigadier general and was appointed military governor in that area. Little is known of his life after this point. In an atlas of Hancock County published nine years after the war, Smith is not mentioned as a subscriber or principle inhabitant.

Did Joseph wound any of the mob with his pepperbox revolver?

Accounts vary. Joseph was using a six-shot pepperbox revolver, which misfired two or three times. One man reported wounded was "an Irishman named Wills, who was in the affair from his congenital love of a brawl, in the arm; Gallagher, a southerner from the Mississippi Bottom, in the face; Voorhees (Voras), a half grown, hobbledehoy from Bear Creek, in the shoulder; and another gentleman." The unnamed fourth "gentleman" was named Allen, but only the first three are known to have been wounded. All four of these men were indicted but fled the county and were never arrested or brought to trial. Parley P. Pratt also named a Mr. Townsend, wounded in the arm, who died from the effects about six months later.

Were the assassins of Joseph and Hyrum ever brought to trial?

In addition to the men mentioned in the previous question, five other men were also indicted: Mark Aldrich, a Warsaw developer; Jacob Davis, an Illinois State Senator; Warren Grover, a captain in the Warsaw militia; Thomas Sharp, editor of the *Warsaw Signal*; and Levi Williams, a colonel in the Illinois militia. Because of their prominence and their confidence in an acquittal, they willingly went to trial. Sharp must be given credit as the leading spokesman for the anti-Mormons and Levi Williams as the leading actor in mob activities. The trial was a farce and the Saints, knowing this, showed little interest in participating and little surprise at its outcome: a verdict of not guilty.

Critics say a martyr doesn't die fighting for his life. True?

Joseph died defending the lives of his brother and his friends as he had previously promised. Willard Richards and John Taylor were both members of the Quorum of the Twelve and his brother was a member of the First Presidency. Their survival was important to Joseph, which was probably also the reason he jumped from the window. He certainly knew he could not escape death in this manner, but doing so might have allowed his friends to survive, and it did.

The definition of a martyr is one who willingly suffers death for his beliefs. It is a fact that Joseph voluntarily gave himself up to Carthage authorities knowing he would die. Thus, he willingly went to his death.

Webster's 1828 American Dictionary of the English Language defines a "martyr" as "one who, by his death, bears witness to the truth of the gospel. One who suffers death in defense of any cause." The dictionary says nothing about doing it without resistance. It is only necessary that there be no renunciation of belief in order to preserve one's life.

Where were the two remaining Smith brothers, William and Samuel, when Joseph and Hyrum were martyred at Carthage?

William, along with his family, was on a mission in the eastern states. His wife had been ill, and he hoped the change in climate would be beneficial. Samuel was living in Plymouth, a small town in the southeast corner of Hancock County. Hearing of threats against his brothers, he had headed to Nauvoo to warn them. He finally made it to Carthage but was too late to save his brothers. The following day, he returned to Nauvoo with Willard Richards and the bodies of his brothers.

Why were John Taylor and Willard Richards at Carthage jail with Joseph and Hyrum? Were they under arrest as well?

Like several of Joseph's friends, John Taylor and Willard Richards volunteered to spend time in jail with Joseph and Hyrum not only for company but as obstacles and, if necessary, witnesses to any illegal actions against the brothers. As several of his friends left the jail on errands, they were refused entry, so that at the time of the attack, only Taylor and Richards remained in the jail with the Smith brothers.

How many times was Joseph shot, according to the coroner?

The coroner's jury, which convened in the jail immediately after the assassination, reported that Joseph and Hyrum had each been shot twice. They apparently did not remove any clothing, so they missed some of the wounds. There was some confusion about the number of wounds others mentioned, possibly because an exit and entrance wound might have been mistaken for two separate wounds. Most accounts agree, however, that John Taylor suffered four wounds and that Joseph and Hyrum suffered four, possibly five, each.

What was the verdict of the coroner's jury investigating the deaths of Joseph and Hyrum as to the identity of the killers?

The jury, composed of twelve Hancock County citizens, determined the

Smith brothers died from wounds "inflicted by some person or persons to the jury unknown." It is highly unlikely that a single member of the jury could have been unaware of the identities of a number of members of the mob who participated in the assassination.

When and how were the death masks of Joseph and Hyrum made?

They were made as the bodies of Joseph and Hyrum were being prepared for burial in Nauvoo by M. Hamlin Cannon, George Q. Cannon's father—who would die two months later—fashioned the molds out of Nauvoo clay, from which plaster casts were made. The molds were destroyed in the process, but Wilford C. Wood purchased the original casts for his private museum in Woods Cross, Utah. In 1990, the masks were donated to the Church Museum. Since that time, copies have been made of the originals and are not that uncommon.

Latter-day Saints have some very harsh feelings about Governor Thomas Ford. Are they justified?

Possibly not. This is a case of our tendency to judge those in the past with our concepts of modern ideal standards of behavior. Remember, this was an era of Jacksonian Democracy in which people commonly believed popular opinion held precedence over Constitutional rights, which were not deeply ingrained at this early stage of U.S. history. Ford was perhaps severe in his condemnation of the Saints, but he was also severe in his scorn for the mobs and their leaders. In a letter to the Warsaw Anti-Mormon Committee he sent only days after the martyrdom, Ford wrote: "I could not believe that so much stupidity and baseness, as was necessary for such an enterprise as the murder of defenseless prisoners in jail would be, could be mustered in Hancock County." Such insulting statements, if he had been part of the conspiracy, would undoubtedly have provoked a response suggesting such collusion.

His major fault may have been his naiveté in believing in the ethics and integrity of the majority of his people, as he later suggested in his His-tory of Illinois. Reed Blake, in his book, *24 Hours to Martyrdom*, paints a dramatic picture of Ford's foreknowledge of the assassinations. Porter Rockwell suggested the same thing in an affidavit made in Salt Lake City twelve years later. Conspiracy theories have always been popular, however, and it is unlikely Ford's supposed involvement will ever be disproved to the satisfaction of all.

Finally, if the Saints truly believe Joseph had finished his work and was to seal his testimony with his blood, Ford would only have been an instrument in the hands of the Lord and must not be condemned too harshly.

Why do some say the Carthage mobs martyred three Smith brothers?

At the time of the Carthage martyrdom, Joseph and Hyrum's brother, Samuel, was living in Plymouth, a small town about fifteen miles southeast of Carthage. When he heard of his brothers' arrest, Samuel mounted a horse and headed for Nauvoo on June 27. Along the way, he learned his brothers were imprisoned at Carthage jail, and he turned his horse toward Carthage. After being spotted by members of the mob, he was pursued for another two hours. Finally escaping, he made it into Carthage only to find his brothers dead. The physical strains of the long and exhausting ride, plus the emotional strain of discovering his brothers slain, produced a severe fever and death within a month. In her book *History of Joseph Smith by His Mother*, Lucy Mack Smith wrote that "being dreadfully fatigued in the chase, which, joined to the shock occasioned by the death of his brothers, brought on a disease that never was removed." The exertions of that day undoubtedly weakened his resistance to one of the common diseases of the time. Nevertheless, he was truly a martyr like his brothers.

Why did the mob let John Taylor and Willard Richards live?

First of all, they probably believed John Taylor was dead. They had undoubtedly seen him fall back inside the window. With the number of shots fired into the room, they probably also believed Willard Richards was dead. Whatever the case, they would have returned to the martyrdom room and possibly have "finished" the assassinations of Richards and Taylor if someone had not shouted "The Mormons are coming!" This cry frightened the mob, and they fled the scene, leaving the two survivors.

Who was the doctor who treated John Taylor's wounds?

His name was Thomas L. Barnes. It is of interest to note that Sheriff Backenstos later supplied a list of "those who took an active part in the massacre of Joseph and Hyrum Smith" and listed a "Thomas L. Barnes, Carthage, Illinois, quack doctor." Obviously, John Taylor did not trust him, but he had no other choice but to allow Barnes to treat him. Barnes later sent John Taylor a bill for his services, which Taylor refused to pay. Only recently, the descendants of John Taylor settled with the descendants of Thomas L. Barnes by paying the sum of one dollar.

Why didn't Joseph send for the Nauvoo Legion when it became evident that the situation was critical? He had the opportunity.

Actually, reports show that Joseph did exactly that, but the officer left in charge of the Nauvoo Legion, Jonathan Dunham, did not make the request public. Though doubtful, this story is just one of the many that floated around after the death of the Prophet, when so many were looking for targets for their wrath. The infamous forger-criminal, Mark Hofmann, took advantage of this story in 1983 to forge a letter he reported to have found from Joseph to Dunham requesting such help. Although later proven to be a forgery, it appeared in 1984 in *The Personal Writings of Joseph Smith* by Dean Jessee.

Joseph knew that the Nauvoo Legion, as numerous and well-trained as it was, was no match in the long run against the entire Illinois militia and mob volunteers. Calling on the Legion would have meant the sacrifice of many lives with absolutely no chance of final victory. Although Joseph likely could have preserved his life, he was not willing to do so at the cost of others. He knew his work was finished and the Restored Church would survive, with or without him.

* *

Why didn't the Legion retaliate after the killings of their leaders?

They did not retaliate for several reasons. First, the assassinations left the Church without immediate unified leadership. Who would have given the orders? Actually, both John Taylor and Willard Richards, the only members of the Quorum of the Twelve in Illinois, did urge restraint. Second, those who might have assumed command of the Legion knew such action could only lead to a war of attrition with little chance of victory. Third, several Church authorities realized public opinion (nationally) favored the Saints in this case. Any retaliation would have jeopardized that opinion. And finally, hadn't Joseph predicted such an end? Wasn't this part of God's plan? It would have been a denial of faith to attempt retaliation.

What personal effects were found on Joseph's body after his death?

J. W. Woods, Joseph's principal lawyer in those final days at Carthage, received from Emma Smith a receipt for items found on the body of the Prophet and returned to the widow:

"Received, Nauvoo, Illinois, July 2, 1844, of James W. Woods, one hundred and thirty-five dollars and fifty cents in gold and silver and receipt for a shroud, one gold finger ring, one gold pen and pencil case, one penknife, one pair of tweezers, one silk and one leather purse, one small pocket wallet containing a note of John P. Green for $50, and a receipt of Heber C. Kimball for a note of hand on Ellen M. Saunders for one thousand dollars, as the property of Joseph Smith, Emma Smith."

Were the two survivors of the martyrdom, Willard Richards and John Taylor, able to identify members of the mob?

Yes. The following list is from the pen of Dr. Willard Richards:

LIST OF THE MOB AT CARTHAGE ACCORDING TO
WILLARD RICHARDS
William Law, Wm. A. Rollason, Wilson Law, Wm. H. J. Marr,
Robert D. Foster, S. M. Marr, Charles A. Foster, Sylvester Emmons,
Francis M. Higbee, Alexander Syrupson, Chauncey L. Higbee, John

* *

* *

Eagle, Joseph H. Jackson, Henry O. Norton, John M. Finch, Augustine Spencer.

In addition to Richards' list, Sheriff Backenstos listed as part of the mob three physicians, a constable, an editor, and four lawyers. He also stated that the "Carthage Greys were nearly to a man parties in the June massacre." Governor Ford, on the other hand, felt that Warsaw citizens were the ringleaders. He probably was making reference to such firebrands as Thomas Sharp, editor of the *Warsaw Signal*.

What was the reaction of citizens outside of Warsaw or Carthage to the assassinations?

Typical responses can be read in major papers throughout the Midwest. The *Springfield Sangamon Journal* doubted the truth of such an atrocity: "The rumor is too preposterous for belief." The *Quincy Herald* wrote, "Their murder was a cold-blooded, cowardly act, which will consign the perpetrators, if discovered, to merited infamy and disgrace." The *St. Louis Evening Gazette* wrote of a "murder of a character so atrocious and so unjustifiable as to leave the blackest stain on all its perpetrators." Such was the general tenor of news reports outside of Hancock County. These reports, while indicating no sympathy for the doctrines of the Saints, did in general demonstrate disgust for the perfidy of the deed.

Why was Sidney Rigdon in Pittsburgh at the time of Joseph and Hyrum's martyrdoms? Had he become disaffected?

He was at least very discouraged—even prophesying that Joseph would die and Nauvoo would fall. Some writers have stated that he had moved to Pennsylvania several months before the martyrdom, while others have insisted he had moved to Pittsburgh merely to campaign for Joseph (he was Joseph's running mate for the Presidency of the United States). Evidence seems to suggest, however, that although no longer an active participant in Church affairs, Rigdon nevertheless was in Nauvoo defending the Church leaders on June 14 when he wrote to Governor Ford claiming the *Expositor*

* *

affair was not the concern of anyone outside of Nauvoo. Fearing for the safety of his family, he apparently moved to Pittsburgh within days of the martyrdom but immediately returned upon news of the Carthage killings.

What was the official legal charge made against the Smith brothers that resulted in their incarceration in the Carthage jail?

They were first charged with inciting riot for the destruction of the *Nauvoo Expositor*. This offense permitted the setting of bail, however, which to the surprise of the anti-Mormons was quickly posted. Before Joseph and Hyrum could leave town, they were rearrested on a charge of treason for their use of the Nauvoo Legion, a state militia, in the destruction of the press and for declaring martial law without the governor's permission. Without taking them before a court on this latter charge, the constable produced a false mittimus, stating the brothers had been brought before a court on that charge and had been ordered to jail, whereupon they were illegally incarcerated. Treason being a non-bailable offense, they would undoubtedly have been remanded to jail, regardless of the improper procedure.

Clothing

* *

Was spinning and weaving still the primary method of providing clothing?

Both were on the way out at the time of Old Nauvoo. The Amos Davis store, only one of several such stores in Nauvoo, sold more than twenty-five varieties of textiles by the yard. With domestic and shirting textiles selling for 25 cents per yard, it did not pay most housewives to spend valuable time spinning and weaving.

Was lace used on women's clothing during the Nauvoo era?

It apparently was. The 1828 *Webster's American Dictionary of the English Language* defines trimming as "Ornamental appendages to a garment, as lace, ribins and the like." In the *Nauvoo Neighbor*, dated May 22, 1844, an advertisement for the Red Brick Store on Water Street listed among their "fancy dry goods" such items as cassimers, satinetts, vestings, kerseys, laces, and so on. Lace was also used on men's shirt bosoms and cuffs.

Were bright colors used in women's clothing of the Nauvoo era?

The colors were generally soft: tan, amber, mauve, rose, teal blue, azure, lilac, apple green, purple, cabbage green, wine red, vanilla, grayed delicate tone, and so forth.

* *

* *

What kind of ready-made clothing, if any, was available to Nauvooans?

Shoes, mittens, shirts, socks, stockings, hats, vests, coats, and roundabouts (wrappers) are some of the articles listed in Nauvoo store day-books. Ready-made clothing was far more prevalent in larger eastern cities or even in St. Louis, where Nauvooans went occasionally to shop. Fashion dolls were available and even clothing patterns were making their appearance.

What exactly were the Millinery shops in Nauvoo?

Millinery shops were shops, often run by women, that made or sold articles by "milliners," which, according to the 1828 Webster's dictionary, consisted of "head-dresses, hats or bonnets, laces, ribins and the like."

Did the Nauvooans commonly wear the type of clothing the missionary guides wear?

As hosts and hostesses, as these guides are, such dress would be quite common in entertaining, "go-to-meeting," and other such occasions. However, in many of the professions represented here, such as milling, farming, and so forth, costumes would be more in line with what you see in the brick yard and blacksmith shop.

* *

Coolidge Home

Where did Coolidge work in the home? Obviously it was not like it is now.

It should be noted that the door used by visitors was *not* the front entrance to the Coolidge home. Modifications have been made around the stairs of the entrance, which fronts Parley Street. The present cooper shop was part of the home. We don't know how much of the north wing, which was used for his cabinet shop, was built and used by Coolidge. There have been a number of remodelings to this building. In 1848, following the departure of the Saints, a German immigrant named Johan George Kaufman bought the building and converted it into the "New York Hotel." It stayed in the family for over a century. According to the Kaufmans, the large brick oven in the north wing was there when they purchased the hotel. The building was remodeled after 1932 and was used as a restaurant for a period of time.

There has been some question over the proper name for the "shaving horse" in the cooper shop. Some insist it is a "schnitzel-bank." Is that the right name?

That is a good German-American name for the object—but this was *not* a German-American home when Coolidge lived here. From colonial times to the present day, in normal English usage, the term has been "shaving

* *

horse," sometimes "shingle horse," and even "draw horse." For anyone in Old Nauvoo who might have called it by the German name, there would have been at least fifty New Yorkers, New Englanders, and Englishmen who used the term "shaving horse."

What are some of the prices of items (for example, a barrel made in the cooper's shop) sold in Nauvoo?

In the 1840s, an average workman's wage was approximately $1 per day. In the Amos Davis store, which was located on Mulholland Street in Old Nauvoo, the day ledger lists the price of a barrel at 50 cents. The ledger doesn't say whether this was a "tight" or "slack" barrel. The type it was would make a big difference in the price of a barrel, which was based on the number that could be made in one day. A cooper with a single helper could make two casks of white oak for liquids (a "tight" barrel) and four or five of red oak for dry goods (a "slack" barrel). The 50-cent price would suggest the one mentioned was a slack cask. A "tight" barrel would be at least twice that much.

The store ledger doesn't mention the size of the barrel, but in normal usage, the term "barrel" was a wooden cask holding 30 to 35 gallons. If it had been larger, it would have gone by another name, such as hogshead, and if smaller, by such names as kilderkin (18 gallons) or the more common firkin (9 gallons).

Were all candles hand dipped? If molds were available, wouldn't they have been easier and quicker to use?

Molds weren't commonly used for a number of reasons. First, they were too expensive to have the number necessary for making a large number of candles at once. Second, it took longer to ready the wicks in the molds than it did for dipping. Third, candles needed to cool in the molds before removing, whereas hand-dipped candles were air-dried, eliminating any waiting time between batches. And finally, molds were usually of one size, and housewives often wanted different-sized candles for different burning times. Hand-dipped candles allowed for greater variety in size.

* *

* *

What were the prices of such items as candles and pottery in Nauvoo stores?

Some of the prices actually listed in the daybook of the Amos Davis store indicate bowls at 12 1/2 cents, a three-gallon stoneware churn at 75 cents, and a one-gallon jug at 25 cents. Because candles came in so many sizes, they were usually sold by the pound at 18 3/4 cents.

Where did the term "cooper" come from?

The word comes from the Latin word *cupa* (bending, hollowness, containing, holding). Such words as "coop" (a pen for chickens or small animals) and "cup" are derived from *cupa* as well. To coop a thing up was to shut it in, imprison it, or cage it. The cage was called a "coop" and the person who made it, the "cooper." Up until the time of Nauvoo, the word "coop" was also another name for a barrel.

I've heard the term "white cooper." Is that just another name for a cooper like Coolidge?

No. A white cooper made wooden containers such as grain measures, sieves, boxes, bellows, and so on. Many of the items he made required curved wood, which he fashioned out of wide strips of thinly shaved bass or poplar. There is no evidence that Coolidge made items such as this. Each type of coopering was specialized in towns as large as Nauvoo.

Many craftsmen bought parts of their product already made. Did coopers?

Yes. When riveted iron hoops began to replace the wooden hoops on barrels around 1800, coopers had to buy those. Even before that, they would often buy or trade for the wood staves farmers would rive out during the winter when farm work was slack.

* *

Entertainment

How was the Cultural Hall heated? Why are there chimneys on the roof but no stoves or chimneys inside?

The Cultural Hall has gone under extensive restoration. It served as a home for many years and even had the top floor removed. Since no fireplaces or chimneys are presently evident inside, the flues may not have been restored. It does seem apparent, however, that the building was heated with stoves whose pipes might well have been connected to flues that ran up the inside of the exterior walls.

What was the size and composition of Pitt's Brass Band?

Pitt's Brass Band first numbered fifteen, including Captain Pitt. Incidentally, the band members all converted at the same time as a result of the missionary work of Wilford Woodruff and Heber C. Kimball in the English Midlands. They stayed together as a group in Nauvoo and emigrated together to Utah. According to Helen Mar Kimball Whitney, William Cahoon, John Pack, Stephen Hale, William Pitt, William Clayton, Jacob Hutchinson, James Standing, and "many more" were members of the choir, and most belonged to William Pitt's brass band.

What kinds of instruments did people play in Nauvoo at this time?

One source described the white-clad band as being proficient on trumpets, French horns, piccolos, clarinets, coronets, bugles, trombones, and bass drums. Other instruments mentioned in Old Nauvoo include the piano and organ as well as melodeons, concertinas, violins, banjos, and flutes. William Pitt owned and played a lyre and a left-handed violin in Nauvoo as well as on the 1847 trek to Salt Lake Valley.

Dances were held on the top floor of the Masonic Hall. What kinds of dances were performed in Nauvoo?

The most common dances were the quadrille (a type of square dance for four couples), French fours, Copenhagen jigs, Virginia reels, Scotch reels, and polkas, which were just making their appearance as the Saints were preparing to leave. German immigrants had brought the waltz, but many Americans considered it too decadent at this time. More staid members, like Sidney Rigdon, preferred "play parties" in which participants marched, skipped, or shuffled to the rhythm of music. Dance objectors justified their participation by not calling this "dancing."

Brigham Young, even more than Joseph Smith, enjoyed music and dancing. He said, "There is no music in hell, for all good music belongs to heaven," even though at times, he seemed to condemn dancing, particularly when he felt such dancing was becoming too unrestrained or when more important work was being neglected.

What kind of songs were the Saints of Nauvoo singing?

The taste in vocal music in Nauvoo was not much different from national taste in the 1840s, being a combination of sacred, sentimental, and comic. Stephen Foster's music was becoming popular, as was the music from the minstrel shows heard on the steamboats along the river. A music hall near the temple was completed in February 1845. To coincide with the April Conference that year, a music festival was arranged that lasted for three nights. A broadside for that festival gives an idea of some of the most popular songs in Nauvoo:

the choir sang "God Save the Band," soloists sang "Isabel," "The Hole in the Stocking," "Lary O Gallagin," "Is There a Heart that Never Loved," "Soldier's Tear," and "O Adam;" a duo sang "The Catholic Priest"; various glee groups sang "Hail Joseph Smith," "Forgive Blest Shade," "Pilgrim Saints," "Hark the Lark," and "Hark the Fisherman."

What does the inscription "M. Helm G.M.A.L. 5843" on the Masonic Hall cornerstone mean?

M. Helm was a member of the medical society in Springfield, Illinois, and a Grand Master in the Masonic Lodge. The Nauvoo Lodge was named after him and thus the inscription means "M. Helm, Grand Master After Light" in the year 5843. This was considered the date of the world in 1843, since the Masons add 4,000 years to our contemporary chronology, believing the earth and its life began 4000 B.C.

The Hall was built for the Masons. How many Nauvooans belonged?

The actual installation of the Nauvoo Lodge took place in the winter of 1842, and by January, Mormon Masons in Illinois totaled 330, outnumbering the non-Mormon Masons in all of Illinois. If we add the Iowa Mormon Masons, we have a total of 506. Fear of domination by the Saints led to the Grand Lodge withdrawing all fellowship with the predominantly Mormon lodges in October 1844, and all LDS members were suspended. In spite of this fact, Brigham Young did not suspend the work of the Masons in Nauvoo until April 1845. The Saints continued to hold meetings, however, until June, and clandestine meetings were likely held until the exodus in 1846.

Was this building originally built as and called the "Cultural" Hall or the "Masonic" Hall?

It was the Masonic Hall. However, "Masonic" is a sensitive word for many Saints who have been accused, unjustly, of adopting Masonic rituals for LDS temple ceremonies. Since the building was used for many cultural

* *

events, the name Cultural Hall is as appropriate as the earlier, more common Masonic Hall.

What features of the third floor are symbolic in reference to the Masons?

Some of the more obvious will be recognized in the windowless north wall (to Masons, north is a symbol of darkness, whereas the east symbolizes light); the domed ceiling, which represents the heavens; and the three windows, which represent the Godhead.

How involved was Joseph personally in the Masonic Lodge in Nauvoo?

Joseph participated in Freemasonry only to a limited extent. We have evidence of his attendance in the Nauvoo Masonic Lodge on just three occasions. It is of interest to note, nevertheless, that his contemporaries commented on his rapid mastery of the tenets and principles of Masonry and his understanding of its symbolism from the very beginning.

Why is some of the symbolism used in LDS temples so similar to the symbolism used by the Masons? Is that where the Prophet Joseph got his ideas?

No. As Joseph explained, they both are derived from the same source— the ritual of the temple of Solomon, which itself was derived from earlier sources. Latter-day Saints believe temple ordinances, including their rituals and teachings, were first revealed to Adam. They were later revealed to Seth, Noah, Melchizedek, Abraham, and each prophet to whom the priesthood was given. Latter-day Saints believe the ordinances performed in temples today are the same as God's ritualistic teachings from the beginning. Masonic rituals and temple ordinances are not identical because some of the Masonic signs and symbols have become misconstrued through the centuries. Joseph was merely restoring the original rites.

* *

* *

Why would Joseph Smith encourage Masonry among the Saints, considering Book of Mormon views on secret societies?

There is an important difference between a "secret society," which keeps its goals and membership secret, and an organization that merely possesses secret rites. The LDS Church does not make public its temple ceremonies, but it is not a "secret society." The same is true of the Masons, whose members readily admit their affiliation and the goals of their fraternal order.

Joseph perhaps thought it was important, in view of the opposition the Church met in Missouri, to join a fraternal organization in Illinois that also included state political leaders. In the event of any future difficulties, such fellow lodge members should be bound by oath to defend member Saints. As it turned out, they did not feel oath bound, because they believed Joseph had violated Masonic doctrine by initiating women into the organization. They had misinterpreted LDS women receiving temple endowments, because of the similarity of some of the rituals.

Why is the front of the Cultural Hall different from the rest of this brick building?

Contemporary newspaper accounts indicated the front of the building was stuccoed to give the impression of a marble front. It was therefore restored the same way.

How extensive was the restoration of the Cultural Hall?

Very. At the time Nauvoo Restoration, Inc. (the NRI) purchased the Hall in 1967, the top floor had been removed and the interior had gone through many remodels, being used first as a mercantile establishment, then a private residence, then a boarding house, and finally an apartment house before becoming vacant for a number of years. In the restoration, the entire interior had to be completely restored to early descriptions, the roof and walls raised to their original height, and the front returned to some of its original appearance. It now has only one front door, whereas it formerly had three.

* *

Emma Smith

Is it true that Emma married her second husband, Lewis Bidamon, on the Prophet Joseph's birthday?

Yes, she married him on December 23, 1847. Many sources list the date as December 27, but when Valeen Tippetts Avery and Linda King Newell wrote an article on Lewis Bidamon for the 1979 spring issue of *BYU Studies*, they acquired a copy of the marriage certificate, verifying December 23.

Why did Emma Smith stay in Nauvoo rather than go west?

Emma probably had a number of reasons not to go west, including her unwillingness to accept the plural marriage doctrine, which was now firmly established, and her unwillingness to accept even more privations without the company of Joseph. The major reason, however, seems her rejection of Brigham's leadership, which, of course, was tied to plural marriage, but there also seemed to be a clash of personalities and mutual dislike. Brigham questioned Emma's commitment to the Gospel for not accepting plural marriage. He, like some of the other loyalists, blamed Emma and the others who had urged Joseph to return from his brief flight across the river to surrender himself to the authorities in Carthage. Emma, on the other hand, justifiably resented Brigham's less than tactful request for some of Joseph's personal property after the martyrdom and his failure to immediately and personally make greater efforts to console her.

We have one interesting insight on Emma's feelings after the death of Joseph. In a letter to her new husband, Lewis Bidamon, when he was in California in 1850, she warned him to beware of the Mormons: "I can tell you they are capable of an infamous ingratitude." This warning indicates she may have felt a lack of recognition for what she believed should have been a more elevated status.

Other factors also entered the relationship, but suffice to say it may have been mainly a Dr. Fell syndrome between her and Brigham. Dr. John Fell was a seventeenth-century Oxford dean who was the subject of a satirical verse by one of his students:

> I do not love thee, Dr. Fell,
> The reason why I cannot tell;
> But this I know, and know full well,
> I do not love thee, Dr. Fell.

Did Emma Smith have children with her second husband?

No. Emma was 43 years old when she married Lewis Bidamon in 1847. She had five children at that time: Julia Murdock Smith, 16; Joseph III, almost 15; Frederick, 11; Alexander, 9; and the baby David, born after Joseph's death, was 2½. Lewis was 45. He had two young daughters, Zerelda, 13, and Mary Elizabeth, 11. His two sons died before 1847. Emma also took in an illegitimate son of Nancy Abercrombie, fathered by Lewis. During Emma's final illness, Nancy helped care for her. At that time, Emma told Lewis and Nancy to marry after her death, which they did. Nancy was much younger than Lewis and ended up caring for him the last eleven years of his life. Lewis died in 1891, twelve years after Emma.

Two men courted Emma after Joseph's death. Lewis Bidamon was one. Who was the other?

In his memoirs, Joseph Smith III reported that during the summer of 1847, two men were paying court to his mother. One was Lewis Bidamon, of course. The other, he said, was James Mulholland, a clerk for Joseph who had died in November 1839. Joseph III either named the wrong man, or there was another James Mulholland.

Was Emma's marriage to Lewis Bidamon one of love or convenience?

Within three years of their marriage, Lewis was in the gold fields of California. One of Emma's letters to Lewis indicates an affection that seems to go beyond the parameters of a marriage of convenience. Addressed to "my ever dear husband," she writes: "I have scarcely enjoyed any good thing since you left home in constant terrifying apprehension that you might be suffering for the most common comforts of life. . . . Neither can I be [content] until you are within my grasp. . . . When, O! When can I begin to think about you coming home?"

Emma's marriage to Lewis was apparently a happy one. Years later, in a letter to her son Joseph III, she wrote that the happiness she currently felt was entirely new and unexpected. It is not clear whether she meant in comparison to her life with Joseph or to what she anticipated after his death.

How well did Joseph's sons accept their new stepfather, Lewis Bidamon?

The three older sons, Joseph III, Frederick, and Alexander, seemed to find no problem, but the younger, more sensitive David seemed to reveal a disgust for his stepfather's drunkenness and foul language. Major Bidamon, as he was called, had a local reputation for both. David illustrated his displeasure in his poem, "Two Fates," which he wrote on August 7, 1865, in Nauvoo:

> An old horse stood by the "grocery" door,
> And a weary long time he had stood;
> His line was half tied, he was aged and poor,
> Yet, he would not depart though he could.
> His master was in at the sloppy bar,
> I felt sad for the weary old horse;

> But felt as I looked at the two, by far
> That the fate of the master was worse.
> The dust was beat up like a scorching bed,
> And the gadflies tormented him sore;
> He was marked with blows, and he hung his head,
> As he stood in the filth at the door;
> But filthier far the words of the man
> As he drained off the glass with a curse,
> And hotter the fever that over him ran,
> Than the sunshine that scorched the poor horse.
> One bore in meek patience what heaven had willed,
> Thus degraded, not by his own will;
> The other with poison and blasphemy filled,
> Cursed fate, and yet willed it so still.
> I passed by the corner and went my way,
> I felt sad for the poor old horse,
> Yet, said to myself, "the best I can say,
> Is, the fate of the master is worse."

This poem is in marked contrast to David's hymn about the father he never knew, which starts with "There's an unknown grave in a green lowly spot, The form that it covers will ne'er be forgot" and then continues on to conclude with:

> The love all embracing that never can end,
> In death, as in life, knew him well as a friend,
> The power of Jesus the mighty to save
> Will despoil of its treasure the unknown grave,
> No more an unknown grave.

Did any of Emma's family ever accept the gospel?

Only one accepted it, although four of her siblings moved to Illinois and lived within fairly easy travel distance from Nauvoo. She visited them but never received a very warm welcome, and they never visited her in Nauvoo. When Emma married Joseph, she apparently became an outcast in her father's family. No correspondence exists between Emma and her family after she left home. Joseph was able, however, to convert and

* *

baptize Emma's nephew Lorenzo, the son of her sister, Elizabeth. Her father's will did not even mention Emma.

Was Emma's life in danger after the fall of Nauvoo in September 1846?

Emma actually left before the surrender of Nauvoo to the mobs. She believed the threats that were circulating—that all members of the Smith family would be killed. She received one threat that she must leave her home or it would be burned over her head, and there was evidence of an actual attempt to do so. Advised to leave Nauvoo for her safety, she rented the Mansion House to a Mr. Van Tuyl and left with her children and a few other Saints for Fulton City on September 12, 1846. She returned the following February, when she heard Van Tuyl was leaving Nauvoo with many of the Mansion House furnishings. She then resided in Nauvoo the rest of her life.

When was the written revelation on plural marriage made known?

The written revelation was not made public until Brigham Young revealed it in Utah in 1852. William Clayton declared it was an exact copy of the original he made for Joseph on July 1, 1843. Although Emma Smith later denied this claim, evidence of the revelation and Joseph's compliance with the doctrine, with his wife's knowledge, has become so abundant that no reputable scholar today would deny it. They might only suggest that it was not truly a revelation.

The fact that her sons questioned Emma about the subject on her deathbed—in spite of their apparent acceptance of her denial—suggests they were never fully convinced of the absence of such a revelation or of their father not practicing the doctrine. Actually, young David returned from a mission to Utah with doubts about his mother's denials. Few today doubt the fact Joseph put the doctrine into practice; it's simply a question of when.

* *

* *

What is the story of the blessing Joseph didn't give Emma?

During one of Joseph's final days, Emma apparently asked him for a special blessing. From Carthage Jail, Joseph sent Emma word to write out the blessing as she would like it and he would sign it upon his return. The interesting question posed by this blessing is fairly obvious: Why did Joseph send a message that he would do it upon his return, which he knew was not going to happen, instead of writing the blessing? A written blessing would be as valid as anything she wrote and he later signed. And he certainly had time to do it while he was incarcerated before his death. The answer may be as simple as him feeling he could not give her the blessing she desired in view of her opposition to the plural marriage doctrine.

* *

****

Exodus

****

Was consideration given to moving any place other than the Rocky Mountains?

Absolutely, but not for the Church headquarters. The Church considered sites stretching all the way from Texas to California to Vancouver Island, but they were to be colonies of Church members. The headquarters, as the Prophet Joseph had prophesied, would be in the stronghold of the Rocky Mountains. It is interesting to note that Brigham carried out the original plans for "colonies," establishing more than 500 communities in his lifetime, more than 300 of which still exist.

Did the federal government truly consider setting aside a "reservation" for the Mormons?

In January 1845, William P. Richards, Esq., of Macomb, Illinois, suggested to Bishop George Miller that a petition should be sent to Congress requesting a 24-square mile land grant in the Pineries of Wisconsin or some other uninhabited portions of public lands as a "reserve" for the Saints.

John Taylor considered the suggestion worthy of a report on the front page of the *Nauvoo Neighbor*. He believed the suggested size was much too small for the anticipated growth of the Church. Instead, he suggested an area at least 200 miles square and if not in Wisconsin, then perhaps in Kansas, Oregon, or West Texas. Whether such a request for a "reservation"

* *

* *

was ever made to Congress as a result of this suggestion is not known.

Illinois newspapers near Nauvoo carried announcements of "wolf hunts." Were wolves that numerous in Hancock County?

"Wolf hunts" in 1845 carried a special significance to the readers of Hancock County newspapers, especially in such places as Carthage and Warsaw. It was a euphemism for night-time raids on outlying Mormon farms and settlements and was a means of calling the mobs together.

Why did the exodus begin in February when the Saints were unprepared, weather conditions were unfavorable, and grass was unavailable for the cattle?

Early in December, Samuel Brannan reported that President Polk's cabinet members "were determined to prevent . . . [the Saints from] moving West . . . [and furthermore] they must be obliterated from the earth." In January 1846, word came from several sources that federal troops were on their way to prevent the Saints from leaving Nauvoo. One was a letter from Governor Ford himself, who wrote to Brigham Young and others to make the Church leaders believe regiments of the U.S. Army would be sent to Nauvoo to arrest the leaders and possibly prevent the migration of the Saints westward. Obviously, Brigham and his advisors believed these sources, prompting the early exodus. In retrospect, little evidence exists that the federal government seriously considered such an interference, but officials such as Governor Ford were merely trying to hurry the Saint's departure.

There is an often-told story of nine babies born under horrible conditions across the river at Sugar Creek at the start of the exodus. Thousands of Saints were still in Nauvoo. Why didn't those expectant mothers stay until after their deliveries?

Actually, the story began with Eliza Snow, who recalled much later, "I was informed that. . . ." Researchers have actually uncovered a notarized statement by a midwife, Jane Johnston, who in a history of her life in 1883

* *

described her experiences in the "Poor Camp" in September 1846, after the remaining Saints were driven out of Nauvoo to camp on the Iowa shore. In her memoirs, she related, "I was the midwife, and delivered nine babies that night." After hundreds of tellings, the Sugar Creek story has replaced the actual events in Mormon folklore.

What was the occasion of Joseph Smith's Rocky Mountain Prophesy in which he told Anson Call, Shadrack Roundy, and others that they would see the Saints become a mighty people in the midst of the Rocky Mountains?

According to Anson Call and later verified by Joseph's recording of it in his history, on August 6, 1842 (being some time after the event; Anson thought it was August 14), Joseph, in company with a large number of others, had passed over to Montrose for the installation of officers in the Rising Sun Masonic Lodge located there. While congregated in the shade outside the building where the installation took place, Joseph told his followers of many things that would transpire in the mountains in the West. He then pointed to Shadrack, Anson, and others and made the prediction.

How did the people manage to feed the thousands of head of cattle, oxen, horses, and so forth?

The spring grass had not yet started and the wagons did not hold enough room to carry all the feed the stock would need, so the animals suffered as well as the people. Whenever possible, Brigham sent wagons to the Iowa settlements nearby to trade for food for the animals as well as his people. In his journal, Brigham Young noted that "two tons of timothy hay were purchased at four dollars per ton, and brought into Camp part for cash and part for splitting rails."

The animals were also forced to browse on bushes, buds, and the bark of branches they found in the hollows or that their owners cut for them.

* *

Why were there still a number of Saints in Nauvoo as late as September?

They were the sick and poor who had neither the means nor the health to leave with the majority. The anti-Mormons had previously agreed to let them remain until the Church leaders made a place for them farther west and had a chance to return for them. Brigham accepted their signed promise, logically believed it, and was making plans for their delivery when the mob, emboldened by the potential lack of resistance and their greed for loot, decided to attack and force the remaining Saints out of Nauvoo.

When the Illinois authorities questioned Brigham Young's intention to abandon Nauvoo, Brigham said he offered proof. What was it?

He said, "I proposed a committee of the whole on both sides, and informed them that we were not sowing any winter wheat, and a greater testimony of our intentions to remove should not be asked." A rural people would have understood this to mean that the Saints were making no preparations for staying another year in Illinois.

Such "proof" apparently did not appease the mobs that continued their depredations throughout that fall and winter. As mob pressure intensified the following spring and summer, it became obvious that the non-Mormons were interested in more than just "proof" of the Saints' intentions to leave Illinois: they wanted plunder.

Were the Nauvoo Saints ever actually "under the gun" during their exodus?

Latter-day Saints who crossed into Missouri or Iowa from outlying towns were often under the gun from roving mobsters who were looting and burning. Within the city, however, the Saints did not come under fire and bayonet until September, when there were too few Mormons left to put up much resistance.

Why were the anti-Mormon mobs so unwilling to let the Saints leave peaceably, even after the exodus began?

By September, the mobs threatening Nauvoo were largely made up of the

* *

* *

most ignorant and violent of Illinois citizens who thrived on mob violence and the opportunity to steal, burn, and commit violence in a quasi-legal manner. Their excuse was that the Saints had voted in the summer elections after promising not to and, of course, the ever prevalent but illogical fear that the Mormons might decide to return. Basically, it was a case of there being too few Mormons left to offer any resistance to mob instincts.

Why didn't the Saints make their homes in the more sparsely settled Iowa after their expulsion from either Missouri or Illinois?

This is a good question, and it might have been a better choice in 1839. Remember, however, that one reason for the later discontinuance of the Zarahemla Stake in Iowa was the persecution in that region. Erastus Snow mentioned in a Conference in Utah that "persecution still followed us in the states of Illinois, Iowa, and Missouri, and finally the Saints fled to these Rocky Mountains where there was nobody to oppose us." Perhaps Iowa was simply much too close to old enemies in Missouri and Illinois for the Church to attempt any settlements there.

Did any loyal Saints remain in Nauvoo after the exodus of the Poor Camp in September 1846?

Very few. Estimates run as high as 3,000 Saints in Illinois who elected not to go west, but most of them became inactive, and many of their descendants today don't realize they have Mormon ancestors. There were a few, like Sarah M. Kimball, the wife of Hiram Kimball, who stayed to dispose of property. This was a major undertaking for the Kimballs, requiring two or three years longer than most of the Saints who went west.

How much daily progress could the Saints make in their trek westward after the exodus?

Because of the initial lack of experience and organization and because of such adverse weather conditions so early in the year, progress was painfully slow. Later, as they traveled from Winter Quarters to Salt Lake City, with

* *

experience and better weather, they could average twelve to fourteen miles per day (oxen moved at about two miles per hour). Crossing Iowa, however, daily progress was at times no more than a couple of miles, and camp time might be extended a few days to dry out goods, make repairs, travel back along the trail to help others, build bridges for others who were following, and so on. Occasionally the travelers would camp at night within sight of the previous night's camp.

What happened to all the possessions and property left in Nauvoo by the Saints?

A very large proportion was, out of necessity, abandoned. The Saints had little choice. Their enemies saw no reason to pay fair prices for things they knew could be had in a very short time for nothing. Some of the more desirable property was sold, but for mere pennies on the dollar. Only the absolute necessities could be taken in the small wagons, and some had no wagons at all. After the Battle of Nauvoo in September 1846, the remaining Saints, numbering 600 to 700, were forced to flee their homes and possessions with little more than they could carry in their hands. Colonel Thomas Kane reported visiting Nauvoo shortly after the exodus and entering homes and shops that looked like the owners had merely stepped out of them for a visit.

The Sugar Creek Encampment, during the exodus, is usually mentioned as six to seven miles into Iowa from the river. Are there any discernible remains?

In 1999, amateur researchers believed they discovered the underground remains of several cabins and as many as 500 graves west of Montrose. Since they seemed uninterested in any excavations, however, the claim is highly suspect. The site is approximately one mile east of Sugar Creek on county road J-72. Admittedly, the original staging area was enormous, probably stretching westward for at least two miles. The "discovered" site is about four miles from Montrose, which means the distance from the river to the main encampment further west would be about six to seven miles. It is conceivable that there was camping on the claimed site, but serious research must be done before claims can be made for proof of discernible remains.

If the Lord told the Saints to go to Utah, why did they send scouts to Texas, California, Oregon, and so forth?

First of all, there was no Utah. The Saints were to find their refuge in the Rocky Mountains, which encompass a vast area. Furthermore, they intended to establish colonies in Oregon, California, Texas, and so forth, so sending scouts to those areas was important. In 1845, Parley P. Pratt wrote a letter for the purpose of explaining the council's plans for emigration. They were not only building up Nauvoo, but they planned to "settle other places too." They still planned on establishing their headquarters in the Great Basin at the center of their colonizing efforts. Proof of their plans was found in a memorial sent by the Council of Fifty to Congress early in 1845. In it, the Council offered to secure areas of the unexplored west all the way from Texas to Oregon "and thus strengthen the government and enlarge her borders." Several Congressmen, including Stephen A. Douglas, supported the memorial, but opposition from key members prevented it from ever reaching the floor for a vote.

One other fact should be noted. When Joseph made his prediction, "California" was a general term for all Mexican territory west of the Continental Divide. Howard Egan, in a journal entry dated April 23, 1845, referred to a popular song throughout Nauvoo, which included the phrase "Upper California, that's the land for me." At that time, Upper California was a vague phrase referring to all of Northern Mexico, included all of the present states of Utah, Nevada, California, and portions of Arizona, Oregon, and Idaho.

In the history of the exodus, the "General Council" seems to have made many of the decisions. Is this term another name for the Council of Twelve?

No. It is a reference to the Council of Fifty (a semi-secret organization—if you can manage secrecy in a group of fifty members). The name itself refers to the political Kingdom of God, whose governing body had been organized on March 11, 1844, by the Prophet Joseph Smith himself. According to one of its members, John D. Lee, this council was "the Municipal department of the Kingdom of God set up on the Earth, and from which all Law emanates, for the rule, government & controle of all . . . People under the whole Heavens." The basic law of this world-government, received through revelation, resembled the constitution of the United States. Since the world was not yet ready for this Council, which included non-members also, it operated primarily as a counseling body for Joseph and later Brigham Young in planning the exodus and settlement of Utah.

One of the most often asked questions by visitors to Nauvoo is "Why were the Latter-day Saints treated with such hostility in Illinois and again driven from a state with little regard for their constitutional rights?"

There was no single reason, but a combination of numerous factors:

- Religious intolerance
- Block voting
- Economic competition
- Destruction of Expositor
- Fear of Nauvoo Legion
- Criminal element of mobs
- Practice of Plural Marriage
- Nauvoo Charter resentment
- Joseph's Presidential candidacy,
- Perceived past reputation
- Apostate betrayal
- Masonic activities
- Weak state governor
- National acceptance of mob violence
- Jacksonian Democracy

In regard to "lack of constitutional rights," this was a period of Jacksonian Democracy, in which most Americans believed that majority opinion prevailed over any law or constitution. Calvin Warren, attorney for the defendants in the assassination trial that followed the killing of the Smith brothers, summed up such beliefs when he told the jury that if the killers were guilty, then so was he, since "it was public opinion that the Smiths ought to be killed and public opinion made the laws."

A major contributing factor one cannot ignore is the lawlessness of the Illinois frontier. This era was one of the most violence-prone in American history, and Illinois was one of the most lawless states. Governor Ford, in his *History of Illinois* written in the 1840s, deals at length with the "mobocratic spirit" in Illinois, admitting it was a major factor that contributed to the Saints' troubles.

We hear of most of the public buildings in Nauvoo being turned into wagon shops in the winter of 1845–46, preparing for the exodus. How many wagons were needed?

There appears to be no definitive answer to this question. The numbers in various sources differ considerably. According to John Taylor, writing in the *Millennial Star* on November 15, 1846, the exodus consisted of 15,000 Saints, 3,000 wagons, and 30,000 head of cattle plus horses, mules, and sheep. Roberts, in the *Comprehensive History of the Church* (2:536), states that "before spring, more than twelve thousand wagons were in readiness." This last figure may have been a misprint in which the figure meant people. Although Taylor's figure of 30,000 head of cattle seems an exaggeration, his figure for the wagons is pretty close to what is the most common figure of 3,500. On November 23, 1845, Brigham Young noted that as of that date, 3,400 wagons were either on hand or started. By spring, we might easily add another 500 or 600 wagons. These figures are also in keeping with the number of families who left Nauvoo for the West. In a letter Irene Pomeroy wrote in October 1845, she described the leaders' plans for the exodus: "They have the arrangements made—we are going in companies of 100 families each, the companies half a mile apart, the wagons two rods apart. They make calculation for 2,500 families." Since many of the families had more than one wagon, the figures of 3,500 to 4,000 wagons sound accurate.

Few writers mention one subject in particular when discussing travel across the prairies or camping at night. What was the procedure when there were no "public restrooms"?

The Saints adopted the rule common to many early travelers: "Gents to the right and ladies to the left." Small trenches were dug far from camp and each person was responsible for burying his or her own waste.

We know what the Church leaders recommended for the trip west, but do we have any detailed descriptions of what a typical wagon looked like or contained?

Perhaps the best description is in a letter by that prolific Nauvoo letter writer, Irene Pomeroy, dated September 19, 1846:

> We started from Nauvoo May 30. We had as good a wagon as any, three yoke oxen, with flour enough for one year, ham, sausages, dry fish, lard—two cans, 100 pounds each of it, sugar, 16 lbs. coffee, 10 lbs. raisins, rice with all the other items for cooking. The bed is long enough for both our beds. They are made on flour barrels, chests and other things. Our wagon is painted red and has 8 bows that are 18 inches apart, a hen coop on the end has four hens. We had 2 webs of thick drilling and put on one cover of that, 3 breadths of stout sheeting over that, and then painted it. The heaviest showers and storms do not beat through, only a few drops now and then. Our tent is made of drilling 16 breadths in a shape of an umbrella. A cord 3 foot long on end of each seam and a pin on that to drive into the ground. The pole in the middle holds it up.

One of the Mormons' most able defenders in their final years in Nauvoo was Sheriff Jacob Backenstos, who repeatedly risked his life defending the Saints. What happened to him after the Saints left?

With the Mormons gone, Hancock County was not a safe place for him, and he joined the army as captain of a rifle company. Fighting in the war against Mexico, he quickly moved up in rank to lieutenant colonel for gallant conduct in the battle of Chapultepec. He later moved to Oregon, resigned his command, and amassed considerable wealth in private business. After some problems with a neighbor, however, he became chronically depressed. After intimating to his wife that he might take his own life, he did just that on the night of September 26, 1857, as units of the U.S. Army were en route to do battle with the Saints in Utah. One must wonder, as Backenstos threw himself into the Willamette River that night, if thoughts of the army in which he once fought going against the old friends for which he once fought had anything to do with his depression.

How many Saints left Nauvoo for the West?

Initially, 3,000 Saints left hastily in February. The majority of the Saints, approximately 9,000 souls, crossed into Iowa from March through June, leaving primarily those too old, too sick, or without the means of travel behind in Nauvoo. A few who elected to stay behind for awhile, and who were for whatever reason left alone by the mob-militia, possibly chose to stay because they had connections with the non-Mormons, or they had not been conspicuous in their Church membership.

Those unable to resist the mobs were driven from the city in September, immediately after the "Battle of Nauvoo," which involved several days of skirmishing from September 10 to 17, with the fiercest fighting taking place on Saturday, September 12, the same day the Prophet's widow, fearing for the safety of her family, left the city. A committee from Quincy mediated a peace with provisions for the Saints' orderly withdrawal. The mob, well-armed and numbering several hundred, however, had other ideas. Ignoring the peace provisions, they forcibly evicted the remaining poor, sick, and disabled from their homes and sent across the river with little more than the clothes on their backs on one of the blackest days in Illinois history—September 17, 1846.

Camping out on the Iowa shore, this group became known as the Poor Camp.

Nauvoo Expositor

Where was the *Nauvoo Expositor* press located?

The building, which no longer exists, was located on the north side of Mulholland Street, between Bluff and Page Streets.

Was there any legal justification for the destruction of the *Nauvoo Expositor*?

Blackstone, one of the most eminent English barristers, whose works were considered standard among American lawyers, declared that the publications of a libelous press may be considered a nuisance; and Nauvoo's own charter, provided by the legislature of the state of Illinois, gave the Saints the power to remove nuisances. By ordering that press abated as a nuisance, the Nauvooans concluded they were acting strictly in accordance with law. Scholars have concluded, however, that Blackstone was referring to the publications, not the press itself, as the "nuisance."

The destruction of other presses during that era, especially emancipation presses like Elijah Lovejoy's and even that editor's death at the hands of Illinois mobs in 1838, was considered justifiable by most of the same people who considered the destruction of a nuisance press by the Saints sufficient reason for the assassination of their leaders.

* *

Didn't Joseph or his advisors anticipate the consequences of their destruction of the *Nauvoo Expositor*?

Not comprehending that the anti-Mormons and even more moderate citizens would make a distinction between the destruction of a press by enraged mobs and one destroyed by the actions of an official government body, Joseph and his advisors apparently did not anticipate the consequences. In hindsight, merely destroying the offending papers rather than the entire press would have been more justifiable. One could say his instincts failed him, but it's hard to argue that the destruction and ensuing arrests weren't part of God's plan.

One of the publishers of the *Expositor* was R. D. Foster. Is it true that the women of Nauvoo drove him out of town after the martyrdom?

Yes. According to Mary Ann Young, the wives of Hyrum Smith and John Taylor, who had suffered so much from the actions of men like Foster, plus the wives of Arthur Milliken (Joseph's sister Lucy) and W. W. Phelps were incensed that one of the men responsible for the Carthage assassinations was still living in Nauvoo. They visited Foster and warned him that if he didn't leave town immediately, they would return the next day with a stronger force. He left that night.

Was the *Nauvoo Expositor* destroyed because its editors denied the Book of Mormon or the prophetic calling of Joseph Smith?

Absolutely not! The front page of one issue of the *Nauvoo Expositor* indicates this fact: "We all verily believe, and many of us know of a surety, that the religion of the Latter Day Saints, as originally taught by Joseph Smith, which is contained in the Old and New Testaments, Book of Covenants, and Book of Mormon is verily true." However, several of those involved in the publication of the paper had been excommunicated or condemned for their own indiscretions and whoredoms. In retaliation, they accused Joseph and the other leaders of the same things of which they were guilty. The paper was destroyed as a "public nuisance" for stating it was "seeking to

* *

explode the vicious principles of Joseph Smith and those who practice the same abominations and whoredoms." Such inflammatory rhetoric could have destroyed the peace of Nauvoo and would have likely encouraged the widespread mob action already at work.

Who made the final decision to destroy the offending newspaper?

After nearly fifteen hours of deliberation, the Prophet Joseph, in his capacity as mayor, gave the order. The city council, relying on what they considered powers contained in the charter and in the legislative powers of the city council, sustained the Prophet and declared the *Expositor* a nuisance and ordered its abatement, which the city marshal, the police, and members of the Nauvoo Legion carried out.

Farming

Are oxen a special breed of cattle?

Any neutered adult male of the bovine family can be called an ox. Today, they are merely beef animals, but during the Nauvoo era they were oxen.

What advantages, if any, did oxen have over horses?

There are several advantages:

- Once trained, they were generally more docile, gentle, and easily guided by a child.
- They were more patient than horses.
- They were less susceptible to disease.
- Unlike horses, they could survive on coarse hay, straw, and husks in the winter.
- If necessary, they could travel several hundred miles without being shod.
- They moved more slowly, but had greater power in starting heavy loads.
- They were cheaper to purchase and much cheaper to harness.
- Native Americans were less likely to steal them.
- They could always be eaten as a last resort.

* *

How many Nauvoo residents, like the Prophet Joseph, had farms on the outskirts of town?

This was an era in which over 80 percent of the American people lived on farms. It was not strange, therefore, that many of Nauvoo's residents felt a strong kinship to the land and wanted farms as security. An estimated one-third of all Nauvooans had farms on the outskirts of the city, including Joseph and Hyrum. In the fall of 1845, as the Quorum of Twelve was negotiating with Illinois authorities for their spring removal, they reminded the officials they had "some hundreds of farms" they needed help in selling. As it turned out, a large majority of these farms had to be simply abandoned.

What kind of fencing did the Mormon pioneers erect, especially on the prairies, where there was little wood for rails?

Near the river, where trees were plentiful, rail fences like those found in the eastern United States were common. On the prairies, farmers made use of their most plentiful resource—sod. A non-Mormon visitor to Nauvoo in 1843 described crossing the prairie a few miles east of Nauvoo. His impressions, recorded in the *Nauvoo Neighbor* in September of that year, mention crossing a prairie about fifteen miles wide, "and as we passed on either hand, showed the work of industry and art. Miles of land are made secure from cattle &c. by means of a handsome ditch and sod fence."

What major crops did Mormon farmers grow?

In 1845, special notice was made of a harvest feast on the community farm known as the Big Field. At that time, an estimated 30,000 bushels of corn waited to be harvested in the field. Corn was probably one of the most important crops in Illinois—as it still is today. Other major crops were wheat, oats, rye, and potatoes. Corn, incidentally, was selling for 20 cents a bushel, so a $6,000 corn harvest on the community farm was an imposing amount to add to Nauvoo's economy. Hemp for Nauvoo ropewalks (rope making facilities) was also a profitable crop.

* *

* *

It has been mentioned that a ropewalk may again be restored by the NRI. Isn't the growing of hemp, which was used in Nauvoo for rope making, illegal?

It is illegal—hemp is more commonly known as marijuana. Many countries legally grow an industrial variety of hemp for cordage, but it is not permitted in the United States without special permission. If permission cannot be obtained for growing hemp in Nauvoo, other fibrous plants such as flax could be used but would not be as authentic or as easily worked.

The Saints were trying desperately for self-sufficiency in food. Did they achieve it?

Since many families left Nauvoo for the west without enough food, we can see that they obviously did not become self-sufficient. We must remember, however, that in the final harvest year of 1845, the mobs destroyed hundreds of acres of crops or otherwise prevented the Saints from harvesting them. The Saints were doing well enough, however, that they were selling food products outside of Nauvoo. On November 4, 1843, Warren Foote wrote in his journal, "Franklin and I took some wheat to Quincy, (which we had taken in for chairs) to sell. We could only get fifty cents per bushel for it in goods."

If the Saints had been allowed to live in peace, there seems little doubt that Nauvoo, with its surrounding Mormon farm communities, would have been self-sufficient by the fall of 1846 or 1847.

What was the "Big Field" mentioned in Nauvoo journals and the Church History?

It was an agricultural cooperative that farmed 3,840 acres of land about six miles southeast of Nauvoo. It provided work and food for those who couldn't afford their own farms or had no means of making a living otherwise. In 1845, this association harvested 60,000 bushels of wheat and corn in addition to other grains and vegetables. In September of that year, the inhabitants of the Eleventh Ward and the members of the association

* *

provided a public outdoor feast at the Big Field in which 616 adults sat down to the tables. Joseph gave a talk to the group and advised them to store their grain in the city. John Taylor remarked of the occasion, "It is a fine thing for the bishops of the several wards to remember the poor."

What was the value of farmlands around Nauvoo in the 1840s?

According to John Taylor (in a letter to the Saints in England published in the *Millennial Star*), farmland on the city's outskirts when the Saints first arrived was $1.25 to $5.00 per acre. John Needham, an English immigrant, wrote a letter to his parents back in England in 1843, in which he detailed the prices of land at that time. He said he was offered a house and 80 acres of fenced and cultivated land for £160, which would have been approximately $400, or he could buy 40 acres at 30s ($3.75) per acre. Uncultivated land varied from 8s to 20s per acre ($1.00 to $2.50) depending on "the situation and title." He mentioned land in the city for as high as £200 an acre ($500) but other city property for as low as $25 an acre.

Did Joseph actually work his farm?

Yes. William Holmes Walker lived as a member of Joseph's family in Nauvoo for three years. He said, "I went into the hayfield with him, and he assisted in mowing grass with a scythe, many a day, putting in ten hours good hard work." John Murdock worked for Joseph on his farm for four years, and a brother, Cornelius Lott, occupied the farm home and looked after things on the farm.

Food and Drink

Did Nauvoo housewives "can" or otherwise process food?

The most common methods of preserving fruits and vegetables were by drying, pickling, or making them into preserves. Meat was preserved primarily by smoking, salting down, or drying. The Saints were canning by this time—mostly fruit. The fruit was bottled or jarred, with corks stuck lightly in them. They were then placed upright in a pan of water and heated but not to boiling. After half an hour, the jars were removed, filled to within an inch of the top with boiling water, and then the corks were replaced tightly. Wax could then be placed around the cork, but it wasn't necessary. The bottles were then placed on their sides to keep the corks from drying out and turned on occasion to prevent fermentation and mold.

Coffee and tea were discouraged as drinks. What were the common drinks?

The Saints drank cider, beer, fruit wines, water, and even combinations such as "switchel." Believe it or not, a historian once said, "Americans discovered drinking water." Their ancestors, often with good reason, considered water a dangerous drink. After awhile, water in the New World, however, was discovered to be far less contaminated than in England or Europe and quite refreshing. It took some time to overcome

* *

the habits of exclusively drinking beer, grog, wine, and so forth, but by the time of Nauvoo, water was not an uncommon drink. Shallow well water, contaminated by privies, stables, and so on, was without doubt a major factor in the high incidence of diarrhea and childhood deaths. Old habits are hard to break, and beer was often considered a healthy adult drink; compared with contaminated well water, it probably was.

With the abundance of wild fruits, game, and fish mentioned in the accounts of early travelers in this region, why do LDS diaries so often mention a shortage of food in Nauvooan homes?

There were three main reasons. First, as the population concentrated in the city, they removed wild fruits and edible plant life to make room for the homes, gardens, roads, and such, and either killed off or chased away the wildlife, which happens in any densely settled region. Second, even before these things happened, most of the Saints were not experienced in gathering or hunting. The Saints, for the most part, were not frontiersmen, but farmers and craftsmen from the East or immigrants from the British Isles. And third, with so many men—the traditional food providers—away on missions or church assignments, families left behind faced difficulties in obtaining even what was plentiful in the area.

Did Nauvoo housewives use cookbooks?

The first American cookbook, *American Cookery* by Amelia Simmons, was published back in 1796, so cookbooks were available. Most Nauvoo homemakers, however, depended on tradition, memory, or collections of "receipts," as they were once called, passed down from mother to daughter. Most authorities on cooking in the 1840s agree there was a lack of variety, an overabundance of meat, and a scarcity of fresh fruits and vegetables for obvious reasons. Also, foreign travelers criticized American housewives for excessive seasoning, little variety of sauces, but especially for the ever-present "bread often doughy and smoking hot."

* *

* *

Were all the deaths in Nauvoo the result of disease or accidents, or is it likely that food contamination played a role?

There is little doubt that throughout the country in the 1840s, improperly prepared and contaminated food played a role in the high fatality rate. Lack of refrigeration, the absence of screens to keep disease-bearing flies out of homes and kitchens, and lack of knowledge about sanitation in cooking and cleaning would have caused a food bacterial content that would give fits to any modern-day public health official. Children had to quickly develop immunity to such microorganisms, or as contemporary death records indicate, they would die young of "summer complaint," "diarrhea," or "bowel consumption."

Add to these sanitation problems the shortages of fresh fruits and year-around vegetables for a more balanced diet and you have an increase in the mortality rate. However, lack of medical knowledge prevents us from knowing in most cases when such elements combined to cause premature death. Logic would certainly make us conclude food contamination was a major factor, however.

What would have been a typical breakfast in Nauvoo?

Actually, breakfast for most Americans differed little from the other two meals of the day. Remember that the early years in Nauvoo were difficult for the impoverished Saints, and they would prepare whatever was available. However, as times improved, they tended to prepare and eat the same types of meals as their fellow Americans, which meant every meal consisted of a variety of meats, fried potatoes, hot buttered breads, and, when affordable, desserts—even for breakfast. One of the few foods that might have been classified as "breakfast food" were griddle cakes, usually made of Indian meal (corn meal) or buckwheat.

* *

The Groves

Were boweries ever constructed in Nauvoo as they were in Salt Lake City?

Boweries would have been most unlikely in view of the fact that outdoor meetings were held in three different groves, depending on the weather conditions. A bowery, when mentioned in the early 1800s, referred merely to a shady place, such as a grove. A bowery was constructed later in Salt Lake City, so many people assume such a meeting edifice was built in Nauvoo. The Prophet Joseph, who used the words "stand" or "grove" for the outdoor meeting place on more than a hundred occasions, never used the word "bowery."

Where were the groves (outdoor meeting places) located?

The West Grove, the most popular outdoor meeting place, was located immediately west of the temple, where the Joseph Smith Academy is now located. This is where Joseph gave the famous King Follett Discourse on April 7, 1844. Edward Stevenson, who attended that day and called it a "grand funeral sermon," described his surroundings: "The weather was lovely and the surrounding river and the Iowa side with its sloping hills looks lovely."

Members held meetings in two other grove locations: one in a hollow immediately south of the temple and the other, referred to as the East Grove, in a hollow about four blocks east of the temple, near the corner

* *

of Robinson and Young Streets. Which ones were used depended upon weather conditions.

Were there any particular seating arrangements in the Groves?

There seemed to be, but they were not consistently followed or enforced. In the October 1841 Conference, according to the minutes, "the several quorums were arranged and seated in order." Ann Pitchforth, in a letter to relatives back in England, described a General Conference: "It was a fine sight. In the center the Twelve Apostles, then the women with hundreds of parasols, then the men. On the outside were the carriages and the horses." Concerning a meeting in the Grove in September 1843, Joseph Smith recorded, "After preaching, I gave some instructions about order in the congregation, men among women, and women among men, horses in the assembly, and men and boys on the stand who do not belong there, &c." (see *History of the Church* 6:34).

How were the speakers heard if the crowds consisted of thousands of people?

Many of the crowd estimates found in newspaper reports and journals were exaggerations. It was fairly common in the nineteenth century to report the size of gatherings anticipated, not the actual attendance. It was a "language of exaggeration," the noted historian Daniel Boorstin explains in his book *The Americans: The National Experience*. The *History of the Church* describes the attendance at the funeral sermon of King Follett as 20,000, another obvious exaggeration. The more reasonable attendance was probably no more than half that number.

Even so, crowds were much larger than speakers would be comfortable speaking to today without electronic amplification. Contemporary reports mention the difficulty many in the audience, especially on the fringes of the crowds, had of hearing the speaker. Furthermore, outdoor speakers did not speak: they yelled. Diaries of that era mention speakers practicing by yelling out talks in secluded places. Joseph would do this along the river early in the morning with a schoolteacher friend. Journals also mention

* *

public speakers being unable to speak above a whisper the day following a lengthy discourse.

Were the Groves still used after the temple was far enough along for members to hold meetings in it?

Although most Church history sources record the first meeting in the temple as being the October 1845 General Conference, this assertion is not technically true. Joseph started preaching in the temple as soon as the first floor was complete enough to hold a congregation. On January 1, 1843, Joseph recorded in his journal, "I preached at the temple on the setting up of the kingdom of God" (see *History of the Church* 5:256). However, since the Assembly Hall was not designed to hold more than 5,000, the Church continued to hold meetings in the Groves until shortly before the exodus.

Were the Groves used year round?

The Saints used the Groves whenever weather permitted. Because of the cold Illinois winters, they seldom met in the Groves in the coldest months, preferring then to meet in several public buildings or homes, including the Prophet's. As could be expected when this occurred, Joseph's home would be so crowded that the windows would be opened and the overflow would stand in the yard to hear their Prophet. When meetings were scattered about the city, the Church authorities would split up and conduct the separate meetings.

Journals often record that members from across the river or on the outskirts of the city would arrive for the normal 10 o'clock meeting, but if the weather was uncertain, they would never know where to meet. If the meeting was held in the Grove, they might attend any other meeting since members did not meet as wards.

Homes and Construction

Was the mortar used in the brick homes of Nauvoo similar to what we use today?

Modern mortar uses Portland cement, discovered in England in 1824. Portland cement plants were not established in the United States, however, until after the Civil War. The mortar used in Nauvoo, therefore, was merely lime mixed with a sand aggregate and water. Much weaker and less stable than modern mortar, lime mortar sufficed, however, due to the thickness of the brick walls.

Where did the Nauvoo builders get the lime they used in their mortar, plaster, and whitewash?

Nauvoo had lime kilns, most of which were located at the upper end of Main Street near the Quarry and the river. Another stood several blocks east of the temple on Brigham Street, one quarter mile north of Young Street.

How did they turn limestone into lime?

When limestone is heated in a kiln, carbon dioxide is driven off. The result is quicklime or lumplime. When added to water, it produces hydrated or slaked lime. When the resulting calcium oxide (slaked lime) is mixed with water for whitewash or plaster and allowed to dry, it will absorb carbon dioxide from the air and return to its limestone hardness but in a different form.

Why did the brick homes have so many reinforcing rods, as indicated by the star washers?

Even though the brick walls were thicker than the modern veneer brick on homes today, the walls would weaken over time because of the inferiority of the mortar and bow out unless strengthened with reinforcing rods.

Was concrete ever used in Nauvoo?

The art of making cement was known in the ancient world but lost after the fall of the Roman Empire. This so-called Roman, or hydraulic, cement was not rediscovered until the eighteenth century, but was still inferior to what we know as Portland cement. American builders were still using Roman cement, which differed from the Nauvoo mortar in that it contained silica. Because it required material and equipment not available in Nauvoo, however, little evidence suggests the Saints used it.

Was the Parley P. Pratt home and store (across from the Joseph Smith Academy dormitories) as large as its present size indicates?

No. Because of the change in appearance from earlier pictures, some historians believe the present building was built on some of the original foundation. Your author believes, however, that the present building on the corner of Young and Wells Streets, has merely undergone extensive remodeling, including an added-on east wing. The roof has also been changed, windows changed and added, and possibly faced with a newer brick.

This store, incidentally, was the location of the tithing office, starting in December 1844.

Why did the Saints continue to work on their homes and plant trees when they knew they were abandoning their city?

Some Saints might have believed, which is human nature, that the exodus

✳ ✳

might somehow not occur. In other cases, continuing home improvement was a matter of pride—that those who came after them, enemies or not, might think more highly of them. Unlike many throughout history who conduct a scorched-earth policy when they must abandon their homes to an enemy, the Saints apparently considered their "city of Joseph" too beautiful and too sacred to be laid waste. And, of course, some must have believed that when their enemies were overcome, the Saints would return to their beloved city.

It is possible that Parley P. Pratt foresaw the restoration of Nauvoo, when, in the October conference in 1845, he told the Saints, "We do not want to leave a desolate place, to be a reproach to us, but something that will be a monument to those who may visit the place of our industry, diligence and virtue." These words appear to be no less than a fulfilled prophesy of Nauvoo today.

Were most homes painted on the exterior and, if so, what kind of paint was used? How was it made?

Paint used on any wood surfaces other than logs was made by the painter. Ready-mixed paints did not appear until after the Civil War. The base of most good paints, including that used on the oak and pine interiors, was ceruse, or white lead colored with pigments. An economical exterior white house paint was made of skim milk, slaked lime, linseed oil, and Spanish white (a white earth from Spain). The variety of pigments added to give the paint the desired color would require the knowledge of a chemist—a knowledge now lost to most house painters—but it included such strange names as realgar, Montpellier yellow, ochre de Berrie, Saxon blue, and so forth. The resulting paint was generally quite good, long lasting, but seldom bright.

If there were so few homes in Commerce when the Saints arrived, how do we account for the need for a store like Hiram Kimball's?

The *History of the Church* identifies a total of ten buildings in the vicinity of Commerce. This number conflicts somewhat with a report by two elders

✳ ✳

who were checking out the opportunities for settlement in that area in January of 1839. They reported about forty empty dwellings in upper and lower Commerce. Both references are to those homes along the river where the Saints first settled.

The Amos Davis Store, which was operating across from the temple site when the Saints arrived in 1839, left a daybook that shows ninety-five heads of families having accounts in his store. Apparently, many farms operated on the prairie east of Nauvoo. The description of the tangled, forested land along the river does not apply to the prairie land that was relatively open with passable roads and where dozens of families lived and took their produce into Commerce by way of the well-known Carthage road.

The northern part of Nauvoo has far fewer homes than the restoration area on the flats. Was it that way originally?

It was not as thickly clustered nor did it contain so many of the finer brick homes that were built on the flats, for two reasons. The more hilly terrain made the northern part of Nauvoo less desirable, and the area was farther removed from the center of commerce on lower Main Street and from the homes of the Prophet and other leading authorities. It thus attracted a poorer class that built less substantial homes that have not lasted or were not desired by the "new citizens." Consequently, more of these were abandoned and allowed to deteriorate.

Why were homes in Nauvoo built so close to the street with little or no front lawns?

Lawns mean mowing and upkeep, and lawn mowers had not yet been invented. The city was designed with self-sufficiency in mind, which meant reserving as much space as possible for gardens, orchards, and animal enclosures. And, finally, it was the custom. A drive through many cities of that era in the eastern part of the country will illustrate the custom of building homes close to the streets.

* *

Homes catching fire in Nauvoo is seldom mentioned. With open fire-places and flueless chimneys, weren't house fires a danger?

The danger was there, but mention of fires was not. First, the homes were mostly new, and fires were more likely to occur in deteriorated chimneys of older homes. Second, the local paper would not report such fires, since being a weekly, the news would be old. That is why one finds little local "news" in weekly newspapers of that era. Third, Nauvoo had strict laws on the care of chimneys and fireplaces, and wardens visited homes to make sure the owners complied. And last, people were very conscious of the danger of fires. The *Nauvoo Neighbor* carried numerous stories of major fires in cities throughout the country, perhaps more so than many papers, making the readers especially conscious of the dangers.

The reconstructed cabins in Nauvoo look quite well made. Are they typical of the original cabins?

Not really. These present cabins were made under better conditions with better tools and better materials. Totally inexperienced home builders, who were pressed to get their families under shelter, most often built cabins under the most primitive conditions. Descriptions from early journals mention dirt floors, leaking roofs, smoking fireplaces, and unchinked walls. Charlotte Haven, a visitor who lived in Nauvoo for a year, described some of the homes as "mere shelters, many built of logs placed cob fashion, some of only one thickness of boards, and others of sod or mud, with seldom any plastering or floors, and minus chimneys, doors, and windows." True, better homes would eventually replace them, but reconstruction of some of the earliest shelters, although more authentically interesting, would undoubtedly be too embarrassing for modern restorers to admit to having reconstructed.

How were log chimneys kept from catching on fire?

NRI has reconstructed a log cabin on Kimball Street with a log chimney similar to some of the earliest cabins built in Nauvoo. To make them

* *

fireproof, they were plastered with mud or mortar. In normal usage, this would suffice for only a short time before cracking, falling away, and becoming a fire hazard. In Nauvoo, however, such homes were normally replaced within a short time by better homes, or at least with brick or stone chimneys. Part of the Nauvoo City Charter provided for the City Council to "regulate the fixing of chimneys, and the flues thereof, and stoves pipes."

How was window glass made in the 1840s, and is any of the glass in Nauvoo today original?

As strange as it sounds, window glass was blown. It started with a large globule that was then opened and spun by the glass blower into a circular flat sheet. When cooled, the glazier would then cut the sheet into various sizes. The first glass factory of importance using this method was the Boston Crown Glass Company, which started manufacturing in 1792. Today, similar glass, with its imperfections, must be imported from Germany. Because it is so close to the original, it is difficult to tell the original from the reproduced, but one could still find some of the original glass in Nauvoo.

Boards for homes such as the Whitney home are produced today by circular or band saws. Were they produced the same way in the 1840s?

Circular saws were known but did not come into use in Nauvoo or its surrounding region until after the exodus. Band saws are even more recent. The early sawmills operated by the Mormons along the river in Nauvoo and in the Pineries in Wisconsin used up-and-down half-inch-thick saw blades operated by offset shafts attached to water wheels. These were called "gate" saws, which operated at about eighty strokes per minute, and when set in gang fashion with more than one blade, could cut 4,000 to 5,000 board feet per day. In the Pineries alone, the Saints had four gate saws going at once, supplied by five lumbering camps.

Saw mills along the river in Nauvoo were needed to cut the logs brought down from Wisconsin and for the logs cut locally. Such mills,

* *

utilizing wing dams built out into the river, were located along the aptly named Lumber Street.

Were kerosene lamps used in Nauvoo?

No. The process for obtaining kerosene from bituminous shale and cannel coal for illuminating purposes did not occur until Dr. Abraham Gesner discovered the process in 1854. Lamps designed to use kerosene did not come about until the 1860s. In Nauvoo, the most common "lamps" used lard oil. Although whale-oil lamps were better, whale oil was not as easily acquired on the frontier.

Was coal ever used as fuel in Old Nauvoo?

Yes. Advertisements in the *Nauvoo Neighbor* soliciting coal indicate its use in businesses and homes in Nauvoo. Eventually, the Church opened a coal mine on the Rock River about 100 miles north of Nauvoo, where it acquired much of its coal. In April 1845, as the Church began closing some of its operations, Brigham Young recorded in the *History of the Church*, "We agreed to advise Peter Maughan and Jacob Peart to return from Rock River whither they had been to work a coal mine."

It is of interest to note that coal was available right in Nauvoo. Opposite the temple site on Mulholland is a depression that was a pit where the Icarians dug coal.

Some historic buildings in Nauvoo have short rods protruding from the ceilings. Are they historic?

These rods were originally installed as part of an NRI security system that sent notice of intrusion to a central office. The system is no longer used.

During the Nauvoo era, a Philadelphia newspaper listed twenty utensils as necessities for a homemaker. What were some of these?

Almost all of them were made of wood and included such items as boards

* *

* *

for kneading bread, slicing bread, and chopping meat; a rolling pin; large wooden spoons; a potato pounder; a lemon squeezer; a mush stick; a washboard; three buckets for sugar; two large tubs; and a small tub for mixing bread dough.

What was the first house the Saints built when they arrived in Commerce? Where was it built and who built it?

On June 11, 1839, Joseph reported, "Elder Theodore Turley raised the first house built by the saints in this place; it was built of logs, about 25 or 30 rods north northeast of my dwelling on the northeast corner of lot 4 block 147 of the White purchase." This would have been between the Mansion House and the Community of Christ Visitor Center, in from Water Street on the west side of Hyde Street, directly south of the Hiram Clark home.

Turley had a shop in Nauvoo where he worked as a clockmaker and gunsmith. Because of his knowledge of guns, he was assigned to help rearm the Nauvoo Legion after the state authorities disarmed it in June 1844. Carrying out his assignment, he was able to purchase a hundred muskets for the Nauvoo Legion in New Orleans. Turley died in the faith in Beaver, Utah, in 1872.

A private home sits on the west side of Durphy Street, opposite the entrance to the State Park. Is this an historic Mormon home?

Yes. George A. Smith, who took over as counselor to Brigham Young after the death of Heber C. Kimball, owned it. St. George, Utah, was named in his honor because of the affection of the people over whom he presided in that part of Utah. George A. Smith's father, John Smith, was the patriarch of the Church. He lived in a room in the home where he gave Patriarchal blessings.

What is the "Widows' Row" sometimes mentioned?

Widows' Row was a long single-story brick building, containing ten comfortable rooms near the southeast corner of Main and Kimball Streets.

* *

* *

It was a tenement owned by a widow, whose tenants were preferably widows, hence its name. Each apartment had a door opening into a garden and was furnished with two windows and a fireplace.

The reconstructed log cabins are made of pine. What about the original log and block cabins?

The first settlers made their cabins out of whatever trees they found locally, including black walnut, yellow poplar, cottonwood, oak, and hickory. Since such trees were limited to narrow strips near the river, they were soon used up. Within a short time, however, the Saints had lumber rafts arriving from their lumber camps in the Pineries along the Black River in Wisconsin. As the name pinery implies, most of these rafts were made up of pine logs or pine lumber. Most of the cabins and blockhouses made in the final years of Nauvoo, therefore, were of pine.

Why does the Winslow Farr home have two front doors?

It was a duplex, with each apartment having one room on the first floor and another on the second. Each first floor room had a steep, twisting stairway that led from the north side of the room to the second floor. Beneath this stairway was a doorway connecting the two apartments. Winslow Farr's son, Lorin, became known for his numerous industrial and construction projects throughout the inter-mountain region. His son, Winslow, pioneered Arizona, and Winslow, Arizona, was named after him. Their daughter, Diantha, married William Clayton, remembered for his pioneer song, "Come, Come, Ye Saints."

Are the stepped gables designed for a practical purpose or are they merely a form of architecture brought from another part of the country?

Much of the architecture of Nauvoo reflects the tastes of the builders for the styles in the area of the country they came from or that appealed to them. This tendency is noted especially in the brick gable ends of such buildings as the Brigham Young home and the Printing complex on Main Street,

* *

which both show the New York Dutch influence. The other main type is the sloping-stepped gable found in the Seventies Hall and the Clark Store opposite the temple site, which reflect the Virginia Federalist style. Some observers have noted that these styles were designed to lessen chimney fire danger, but the evidence for this assertion seems scanty in view of the fact that in later years, many of these stepped gables were removed.

Why did later owners remove the gables of many of these Nauvoo homes?

Roofs on such homes have a tendency to leak more easily when the shingles are butted against the brick ends. By removing the brick gables, the roofing can be carried out over the edge, and there is no concern with sealing where the roof and the stepped gables meet. If you look carefully at the Print Shop, for example, you can see where the stepped gables have been restored.

Was ice cut, stored, and used for food preservation in Old Nauvoo?

Before Nauvoo, use of ice for food preservation was found only among the more affluent who could afford the construction of what were known as ice houses, which were both expensive and impractical in Nauvoo. Ice boxes for home use were just being introduced when Nauvoo was founded. In spite of easy access to river ice, we find no evidence of any ice industry in Nauvoo. River ice was cut years later, however, in such nearby river towns as Ft. Madison.

Because of the lack of such refrigeration for foods, most meats were dried, smoked, or salted down, and most milk was made into cheese. When cooling was desired for short periods of time for easily contaminated foods, people might lower such foods into the well or merely place them on the "cellar bottom."

Most wells look like they had buckets for drawing water. Did any wells in Nauvoo have pumps?

Most wells did have buckets and windlasses. Pumps, although they existed,

* *

were more complex and expensive and would freeze more easily in the winter. Pumps did exist in Nauvoo, however. When Joseph and Hyrum's bodies were removed from the Mansion House under the cover of night, they were reportedly taken "through the garden round by the pump, and were conveyed to the Nauvoo House." There is a pump in the backyard of the Heber C. Kimball home, but that is probably a post-expulsion addition.

Why did Joseph originally plan homes with full acre lots? Isn't that excessively large for a city lot?

There were two main reasons. First, planning a new city was an opportunity to provide the attractive spacious feeling that would be in keeping with the beauty of the gospel the Saints were teaching. Second, always with a mind for self-sufficiency, Joseph expected such lots would provide a livelihood for the owners. They would have plenty of room for large gardens as well as large and well-planned orchards. Unfortunately, with the city growing faster than even Joseph had anticipated and with the owners having free agency to subdivide their lots, the original plan was not followed.

What are those shallow, wooden, upside-down boxes on some of the Nauvoo home roofs?

One can see such boxes on the Farr and Yearsley homes. Called "scuttle" doors, they were designed to provide easy access to the roofs by way of "scuttle" stairs through the attics. In the days when wooden shingles could loosen and leak so easily and chimney fires were such a risk, fast and easy access to the roofs was essential.

Prairie sod was so deep and compact. Was it ever used for building sod homes during the Nauvoo era?

In 1843, Joseph gave some land at the Big Mound (seven miles east of Nauvoo) to John Marriott and Christopher Layton, immigrants from England. There the two men built a one-room sod house for their families.

* *

✳ ✳

Brother Layton later wrote, "When it was pared down it looked pretty well. The first winter we had quilts for doors; we had a dirt floor, and when the beds were made down they just about filled the room"

In 1843, David Nye White of the *Pittsburgh Weekly Gazette* visited Nauvoo for an article in his newspaper. He described both the city and its outlying areas: "Quite a number of the houses or huts in which the inhabitants on the prairies live, are also made of turf, and covered with clapboards." White didn't explain how the boards were attached.

Sod homes in Illinois likely didn't last nearly as long as they would have in the drier western states, but they were built and lived in—at least until better homes could be built.

✳ ✳

Kimball Home

Why does the temple print in the hallway of the Kimball Home show figures on the tower and a winged angel?

The print was made circa 1890 by a Mr. Murphy. It is merely an artist's conception made forty-two years after the temple's destruction by fire and is understandably inaccurate as were so many historical renderings of that period.

What is the significance of the indenture in the study?

This is a land contract for property on Block 121, which lies southeast of this property, across the highway, and is now part of the State Park. It is an authentic document of Old Nauvoo signed by such prominent figures as Joseph's attorney Almon Babbitt, but most interestingly, by Robert Smith, a Carthage official who illegally assigned Joseph and Hyrum to jail after their surrender in June 1844 on charges of treason. He was also captain of the Carthage Greys, the principal participants in the martyrdom.

Was the artist Frederick Piercy, who drew the artwork in the hall, a member of the Church?

Although Fawn Brodie, author of the infamous book *No Man Knows My History*, claimed Piercy was not a member of the Church, there is a record of his baptism in England. In 1853, at the age of twenty-three, this painter journeyed to Utah, making sketches and watercolor drawings along the way to illustrate an emigrant guide book, *Route from Liverpool to Great Salt Lake Valley.* This book is one of the earliest visual records we have showing the Mormon route. Several of those original paintings and drawings are in the Boston Museum of Fine Arts. Piercy later became alienated from the Church and was excommunicated in 1857, when he failed to come to Utah as Brigham Young requested.

Who made the engraving of the General Authorities just inside the front door?

This is also a Piercy engraving. Some have asked questions about the seniority arrangement, which shows Orson Hyde and the Pratt brothers ahead of John Taylor and Wilford Woodruff. Parley P. Pratt was assassinated, and his brother Orson and Orson Hyde were at one time briefly removed from the Quorum. When they returned, they were placed further down the list in seniority. Wilford Woodruff is shown ahead of John Taylor, which merely seems to be a mistake on the part of the engraver.

How did Heber C. Kimball make enough money to have a home like this when he spent so much of his time on missions for the Church?

Stanley Kimball, in an article in the summer 1975 issue of *BYU Studies*, states,

> The sources are obscure regarding how Kimball supported himself in Nauvoo. He had been working full time for the Church almost since his arrival in Kirtland in 1833. We know that his brick home in Nauvoo was built for him by the Church, or at least by its members. We also know, for example, that on 25 January 1845 Brigham Young gave him five pounds sterling ($25.00) and that he occasionally received money and provisions from the Church. There is evidence that he did some work as a potter in Nauvoo. . . . From comments in his correspondence with Vilate, and a few other sources, it is clear that Kimball also bought and sold some building sites in Nauvoo from which he may have derived some income.

Since Heber was an astute businessman, we might also assume that as a formerly successful potter, he might very well have had a pottery in operation, even when he was not present in Nauvoo. There was also good money in land speculation; he might have made more in that manner than Stanley Kimball implies.

Do we know which part of the Kimball home is the oldest?

After returning from his second mission to England, Heber built a large log home on the site of the present two-story west wing of this home. In 1843, he added a small brick wing to the east. In June 1845, he tore down the log portion on the west and built the larger two-story portion in its place. He finished it in November 1845, only a few months before the exodus. Unless, for some unexplained reason, the smaller east wing was later replaced, this current east wing would be the oldest portion of the house. Heber is unlikely to have razed a standing brick portion of his house, which was only two years old. A more feasible scenario is that later owners merely remodeled the older east wing.

If the Widow's Walk and the porches were not contemporary with Heber, why were they included with the restoration of his home?

When Dr. Leroy Kimball was restoring his ancestor's home, it was only to be a summer home for himself. Others had added the features, and apparently Dr. Kimball liked them. He did not feel the need to be so historically accurate since he intended to live in the home. He opened it to the public only after he discovered the interest it provoked when it was completed. Since it became NRI's first restoration, and the founder of NRI was the restorer, he decided to leave it as it is.

If the Kimball home was the catalyst for the organization of NRI, why was the Church buying up property in Nauvoo as early as the 1930s?

At the time Wilford Woodruff purchased the first property for the Church in Nauvoo, he and other far-sighted Church leaders recognized the value of preserving the historical legacy of the Church. The acquisition of early Church sites began in 1903 under the direction of President Joseph F. Smith, with the purchase of Carthage Jail. Further purchases of property in Nauvoo was merely the continuation of preserving historic Church property while it was still available, its utilization to be determined later.

We cannot give too much credit to citizens like Brother Wood who purchased historic properties with their own money and held them until the Church decided to acquire them for preservation purchases.

Who owned the Heber C. Kimball home before Dr. LeRoy Kimball bought it?

In 1954, according to Hancock County records, Dr. LeRoy Kimball bought Lot 3 on Block 106, which includes the Heber C. Kimball home, from an owner by the name of K. E. Jones.

King Follett Discourse

Why was the King Follett Discourse called a funeral sermon if it was not given at King Follett's funeral?

Joseph Smith spoke on genealogy and temple work on the day of the funeral. In that March 10 sermon, the Prophet stressed that the living cannot be saved without their dead, elaborating on the mission of Elijah. Less than a month later, however, the family of King Follett again prevailed upon the Prophet to speak in honor of their loved one. During this conference, on April 7, 1844, Joseph delivered what has become traditionally known as the King Follett Funeral Discourse. Often overlooked is a statement the Prophet made at the beginning of his talk: "I have been requested to speak by his [King Follett's] friends and relatives, but inasmuch as there are a great many in this congregation who . . . have lost friends, I feel disposed to speak on the subject in general" (HC 6:302).

Where was the King Follett Discourse given?

All contemporary references to this sermon mention it being given "in the grove," a term usually applied to the West Grove. Since the other two grove sites were used less often, records generally specify when they were used. For example, on June 16, nine days after the King Follett Discourse, Joseph gave a sermon on the Christian Godhead, and records specifically mentioned it took place in the grove east of the temple. It is also of interest to note that on April 6, the day before the discourse, the meeting, according to Joseph's journal, was in the East Grove. He says a "brisk" breeze was blowing that day, which would have encouraged the authorities to move that day's meeting to the West Grove. On the day of the discourse, he does not mention the breeze or the East Grove. Furthermore, an attendee, Edward Stevenson, recalled in his journal, "The weather was lovely and the surrounding river and the Iowa side with its sloping hills looks lovely." Such a view would be possible only from the West Grove.

Discourses like the one honoring King Follett were not written out or taped. How do we therefore have such complete records of them?

How complete they are is still unknown today, but we have reason to believe they are as accurate as we will ever be able to discern. For example, as Joseph spoke during the King Follett sermon, four of the most capable penmen in Nauvoo recorded his words. Thomas Bullock, as Joseph's personal clerk, and using some shorthand elements, wrote 3,990 words. William Clayton, another of Joseph's private secretaries, recorded 2,596 words. Willard Richards recorded a summary in Joseph's daily journal, and Wilford Woodruff recorded 2,486 words for his own personal journal. The current published version is a studied amalgamation using elements from all four scribes.

What major doctrines did the King Follett Discourse contain?

Actually, several of the significant doctrines had been revealed previously in bits and pieces, but in this great discourse, Joseph tied them all together. Some of the most significant of those were: Men can become gods, there is a plurality of gods, and God was once as man now is. Other doctrines he discussed were the nature of God, the co-eternal existence of man and God as intelligences, eternal progression, and the saving links between the living and their progenitors.

Do we know whether the Saints enthusiastically accepted or understood the doctrines in the King Follett Discourse?

* *

Of the thousands who heard the discourse, we have record of relatively few who recorded their impressions. And of those who, for the most part, were positive were the very ones who followed the leaders west and accepted the doctrines. We have few diaries or journals mentioning dissent or rejection of the doctrines in the discourse. Such potential writers simply left the Church, most of them not wishing to record or remember their experiences in the Church.

Joseph had a way of making doctrines understandable, but he was still continually complaining about the inability of his generation to understand the doctrines of the kingdom. "Getting anything into the heads of this generation," he said, was "like splitting hemlock knots with a corn-dodger for a wedge, and a pumpkin for a beetle." All in all, it was perhaps less a case of understanding than willingness to readily accept doctrines so different from "traditional" Christianity.

Why would Joseph deliver such important doctrines on the occasion of a service dedicated to the remembrance of a deceased friend?

First of all, the sermon was directed, in his mind, to all those who had lost family members and friends, not just to the memory of King Follett. Joseph knew his time was short and that the Lord still had much he wanted His people to more fully understand. The doctrines Joseph revealed, he knew, could be a comfort to not only the Folletts but to all those (and there were many in Nauvoo) who, after losing loved ones, wanted answers to their questions about eternal life.

If not for the Discourse, how well would King Follett be known among the Saints today?

His only other significant "claim to fame" in LDS history was his distinction as the last of the prisoners to be released from Missouri incarceration. This distinction and his friendship with Joseph would certainly not have been enough to give his name the veneration it carries in Mormon circles today.

* *

* *

To what extent did the King Follett Discourse encourage the apostasy of members such as the Law, Foster, and Higbee brothers?

Some who heard the King Follett Discourse were converts who had arrived in Nauvoo knowing only the first principles of the gospel and, of course, the Book of Mormon. The idea of the plurality of gods, potential Godhood, and other "mysteries," which Joseph taught in the King Follett Discourse, would have been blasphemous in the religions from which they came.

Prior to the spring of 1844, some of these members were showing dissatisfaction with Joseph and the new doctrines and apprehension over the rising tide of anti-Mormonism. Such leading figures as the Laws, the Fosters, and the Higbees, themselves at odds with Joseph and other Church leaders for personal as well as doctrinal reasons, took advantage of such growing public dissatisfaction to lead what they thought was a much larger group of dissenters than actually existed. Nevertheless, they were effective in generating even greater animosity among the anti-Mormons and were to a major extent responsible for the assassinations in the Carthage jail and the forced exodus of their former friends.

* *

Law and Order

Did Nauvoo have a jail?

During the Mormon occupation of Nauvoo, the nearest jail was in Carthage. Crimes in Nauvoo—seldom and minor—were settled in Church courts or Mayor's courts, in which the sentence was normally either restitution, work, or both.

In 1844, a visitor to Nauvoo, Edwin De Leon, reported that he had spent two weeks in Nauvoo, during which time he heard of no crime and saw no pauperism. He credited this fact to city law enforcement and to the Relief Society for helping control pauperism and immorality generally. If any serious crimes were to occur, the Hancock County authorities would handle them. It is interesting to note that after the Saints left and the Nauvoo population dropped to approximately one tenth of its original size, a jail was constructed in the basement of the Yearsley home in 1854.

Did Nauvoo have a paid police force?

Under the terms of the city charter, Nauvoo was permitted to establish a police force, which it did. As the city grew and external forces threatened, a city ordinance expanded the police force in December 1843 to forty policemen with various ranks. Although not mentioned, the pay was apparently rather meager. In 1844, Brigham Young, Heber

* *

C. Kimball, George A. Smith, and Hiram Kimball relinquished their stipends as city councilors in order to lessen taxes and pay the police force. At the time, the police captain, Hosea Stout, said, "The police only want to live."

When was the stone jail near the water tower built and used?

After a tornado toppled the temple walls in 1850, the site was used as a quarry for other buildings in Nauvoo. The jail built to replace the Yearsley home jail was constructed of these stones.

Could lawyers make a living in Nauvoo? If so, what did they do?

The city of Nauvoo, at its peak, boasted nine law firms. They were able to make a living, but it was not as profitable as in eastern cities such as New York, where a beginning lawyer could make $3,000 annually. A brief perusal of the court and land records in Carthage reveals a sizable amount of legal work performed during the Church's seven-year tenure. Lawsuits brought by Hancock County anti-Mormons were a constant source of harassment. There were also land transfers, divorces, and necessary legal advice to be sold, but due to the presence of Church courts to settle disputes that might otherwise go to a civil court, and because of the opposition of Church leaders, especially Joseph, to lawyers in general, business for lawyers in Nauvoo was not good. For these reasons, attorneys such as George P. Stiles and O. C. Skinner found it necessary to advertise their services in the local newspaper. These factors may also have played a role in turning such lawyers as C. L. Higbee and R. D. Foster against the Prophet and involving them in his death.

Until the 1860s, few people in America had only one occupation. Most were jacks-of-all-trades, even professionals such as doctors and lawyers, although it was less true in those professions than in most others. It is interesting that the apostate lawyer R. D. Foster was arrested and fined for gambling, perhaps in an effort to supplement a meager income.

* *

* *

Didn't the Nauvoo Charter give the city almost total sovereignty in matters of law? Was that normal for cities like Nauvoo?

Yes, Nauvoo was granted almost total sovereignty. That is, the authority to pass any laws not repugnant to the Constitution of the United States or the Constitution of the State of Illinois. This permission meant city ordinances could be in direct conflict with state laws as long as they weren't in conflict with the constitution of either the state or federal governments.

This sovereignty was not abnormal. Several other Illinois cities had similar charters, including Chicago, Springfield, and Quincy. The difference was the tendency of the Saints to assume the powers that, according to the charter, they believed had been granted them, especially the power the city assumed in issuing writs of habeas corpus. The state was helpless in curtailing the powers of the city of Nauvoo as long as the charter existed. In the end, the legislature felt its only recourse was to revoke the charter, which many legal experts at the time believed had been issued in perpetuity. In 1870, the Illinois State Constitution was amended to forbid the granting of "any exclusive privilege, immunity or franchise whatever" to any "corporation, association, or individual."

To protect themselves against what happened in Missouri, the Mormons had only taken advantage of what was legally the privilege of several Illinois communities—communities that had never felt the need to make use of those privileges.

Joseph was wrongly accused numerous times of violations of the law. Once, however, he insisted on being fined for a violation. What was the occasion?

On August 1, 1843, Joseph had a confrontation with a tax collector who called Joseph a liar and picked up a stone to throw at the Prophet. Joseph struck him, and when Daniel Wells separated the two men, Joseph asked Wells, a justice of the peace, to fine him for the assault. When Wells refused, he rode to Alderman Whitney, related his story, and insisted on a fine, which Whitney imposed and Joseph paid. Joseph

* *

had experienced too many instances of lawbreakers escaping justice that his sense of honor would not allow him to risk being accused of the same thing.

Anti-Mormon mob activity suggests a rather lawless frontier environment in Illinois. Was this kind of extra-legal activity unique in the United States at that time?

No. During the Nauvoo years, there were a number of major riots throughout the nation that were also directed against religious or ethnic groups such as the Catholics or the Irish. One historian of American violence believed "the period of the 1830s, 1840s and 1850s may have been the era of the greatest urban violence America has ever experienced." In his book *Frontier Violence*, Eugene Hollan wrote, "Mob violence not only increased markedly but also became a feature of American life." The major difference with anti-Mormon violence was that in both Missouri and Illinois, the violence earned the support of the local governments or their leaders, who justified such violence under the rationalization of majority—otherwise known as democratic—support.

There were numerous charges by the anti-Mormons of counterfeiting in Nauvoo. Was there any element of truth to these charges?

There *were* counterfeiters in Nauvoo. Some non-member criminals set up shop in the city or vicinity, believing accurately that the Mormons would be blamed for their activities. Occasionally, some would join the Church, expecting the Church authorities to protect them. One young member, Therin Terrill, was arrested with several counterfeit coins on him. He claimed another Mormon, George Reader, had given the coins to him. When such members were discovered, they were quickly excommunicated. All in all, however, the charges of illegal activities in Nauvoo were grossly exaggerated. Anti-Mormons wanted to believe any negative thing about the Saints, and papers such as the *Warsaw Signal* were willing to print any rumor that pleased their readers.

* *

Anti-Mormons claim the Avenging Angels or Danites were still active during the Nauvoo years. Were they?

The story of the Danites in Missouri has been so distorted that few writers are able to find the real story. The Danites started out in Missouri as a public organization that involved the entire LDS community working for the defense and welfare of all members. Sampson Avard was able to subvert some members who were growing tired of the defensive posture of the Saints. He was later able to implicate—at least in the minds of the public— the Church leaders because they had openly espoused the original public organization. After this implication, the imagination of fiction writers took over, including such writers as Arthur Conan Doyle, Zane Grey, and Robert Louis Stevenson, thus fixing public opinion for the next century.

Was any extralegal group operating among the Saints in Nauvoo?

Yes. During the Missouri troubles, two or three small bands of mounted horsemen conducted raiding expeditions in an effort to acquire firearms, horses, and so forth, especially from those responsible for their maltreatment. Although the Danites had been disbanded, these "fur companies," a name carried over from such groups in Missouri, continued in Nauvoo, guarding the city and maintaining order.

We hear of tarring and feathering being a fairly common mob activity during the Nauvoo era. Did this ever happen in the city of Nauvoo?

There is one recorded instance mentioned in a letter of complaint from General Douglas Knox of the Warsaw militia to Willard Richards, dated July 25, 1844. Joseph and Hyrum had been killed only four weeks previously, and the women of Nauvoo, more incensed perhaps than the men, decided to retaliate. Knox reported that some Nauvoo women banded together to tar and feather some undesirables who had come into the city. It is rather difficult to imagine Willard Richards—who had seen his friends killed by such "undesirables" only a month previously—giving any consideration to chastising the sisters as a result of this complaint.

* *

Lucy Mack Smith

A common story associated with the furnishings in the Lucy Smith home states the dishes belonged to her sister-in-law Polly, who was married to Isaac Pierce. According to Lucy's history, however, Pierce was married to Mary, the sister of Joseph Smith Sr. Who was his wife?

Lucy's history is right; the story is wrong. What is interesting is that Joseph Smith Sr.'s sister, Mary, and her husband Isaac were very hostile to the Church and demonstrated this hostility to Lucy. Whatever the case, an interesting question would be why Lucy would have ended up with the dishes that belonged to her hostile in-laws, the Pierces?

Lucy Mack Smith dictated the biography of her son. Who actually wrote it?

A 23-year-old highly literate scribe named Martha Jane Coray, whose husband, Howard, was known as the Prophet's first scribe in Nauvoo, wrote the biography. Howard was teaching school when the dictation started but soon quit to join his wife in revising the preliminary manuscript. Most of it was apparently dictated while Lucy was living in the abandoned Jonathan Browning home in the winter of 1845–46 after the Brownings returned to Quincy to settle some affairs.

* *

When and where did Lucy die?

Lucy died on May 14, 1856, while living with her daughter-in-law Emma in the Mansion House.

How long did Lucy live in the Noble/Smith home and why did she leave?

Few sources agree on the answer to these questions. At the time of the exodus, for safety reasons, Lucy moved with her daughter and son-in-law, the Millikens, to Knoxville, Illinois, about sixty-five miles northeast of Nauvoo. After three years in Knoxville, the family moved to Fountain Green Township near Colchester, where Lucy's daughter (also named Lucy) and her husband Arthur remained the rest of their lives. Lucy Mack, however, moved back to Nauvoo, and at this point, the disagreement over history begins. What year did she move back to Nauvoo, and did she move back into her own little home or did she join Emma and Lewis Bidamon in their home? Evidence seems to suggest, because of her poor health, she moved in immediately with Emma and the probable date was around 1851 or 1852. All this would mean she lived only briefly in her little home on the corner of Hyde and Kimball Streets.

Did Brigham Young actually try to suppress Lucy's biography of her son, Joseph?

Actually, the original title for Lucy's book was *The History of Mother Smith by Herself*, but throughout most of its history, the title has been *The History of Joseph Smith by His Mother, Lucy Mack Smith*. It was first published in England by Orson Pratt without authorization, and Brigham Young sought to suppress it because of what he considered a number of errors. When he set George A. Smith and Elias Smith to correcting it for another publication, they found relatively few errors in it. Mother Smith's memory was much better than Brigham and other leaders believed it was. Most of the changes revolved around Lucy's characterization of her son William, who was more of a scoundrel than a typical mother was inclined to describe.

* *

* *

Why didn't Lucy go west with the Saints?

Lucy wanted to go and said she would if her son William and the husbands of her daughters would go. She was quite feeble and crippled by arthritis, however, and dependent on her daughters and Emma, who elected not to go. Unlike Emma, Lucy apparently liked Brigham and was willing to accept his leadership of the Church.

* *

Lyon Drug Store

Is there a special name for the straw beehive in the Lyon Drug Store that has become the symbol of Deseret?

These primitive hives are called "skeps" and were most common in the northeastern United States, where so many of the Mormon Pioneers were from. These were normally made of twisted and wrapped rye straw. Because honey could not be removed from such hives without destroying the hive itself, these skeps were replaced with the more familiar box hives that could be used over again.

Did Windsor Lyon need training or a license to recommend, mix, and dispense medicines?

In the British Isles, apothecaries had to make up their standard medicines according to government-approved formulas. Inspectors, who had the authority to destroy medicines they considered unfit for use, visited such shops periodically. The United States at this time had no such laws. Patients could only be guided by the recommendations of honest physicians.

New York and Philadelphia had colleges of pharmacy, but one did not need to graduate or even attend them in order to dispense drugs. However, the public was becoming aware of the importance of degrees from these colleges and tended to patronize their graduates when possible. We have no evidence that Brother Lyon had such training. He was a druggist, not an apothecary.

* *

What is the difference between a druggist and an apothecary?

A druggist is the dealer of a much more comprehensive line of merchandise including not only medicines but spices, dye-stuffs, and paints. An apothecary, on the other hand, compounds and sells medicines only.

Weren't there more dramatic store signs than what we see today in Nauvoo?

Yes. As a matter of fact, Lyon Drug Store had a large sign with the image of a lion on it. It can safely be assumed that Nauvoo was no different than any other city in the country, all of which had a variety of hanging signs for advertising the wares inside the stores. Nevertheless, the business sections of such towns would still be a far cry from the lavish display of advertising we see today.

Since the Thompsonian system of natural medicine was prevalent in Nauvoo, we can assume Lyon sold herbal medicines. Did he grow his own herbs?

Lyon would have had an herb garden, as did practically every household in Nauvoo. It didn't take the prompting of Thompsonian enthusiasts to encourage the use of herbs. Wives and mothers had used them for centuries, and belief in their curative powers was not lost upon the women of Nauvoo, especially with their Prophet urging greater reliance on them.

How was the sugar processed that came in the hard cones (sugar-loaf)?

The crushing and boiling of sugar cane extracts the sucrose or sugar. The simplest and least refining process results in molasses. The greater the refining, the greater the expense, and the whiter the sugar. Near the end of the processing of the juices from the cane, the brown sugar, after being discolored with bone char filters, ended up as white crystals. To simplify handling and shipping in the days before inexpensive containers were

* *

* *

available, the crystals were mixed with pure white syrup (derived from one of the earlier processing steps) and molded to the desired cone shape.

Thus the sweetness, whiteness, and price of sugarcane products depended upon the number of times the raw juice was boiled, adulterated with water, and the sugar removed. White cane sugar cones are the most expensive but have the least vitamins and minerals. Blackstrap, the first refining, was not only the healthiest but also the cheapest and thus most often used by Nauvoo housewives.

* *

Maid of Iowa

How large was the Church-owned steamboat, the *Maid of Iowa*?

Actually, it was renamed the *Iowa Twins* when purchased by the Saints in 1843, but most Saints continued to call it the *Maid of Iowa*. It was a stern wheeler and quite small compared with most Mississippi river boats. Designed specifically for the upper Mississippi with its many rapids and the lesser tributaries, it weighed only 60 tons and measured 115 feet in length with a draft of less than two feet. It cost just over $4,000 when it was built in 1842. Although basically a freight steamer, it could handle as many as two hundred passengers, with cabin accommodations for about thirty.

What was the *Maid of Iowa* used for?

Although used briefly as a ferry between Nauvoo and Montrose when it was first purchased in 1843, it went into the more lucrative business of freighting. It brought coal from Iowa, lumber from the north, lead from Wisconsin, military supplies from Missouri, and carried south such items as Illinois wheat, corn, and pork. It also served as an excursion boat, a meeting place for Church services, and in bringing converts to Nauvoo from New Orleans and transporting missionaries from Nauvoo.

* *

What happened to the *Maid of Iowa*?

Knowing the Saints were leaving Illinois, Brigham Young ordered the steamer sold "for what could be gotten for her." Captain Peter Hoelting of Wisconsin purchased it to haul freight on the Fox and Wisconsin rivers. It was last reported carrying freight on Soap Creek in Iowa in 1851. Local legend maintains it came "home" to Nauvoo and was caught in an ice jam off Dundey Landing on the end of Parley Street where it wrecked. The story goes that the hull lay in the river until it rotted away. Legends should be ignored by historians, but this one was too good to ignore.

Who was the captain of the *Maid of Iowa*?

Daniel Jones was not only the captain of the steamboat *Maid of Iowa* but also part owner along with Joseph. Joseph had converted him, and he was at Carthage jail with the Prophet the night previous to the martyrdom. There he asked the Prophet if his time had come to die, to which Joseph replied, "You will yet see Wales and fulfill the mission appointed you before you die." Jones lived to not only serve two missions to Wales, but he also deserves credit for more than 6,000 convert baptisms, leading the emigration of many of those converts to Utah (including the nucleus of the famed Tabernacle Choir), and for numerous other accomplishments. He died firm in the faith and is buried in Provo, Utah.

* *

Medicine and Death

Do we know how many residents died during the Saints' seven-year sojourn in Nauvoo?

From September 1842 through September 1845, the *Nauvoo Neighbor* published the sexton's death list. The total deaths during that time period was 832. Since that accounts for less than half the approximate time the Saints lived in Nauvoo, we can roughly estimate the total deaths, assuming they were similar in the unrecorded period of time, at no less than 1,700 men, women, and children. Children five and younger made up 44 percent of these deaths.

To put these deaths into perspective, imagine living in a relatively small town of 6,000 or 7,000 people (the average size of Nauvoo during its seven years) and witnessing five or six deaths each week. It would be unusual not to experience the death of a friend or relative several times in those few years.

Did Nauvoo have an unusually high death rate compared with the rest of the nation?

Yes. The crude mortality rate for the nation in the 1830s has been estimated at 13.8 per thousand. In the first five years of Nauvoo's existence, the death rate varied between 22 and 26 per thousand. By 1845, the rate had dropped below 20 but was still higher than the national average.

* *

If allowed to stay in Nauvoo, the Saints would have been able to lower the death right considerably by draining the swamps, building more substantial homes, and acquiring more abundant food.

What were the major causes of death in Nauvoo?

By law, the city sexton had to keep a record of all deaths, including the name of the deceased, his age, and the date and cause of death. Because of the primitive state of medicine in the 1840s, the cause was not always known, so the sexton would often list merely a symptom, for example, "fever." From these symptoms, we can often determine the disease itself.

The most common disease in Nauvoo was "ague and fever," known today as malaria. Typhoid was undoubtedly present, although it might easily have been confused with ague. Brain fever was also mentioned, which was probably meningitis. Other common causes were "consumption," or what we would call tuberculosis; pneumonia, which was probably the cause of Don Carlos's death; whooping cough, especially among the very young; inflammation and diarrhea; measles; scarlet fever; diphtheria; and canker, which according to contemporary dictionaries simply meant to "waste away by means of any noxious cause." And there were many "noxious" causes in those days.

Contrary to popular belief, less than 1 percent died during childbirth; the midwives were very talented. Also contrary to legend, the sexton's list indicates no deaths as a result of women's long dresses catching fire in the open fireplaces.

Did all burials take place in the Pioneer Cemetery on Parley Street?

There were no laws respecting where a burial had to take place. Consequently, some burials took place in the yards of homes. Examples are the small burial found behind the Browning home and the burial of Jenetta Richards alongside Durphy Street, north of the Woodruff home.

Most burials, however, were in one of four major burial grounds, with the majority being in the Church-owned Pioneer Cemetery on Parley Street. Another was the Dundey family burial ground located near the river, north

* *

* *

of the Parley Street Landing. One of the first burial areas was the Durphy Street burial ground, where most of the Saints were buried until the opening of the Parley Street Cemetery in 1842. Most of these burials were disinterred and moved to the Old City Cemetery when Durphy Street was straightened and built through the grounds. The Old City Cemetery east of the city was laid out within two years after the exodus.

What was the "sickly" season so many journal writers mentioned?

This was the summer and early fall, especially August and September, and coincided with the prevalence of ague and fever (malaria), which, unknown to the Saints, was caused by mosquitoes. Ague and fever was so common along the entire Mississippi during this period that many did not even consider it a disease but merely a consequence of a change of seasons along the river. It was not uncommon to hear the phrase, "He ain't sick—he's just got the shakes."

Malaria, incidentally, was not a native disease in the United States. Experts believe it was imported with the slaves into America and moved west with the frontiersmen. It became so virulent in the beginning of the nineteenth century in the American Bottoms of Illinois, around St. Louis, that the area became depopulated as settlers fled the disease. Just a few years before the Saints arrived in Illinois, many questioned whether this part of the Mississippi Valley would ever be settled permanently.

Willard Richards was a physician. Did he practice medicine in Nauvoo?

He was practicing medicine near Boston when he encountered the Church, and after reading the Book of Mormon and becoming convinced of its truth, he settled his accounts and sold his medicines. From the time he joined the Church until he died in Salt Lake City in 1854, he was totally involved in Church work as a clerk for Joseph, as a Church Historian, and as one of the apostles. He simply had little time to practice the traditional medicine he had been taught. His brother Levi practiced botanical medicine in Nauvoo.

* *

* *

Did Nauvoo physicians perform surgery?

Few records exist regarding the extent of this practice. In July 1841, the Prophet recorded in his journal, "Brother William Yokum had his leg amputated by Dr. John F. Weld, who operated free of charge; he was wounded in the massacre at Haun's Mill, October 30th, 1838, and had lain on his back ever since; and now it was found the only chance to save his life was to have his leg cut off. He was also shot through the head at the same massacre." Some of Dr. Weld's medical equipment is on display at the Nauvoo Historical Society Museum on Mulholland Street.

Was bleeding still a common practice in Nauvoo?

In the early nineteenth century, physicians trained in the orthodox methods of medicine relied heavily on bleeding and "purges" such as calomel (a common preparation of mercury) that could easily prove fatal. Joseph's older brother, Alvin, died in this manner, and from experiences such as this, Joseph often preached against this type of "heroic medicine." He instead recommended Thompsonian medicine, an herb-based system of medicine named after its founder, Dr. Samuel Thompson. Due to the Prophet's promptings, bleeding and other forms of heroic medicine were less common in Nauvoo than in other parts of the country. Otherwise, the death rate in Nauvoo might have been even higher.

It's interesting to note, however, that in treating sick animals, bleeding was still a fairly common practice in Nauvoo.

Were the dead embalmed?

Modern embalming, called arterial embalming, was still being perfected at the time of Old Nauvoo and wasn't often used in the city. Its widespread use began with the Civil War as a means of preserving the bodies until they could be brought home from the battlefield. Washing the body, wrapping it in winding cloths or a shroud, and prompt interment was the usual practice in Nauvoo, and was particularly necessary considering the number of deaths occurring there.

* *

✳ ✳

There are stories that Joseph, anticipating an early death, had prepared a tomb for himself. Are these stories true?

In both the *History of the Church* and *Journal of Discourses*, Brigham Young makes reference to hearing Joseph speak of "the tomb I (Joseph) have prepared." Brigham stated frankly that Joseph had "built a tomb for himself in the city of Nauvoo." On August 22, 1842, Joseph recorded in his history: "Let my father, Don Carlos and Alvin and children that I have buried be brought and laid in the tomb I have built. Let my mother and my brethren and my sisters be laid there also; and let it be called the tomb of Joseph, a descendant of Jacob; and when I die let me be gathered to the tomb of my father."

After the death of Joseph and when relations became strained with Emma, Brigham stated in a public speech, "And we will petition Sister Emma in the Name of Israel's God, to let us deposit the remains of Joseph according as he commanded us." Joseph said "the tomb I have built." One doesn't "build" a grave. One builds a vault, and Emma did not move the bodies into a vault but merely had them reburied.

Evidence also indicates that the tomb was capable of being entered after the "burial." James Monroe, the Smith family tutor, wrote in his diary on May 28, 1845, four days after the funeral of William Smith's wife Caroline, "I took Melissa (Lott Smith) out this afternoon in the carriage and visited Mrs. (Caroline) Smith's tomb, in company with William (Smith) and Miss Grant. The body does not seem to have decayed much." At the time of Caroline's funeral, her remains had been "deposited in the tomb of Joseph."

Gracia N. Jones, in her book *Emma's Glory and Sacrifice*, states that on October 4, after Joseph's death, the brethren made a personal visit to Emma at which time she expressed good feelings toward them but "she was adamant that Joseph's body not be moved to the tomb by the temple." Unfortunately, her footnote for this source does not match her information, which may be nothing more than a printing error.

So the question remains about where that tomb was constructed. Church historians have different theories, but they have so far found no definitive evidence of the location of that tomb.

✳ ✳

* *

Why were the remains of Joseph and Hyrum exhumed in 1928?

The Saints believed the rising water of Lake Cooper (resulting from the construction of the Keokuk Dam) would inundate the graves. By 1928, no one knew the exact location of the graves, which prompted the title of the poem by Joseph's youngest son, David, "The Unknown Grave." Thus, the Community of Christ Church, which owned the property, after some trenching, discovered and removed the bodies, reburying them in the Smith family cemetery southwest of the Homestead where they are today.

What were the average life spans of those who lived in Nauvoo?

The average span for women in America during the early nineteenth century was forty years; for men it was thirty-eight. On the frontier, and especially a malaria-infested place like Nauvoo, it was even less. The major reasons for such a short life span, especially under frontier conditions, were the rigors of life, little medical knowledge (about such diseases as malaria and tuberculosis, for example), unhealthy diets, and lack of sanitation.

In Nauvoo, because of its short history, average life span would have little meaning, but we would be safe in assuming those seven years, because of the impoverished condition of the Saints on their arrival and the malaria-prone town site, would have shortened the natural life spans of the Saints to some extent.

Did Nauvoo have dentists, and, if so, what kind of dental work did they do?

Although Nauvoo had a number of physicians, they did not have many dentists. One who did set up practice in Nauvoo, although he had to do other things to subsidize his income, was Alexander Neibaur, a surgeon dentist from Prussia who was converted in England. He advertised in the *Times and Seasons*, in August 1842, noting that he could be "consulted, daily, in all branches connected with his profession, Teeth cleaned, plugged, filed, the Scurva effectually cured, children's teeth regulated,

* *

* *

natural or artificial teeth from a single tooth to a whole set inserted on the most approved principle." Although he didn't mention it, most of his business was extractions. He noted in his ad that Brigham Young gave him permission to use the Young residence, or he would make house calls. He mentioned the charges were "strictly moderate."

Did Nauvoo physicians only do house calls or did they have offices and examination rooms?

A large number of physicians resided in Nauvoo, and several advertised the locations of their offices. Dr. Jesse C. Braley advertised in 1845 that he had an office in the Seventies Hall. Dr. Charles Higbee offered his services from an office in the Masonic Hall, and Dr. W. B. Brink, who advertised a cure for cancer, advertised his place of business as a few rods west of the Nauvoo Temple. That so many doctors were advertising and that several physicians simply were not practicing their trade in Nauvoo suggests traditional medicine was not a profitable profession. There were still too many unscientific practices, too much quackery, too much competition from herbal practitioners, including midwives, and too much criticism from the Prophet and Church leaders about the dangers of traditional medicine to make it a popular profession.

In fact, an editorial in the *Times and Seasons* on April 1, 1845, frankly stated, "Nor are the services of physicians held in so great repute in Nauvoo, that the saints confide in medicine; but rather the commandments of God are looked to as being far more safe than trusting an arm of flesh. There is but one Doctor that does much business in his profession, and that is surgery." This reference may have been to Dr. Weld.

If so many were buried in the Pioneer Cemetery, why do we find so few markers?

There are three major reasons. First, burials were so common that the graves were often left unmarked with the expectation of later putting up a marker, and in the process, the location was sometimes lost. Hosea Stout records in his diary of looking for the grave of his daughter and being

* *

* *

unable to find it. Being impoverished, many families could afford nothing more substantial than a wooden marker, which lasted only a few years with no family left in Nauvoo to care for the grave. And finally, for many years, the cemetery was abandoned to farm animals that trampled and destroyed many of the more fragile markers.

In recent years, under the care of the LDS Church, the cemetery has been cleaned up and stabilized. Unfortunately, it is too late to restore the numerous "lost" grave markers. Knowing the names of many of those in unmarked graves, new markers could be erected, but to do so would destroy the historical sanctity of this site and make it nothing more than a memorial garden.

One hears little of folk medicine among the Saints. Did they make use of such remedies in Nauvoo?

They certainly did, but most journals and memoirs, possibly because of the writers' embarrassment, make little mention of them. An exception is the reminiscences of Helen Mar Whitney. She remembered, "Every remedy that could be thought or heard of was tried; we even resorted to tricks and stratagems, some of which were ludicrous in the extreme and afforded considerable fun and amusement."

She described trying to bargain away the ague to the ones who were willing to risk their chances for some remuneration. Another remedy they tried when they felt oncoming symptoms was to run across the floor as if going onto the bed, but to go under instead, thus cheating the "old gentleman," who would go, as usual, onto the bed. She also mentions rattlesnake skins wrapped around the head for headache. Other remedies were as varied as the people who moved to Nauvoo.

Don Carlos was the first of the Smith brothers to die in Nauvoo. Where was he buried?

Don Carlos, a Mason, was buried with Masonic and Military rites. Helen Mar Whitney, who marched with her father, Heber C. Kimball, in the Masonic procession, described the burial place: "Those of the Masonic

* *

fraternity marched next to the family to the grave which was in a little grove at the foot of the hill south west of the temple." Eliza Snow described the funeral procession disappearing among the dwellings "near the river's edge." Although another burying ground lay north of the Parley Street Landing along the river's edge, Sister Snow was probably using poetic license. Helen Mar's description most closely matches a burying ground around which Durphy Street passed as it ascended the bluff. To permit the straightening of Durphy Street, that cemetery was later closed and the bodies disinterred, many of them moved to the city cemetery directly east of the city. Apparently, the body of Don Carlos was also disinterred and is now listed as being in the Smith family plot on Water Street.

Were all babies in Nauvoo delivered by midwives?

Letters and diaries from Old Nauvoo suggest most of them were. During this time, people widely believed that the use of male doctors for delivering babies undermined the "foundations of public virtue," as one Boston physiologist wrote in 1848. The well-publicized malpractice suit in Nauvoo against Dr. W. B. Brink, which he lost, for permanently injuring a woman during a delivery, did little to encourage women to use male doctors, whereas the success of the many midwives in Nauvoo certainly encouraged their use. The number of midwives kept busy in Nauvoo and the constant advertising by physicians also suggest the universal use of midwives for delivering Nauvoo's babies.

Did midwives practice any medicine other than obstetrics?

We know they practiced botanic medicine. Joseph Smith set apart Ann Green Duston Carling (an English convert from Herefordshire), like several other sisters in Nauvoo, for her midwifery duties. The Prophet told the popular Nauvoo midwife she would be successful if she used herbs exclusively, which suggests she was doing more than just delivering babies. In fact, she was known in Nauvoo as the "Herb Doctor." The Prophet personally set Harriet Johnson apart as a midwife, and we can be assured he would have given her the same advice. In forty years of practice, Sister Johnson delivered 4,000 babies.

How successful were midwives in the early 1800s? Were they prepared for complications in childbirth?

Although Nauvoo reportedly had an unusually high infant mortality rate, the sexton's death lists indicate these to be children and not newborns. Consider thirteen randomly selected weekly sexton's death lists, which indicated ninetey-seven deaths in those weeks. Of these, sixty-two were children in their teens or younger. How many newborns were lost as a result of birth complications is unrecorded, but journals indicate midwives were quite proficient in their handling of complicated births. On the list of over 800 names on the sexton's list, only ten women died from childbirth complications.

We cannot overlook the fact that midwives had a greater compassion for their patients and could elicit greater faith than male doctors. As most of them had given birth themselves, midwives more easily identified with the expectant mothers and treated them accordingly.

We hear much of Patty Sessions, probably because of her published diary. Who were some of the other popular midwives in Old Nauvoo?

Sarah Marinda Thompson, who arrived in Nauvoo in 1841, and Elizabeth Fife Blair from Scotland were two popular midwives who made wide use of herbs. Jane Johnson Black, the only woman on the scene in support of the defenders in the Battle of Nauvoo, was, at the end of her life in Utah, credited with delivering more than 3,000 babies. Others were Harriet Matilda Johnson, Pauline Phelps Lyman (a plural wife of Amasa Lyman), Elizabeth and Mary Ann Ransay, Mary Elizabeth Robinson, and Elizabeth Degen Bushman, a convert from Switzerland who received $2.50 for each delivery.

Miscellaneous

What happened to the homes and furnishings after the Saints left Nauvoo?

The Saints tried to sell their homes and the goods they could not take with them—and they were able to take very little. With so many homes and furnishings up for sale at the same time, however, the market was glutted and the Saints were usually able to get only pennies on the dollar for their possessions—if anything at all. A classic example is the home of John D. Lee, which cost him $8,000 to build and which the Church Committee was able to dispose of later for $12.50.

Thomas Kane, who visited Nauvoo after the exodus and was a well-known benefactor of the Mormons, describes entering homes still furnished, looking like the owners had merely arisen from their tables and walked out the door. By the time of the Battle of Nauvoo in September 1846, many of the homes had been taken over by the "New Citizens," some of whom fought alongside the few remaining Saints against the mobs. With the population of Nauvoo dropping to one-tenth of its pre-exodus size, we can visualize as many as nine out of every ten homes vacant and ready to begin their process of decay.

What was the major source of water for the Nauvooans?

Dug wells. The shallow wells of Nauvoo, however, were so highly

* *

impregnated with lime that they left clothes with a grayish hue. Most homes, therefore, had cisterns in which to store the soft rainwater.

After the death of the Prophet Joseph, Emma had a well dug, and we have a record of the connected expense. The record tells us much about wells in Nauvoo, their depth, construction, and so forth:

Digging & walling 56 ft. @ 62½	$35
Bricks	$13.25
Boarding well diggers (2 hands 2 weeks)	$6.00
Well rope, chain	$2.00
Bucket & ironing	$1.50
Crank for windlass	$1.25
Ten lbs. nails for roof and well	$70
Lumber & building curb	$6.00
Total	$65.70

What kinds of stoves were used in Nauvoo?

The stoves in Nauvoo—and there were not very many—were called box stoves, shaped as the name suggests. Europeans and New Englanders had been using such stoves since the mid-1600s. They were normally never over three feet high, were shipped as flat metal plates the homeowner had to put together, and cost as much as a month's wages.

How much of the original city was inundated by the river when the Keokuk Dam was complete?

Relatively little. Photos of the boat landing at the Nauvoo House before the completion of the dam indicate practically no loss there whatsoever. There was originally a steep bank along that side of the city and the water apparently rose up the bank rather than inundating much land. Evidence of this can be found in the collected discourses of Joseph F. Smith, who remembers his father and Uncle Joseph returning from their initial attempt to escape to the west before their fatal trip to Carthage:

"[I] watched them till they landed at the bank of the river near the old *Times and Seasons* printing office, watched them as they walked up the

* *

bank of the river on to Water Street, and walked along and come into our house." Photos taken in 1907 by photographer and missionary George Anderson show such a bank.

At the foot of the embankment along the southwest portion of the city ran Lumber Street, which connected the mills along the river and was named for the lumber unloaded along the shore. That street, as well as the mill sites, was inundated, but it didn't amount to much actual area. North of the Parley Street landing was the sparsely settled Munson Lands, and so any loss of river side there was relatively unimportant and still rather small in area.

Did the Saints in Nauvoo really cross out the name of Abraham Lincoln when he was running for the State Legislature in 1840 and vote for a Mr. Ralston?

This is a common story in Mormon circles. During the presidential election of that year, a candidate from Fountain Green, a Whig justice of the peace named Abraham Lincoln (but not *the* Abraham Lincoln), ran for elector. The Saints crossed out his name and voted for his opponent, James H. Ralston. Those who repeat the story usually do it to show the magnanimous character of the Abraham Lincoln who aided in the passage of the Nauvoo Charter and later congratulated the Saints on the bill's successful passage. It was his name they crossed out.

Why didn't the federal government play an active role in defending the Saints from mob rule?

Throughout American history, there has been conflict over states' rights, with the states jealously guarding what they consider to be their sovereign rights and responsibilities. Law enforcement was considered the states' responsibility. Not until federal marshals were sent into Little Rock in 1954 did the federal government take the initiative in protecting the "civil rights" of citizens. In the 1840s, few challenged the thinking that federal authorities were powerless to infringe on the traditional responsibilities of states.

* *

Why didn't the state of Illinois and Governor Ford play a more active role in defending the Saints from mob rule?

Certainly the state of Illinois had the means and the legal right, but times don't change much when politics are involved. Governor Ford, an elected official, was not about to seriously challenge the popular feelings of those who elected him. Jacksonian Democracy was at its height during this era, when "law" or the Constitution came in second to the popular "will" of the people, regardless of the legalities or morality of that "will." For this reason, the 1830s and 1840s have often been called the most violent decades in American society, as resentment grew against "unorthodox" immigrant groups and "un-American" beliefs. Even though bigotry might have been the motivating cause of mob action against such groups, it was "justified" because it was the "will" of the people.

Why did Thomas Sharp, the Warsaw editor, hate the Mormons so much?

The enmity started as political rivalry between Nauvoo and Warsaw, both river towns with much economic and political potential in a very young and rapidly growing state. Sharp, as editor of the *Warsaw Signal*, began using the power of the press to disparage a rival town. Unfortunately, William Smith, as editor of the *Nauvoo Wasp*, pulled few punches in his attacks on Sharp, including personal attacks, and the hostility escalated. By the time John Taylor took over editorship of the Nauvoo paper and Joseph changed the name to a friendlier sounding *Nauvoo Neighbor* in May 1843, the fight had advanced too far. Sharp, a bigoted but well-respected leader among the anti-Mormons, was able to use his press to inflame public opinion in Hancock County to an irreconcilable point.

Another factor that cannot be overlooked is simply one of business competition. Most weekly presses during the Nauvoo era depended on job printing as a source of income. When the Saints gained some political control of Hancock County, they were able to divert much of the county's job printing business from the *Warsaw Signal* to the *Times and Seasons*.

* *

* *

Why did so many non-Mormons desire to live in a city so dominated by Mormon theocratic rule?

A simple answer would be, "They found it a delightful place to live!" As true as this could have been, there were other reasons. Any large city, throughout history, has its attractions: culture, shopping, entertainment, socializing, business possibilities, and so on. Nauvoo had all of these, and despite their dislike of Mormonism, the non-Mormons found religious toleration and a relatively secure environment on a rather lawless frontier. Governor Ford himself mentioned the lawlessness of the Illinois frontier, which ironically attracted a different sort of people to Nauvoo: criminals who believed they could carry out their illegal activities and blame them on the Mormons. Removing such elements was a continual problem for the Saints.

Reading the letters of non-Mormon resident Charlotte Haven, who lived in Nauvoo for over a year, is very informative. The letters, although mocking and sarcastic, reveal her delight in her short stay in the city and are especially telling coming from a young, educated woman from the East.

With so many horses in Nauvoo, how were the streets kept clean?

If the streets had been paved as they are today, there would certainly have been a problem. The streets were for the most part dirt, however, and when it rained they became muddy. As unpleasant as this may have been, it did serve the purpose of easily mixing and thus disposing of what might have made the streets odorous and objectionable thoroughfares.

The Church has received some criticism from purists for constructing such a pristine-looking town with manicured lawns, and so on. How authentic is this look?

Every restoration has the same problem: whether to make the restoration realistic and turn off many visitors with the dirt, mud, smells, weeds, and so forth, or to compromise by being as authentic as possible with the restored buildings but taking some license with the surroundings by paving, mowing lawns, planting more flowers and shrubbery

* *

than existed, and so on. Authenticity is a perpetual concern of most restorationists, so we are fortunate to have our critics to keep us from making too many compromises. One restoration in upstate New York that attempted to be totally authentic was a failure because it appeared neglected and on the verge of financial collapse and could not attract visitors.

What kinds of produce did gardeners grow in Nauvoo?

We can assume gardens then would have been similar to today's gardens: beans, melons, corn, peas, beets, cucumbers, turnips, onions, carrots, and so forth. Tomatoes were just being popularized as safe and healthful. Grapes and various kinds of berries were common. The large areas formerly set aside for gardens and orchards were rapidly utilized by the huge influx of immigrants, and lots were divided and subdivided. Letters from Bathsheba Smith to her husband George A., and Hannah Ells to Phoebe Woodruff, and the diaries of Mary Ann Maughan and Louisa Barnes Pratt confirm the sad fact that the homes of Nauvoo never had an abundance of food. If the city had developed as Joseph envisioned and with a few more years of peace, the Nauvooan countryside would truly have been a land of abundance.

How many of Nauvoo's residents were immigrants from the British Isles?

An article titled "Migration of English Mormons to America," published in the *American Historical Review*, mentions 4,733 British converts between 1837 and 1846 who gathered "primarily to Nauvoo." If this figure is reliable, and subtracting those who didn't make it all the way or who became discouraged and returned, we are still left with a figure that represents approximately one third of Nauvoo's population, higher than most historians would suggest. Since many of the English actually settled outside of Nauvoo in places like Warren, Big Mound, and Stringtown, we suggest the number of Nauvoo citizens from the British Isles would have made up to 20 to 25 percent of Nauvoo's population.

* *

How actively was Christmas celebrated in Nauvoo?

Christmas wasn't much different than any other day. There were no Christmas trees, no mention in journals of exchanges of gifts, nor mention in local newspapers of Christmas celebrations, gifts, or decorations. There are reports of adults gathering in the evening for dinners and, on occasion, serenading some homes in the night. Other than that, Christmas seems to have passed relatively unnoticed among a people who believed Christ was born in April anyway.

In April 1843, some metal plates, excavated in Kinderhook, Illinois, about seventy miles south of Nauvoo, were presented to Joseph Smith, who authenticated and translated the plates, in spite of the fact that the plates were later proven a fraud. Is this true?

No. The so-called Kinderhook Plates were later proven a hoax, but no translation exists, nor did the Prophet ever pen any words to suggest he considered them genuine. The translation attributed to Joseph was an excerpt from the journal of William Clayton, who may have been influenced by the opinion of John Taylor and what he expected the Prophet to say. John Taylor, a close personal friend of the Prophet and editor of the *Times and Seasons*, took the find seriously and suggested in an editorial that the Prophet could give a translation of the plates. It was not uncommon in the early nineteenth century for reporters and others to anticipate the results of an event or what was expected to happen and report such things as fact. Communication was so slow that such writers or reporters did not have to expect correction soon if at all.

Note also that Joseph showed no further interest in the plates and that the hoaxers never stepped forward at the time to "expose" Joseph, which would suggest the Prophet knew they were a hoax.

Did a match factory in Nauvoo become the genesis of the Diamond Match Company?

Yes, but it was not a Mormon factory. Emma Smith's second husband,

* *

Lewis Bidamon, sold an iron foundry in Canton, Illinois, to the McCormick interests and started a match manufacturing business in Nauvoo, which became the Diamond Match Company. Nauvoo historian Ida Blum claimed Nauvoo had three match factories.

How did wives survive when husbands were called on extended missions?

With difficulty. Only within the past few years has more attention focused on the sisters of Nauvoo, who usually, without complaint, did the work that in most frontier communities would require the efforts of both the men and the women. With so many men away on missions or involved in Church business or temple building, it fell to the women to not only bear and raise the children while attending to all the other household duties, but to also take up the wide slack left by absent husbands in the more typical male responsibilities.

This meant supervising the construction of the new homes or even working on them themselves. It meant operating businesses, caring for farm animals, and finding the means of putting food on the table for their children. Few times in American cultural history have such heavy burdens fallen on the women of any American community as they did on the sisters of Nauvoo.

What was the average age for marriage for both women and men?

There are no statistics available for such figures, but, historically, LDS couples have married at an earlier age than those in the general population. And in the early nineteenth century, "child" brides were relatively common, with letters, diaries, and family histories mentioning brides as young as thirteen. With the assumption that a young man should be able to support a wife, men would marry later, of course, but waiting was not a requirement for girls. All that was required of them was the ability to "keep a home" and have children. Few girls would surpass seventeen or eighteen without marriage proposals, and young men would, in general, propose by the age of twenty. An exception to this general rule was the case of Joseph Smith's youngest brother, Don Carlos. He married when he was nineteen. His bride, Agnes Coolbrith, was twenty-

* *

four. Note that the city of Nauvoo even dealt with marriage regulations. In February 1842, Nauvoo passed an ordinance that permitted girls of fourteen and boys of seventeen to marry with their parent's consent.

How common was divorce among the Saints at this time?

Illinois had the most lenient divorce laws in the nation, allowing divorce for almost any reason. Still, contemporary news articles suggest abandonment as the most common form of marital separation. Brigham Young's second plural wife, for example, was 41-year-old Augusta Adams Cobb. She left her husband and five of her children in Boston, coming to Nauvoo with two of her children, one of whom died on the way. It was not uncommon for newspapers such as the *Nauvoo Neighbor* to carry official notices that a spouse would not be responsible for the debts of a departed mate.

As time went on and official records became of greater significance in the lives of the average American, divorce became far more common. By the time of Brigham's death, for example, ten of his plural wives had received divorces.

What happened to all the widows of the Smith Brothers?

Emma, of course, married Lewis Bidamon and stayed in Nauvoo, no longer active in the LDS Church. Hyrum's widows, Mary and Mercy, went to Utah with the Saints, and there, Mary's son Joseph Fielding later became a President of the Church. Samuel's widow, Lavira, also went to Utah, taking along not only her children, but those of Samuel's first wife, Mary Bailey Smith. There they continued to be active in the Church. The widow of Don Carlos, Agnes Coolbrith Smith, went to St. Louis with Lucy and Emma at the time of the exodus. After a brief stay, Lucy and Emma returned to Nauvoo, but Agnes married William Pickett, a lexicographer, who took her west to California. There she lived the rest of her life, no longer active in the Church. Her daughter, Ina, a daughter of Don Carlos, took her mother's maiden name, becoming in her later years the first poet laureate of California.

* *

* *

We hear much of the Icarians who "took over" Nauvoo after the exodus. How extensive was their "take over?"

The Icarians, a French communistic society of 260 people under Etienne Cabet, came to Nauvoo in 1849. The following year, a census showed 276 Icarians occupying sixty-nine houses. Six years later, Cabet was dead and the group began its decline. The Icarians are remembered, therefore, not for their numbers but because they were another unique communal society that followed so close upon the heels of the Mormons and just happened to buy up some of the property the Saints left, in particular, the temple site.

How long did it generally take to travel from the British Isles to Nauvoo?

The time would vary, of course, depending on the ship and the weather conditions, but the trip from England to Nauvoo by Alexander Neibaur, a Nauvoo dentist, would have been fairly typical. As he recorded in his journal, his trip across the Atlantic to New Orleans and up the Mississippi River took seventy-one days and four boats.

Other immigrants landed on the East coast and came overland from such ports as Boston, Philadelphia, or New York. If they landed in New York, they could take the Erie Canal to Buffalo and a lake steamer to Cleveland and then travel overland from there. Or they might travel the entire distance by stage. Whatever the case, the time would probably be no greater than by ship and riverboat all the way to Nauvoo and perhaps ever shorter.

Many Saints arrived in Nauvoo with few resources and others were even impoverished. What steps did the Church leaders take to help such people?

The Church did not ignore such members, as many critics like to suggest. Joseph, trustee for the Church lands, often sold cheaply or gave away town lots and country acreage to the immigrants, depending on their circumstances, as mentioned in the History of the Church: "Sunday,

* *

19—The High Council at Nauvoo voted to donate a city lot to Brother James Hendrix, who was shot in Missouri; also voted to build him a house; also donated a house and lot to Father Joseph Knight."

The Church originally took collections for the poor, but being too haphazard, the care of the poor was soon given into the hands of the bishops. This care was their primary responsibility in Nauvoo, and the First Presidency directed them to set up storehouses from which the poor might draw supplies. Heber C. Kimball's daughter, Helen Mar, remembered her mother calling upon the Bishop for assistance. She accompanied her "to see the Bishop [Vinson Knight], who was living in Upper Commerce, where the storehouse of the Lord was kept." This storehouse was the temple store, which functioned much like the bishops' storehouse does today. Members donated goods to the store in the form of tithing, which would then be distributed to the full-time temple workmen as pay as well as to the impoverished citizens. Such workmen were often those who could not find other work and would have descended into poverty without the temple work and store.

In his journal on October 15, 1843, Joseph noted, "Some say it is better to give to the poor than build the temple. The building of the temple has sustained the poor who were driven from Missouri, and kept them from starving; and it has been the best means for this object which could be devised."

The Church also had a farm, called the Big Field, where the poor could find work and food. Probably no community in the nation was better organized to care for their poor than Nauvoo.

Historical records indicate figures as high as 12,000 Saints being driven out of Missouri in the winter of 1838–39, but only 5,000 to 6,000 crossed to a welcome in Quincy. Where did the rest go?

The 12,000 figure may be a little high and the 5,000 to 6,000 figure a little low. However, all of those driven from Missouri did not end up in Quincy. Many of the Saints merely passed through and settled in the sparsely settled regions east of Quincy. Governor Lucas and the Iowans extended a welcome to the Saints, and many traveled

* *

northward and settled in Eastern Iowa from Keokuk to Fort Madison. Others were still moving from Missouri in the spring, about the time the Church purchased land in Commerce and the Saints started settling there. By the time the Saints understood the gathering was to be primarily in and around Nauvoo, many of them had established homes throughout much of Illinois and in Eastern Iowa. Quincy was still the major destination for the exiting Saints from Missouri, but it was not the only one.

Joseph mentions riding out to "Big Mound." Where was it and how did it get its name?

Big Mound was a settlement of British converts about seven miles east of Nauvoo. There are many Indian mounds in the Midwest, but this mound is merely a low-lying, broad-based hill. Relative to the flat farmlands around it, however, it could be defined as a "mound." Today, a farmhouse is built on the crest, but there is no evidence of the large community clustered there during the Nauvoo years. This mound has also gone by the name of Davis Mound, named after a Nauvoo merchant, Amos Davis, who had a home at the mound and died there in 1872.

Who or what was "Jo Duncan," a name often associated with Joseph Smith?

This was the name of one of the Prophet's favorite horses, a sorrel he purchased in July 1842. It was also the name of a former governor of Illinois who again became a candidate for that office in 1842 but lost to Thomas Ford. Why he named a favorite horse after a politician who was far more outspoken against the Mormons during his campaign than Thomas Ford, Joseph never said.

Joseph had another favorite mount named Charlie, a black horse with a prominent white star on its forehead. The Prophet often blackened the star so his enemies would not so easily identify him.

* *

* *

What is the importance or significance of Nauvoo being designated a National Historic Landmark, as it was in 1961?

If this property were privately owned and taxable, there would be tax credits available. However, since it is non-profit, this benefit does not apply. Therefore, the major advantages become, in this case, only two-fold. The designation protects the property from potential public projects on a state or federal level that might otherwise find a need to disrupt or destroy the historical significance of the site. The second advantage is strictly honorary and informs the public in general of the historical importance of this site. At the time of the designation, the National Historic Landmark Commission called Nauvoo one of the ten most significant historic landmarks in the country.

How could the Saints, impoverished after being driven from Missouri, afford to buy so much land in Illinois?

The Church purchased most of the land on long-term credit from such speculators as the White sons, Isaac Galland, Horace Hotchkiss, George Robinson, and Hiram Kimball. The land was then subdivided and sold to Church members, with the proceeds going to pay off the creditors. Since the refugees from Missouri had little cash, much of the money had to come from new converts moving into Nauvoo. Because of the Saints past reputation as an industrious people, land owners were quite willing to extend credit to them.

The early maps show a Commerce and a Commerce City where Nauvoo was built. Why were two separate towns laid out?

Actually, there were three town sites. The first settlement was Venus, made by James White and his sons in the southwest section of the peninsula. The first post office in Hancock County was established in Venus. Land speculators soon followed and laid out the town sites of Commerce and Commerce City north of Venus, both of which were primarily paper towns. By the time the Saints arrived in 1839, the entire area had become known as Commerce.

* *

* *

Why do we hear so much about Isaac Galland, as though all the land was purchased from him?

He did own much of the land, especially across the river in Iowa where the Saints also settled. Much of the reason he is so prominent in Church History, however, is because he joined the Church in 1839 (probably for business reasons) and served as land agent for the Saints. He was also generous, charging the Saints no interest on the lands he sold them and being a staunch defender of the Saints until he withdrew from activity in 1842, about the time he no longer found his association profitable. After a brief stint in California, he returned to Ft. Madison, where he died in 1858.

Why were the Saints so welcome in Illinois in 1838–39—in view of their expulsion from Missouri—with the widespread approval of the people of that state?

There were welcome for two major reasons. First, the relationship between the citizens of Illinois and Missourians was contentious. Illinoisans considered many of the settlers in frontier Missouri the riffraff from the southern states, whereas the people of Illinois, mainly from the Northeast, considered themselves higher class. In fact, Illinoisans commonly called Missourians "pukes." Welcoming the Saints into Illinois would "prove" to the country the difference between the law-abiding, tolerant citizens of Illinois and the low-class, bigoted "pukes" of Missouri.

Second, communities in Illinois needed the industrious Latter-day Saints. The communities were vying with each other for population, industry, and political prominence. The state also needed a larger tax base to help pay off the huge state debt that had been extended for "internal improvements." The Governor of Iowa was equally anxious to welcome the Saints for the same reasons. A large influx of Mormons could have given either of these states the financial and political advantages they needed.

This answer is not intended to diminish the hospitable nature of the people of Quincy, which was real. This hospitality was proven by their sympathy throughout the Mormon stay in Illinois and especially their generous relief of the Poor Camp after the last of the Saints were driven

* *

across the river following the "Battle of Nauvoo" in September 1846.

Why didn't the Saints select Iowa rather than Illinois when they were expelled from Missouri?

This is an excellent question and, in fact, many Saints did select Iowa, but not the majority, by any means. Governor Lucas of Iowa had welcomed the Saints if they desired to move there, and choosing Iowa would certainly have been advantageous, as later events proved. At the time, it was more sparsely populated, and thus opposition, if it arose, would have been less. Iowa was easier to reach and would have been farther from the more settled communities east of them where so much opposition was to occur.

A more important reason, however, was voiced by Isaac Galland in an 1839 letter to David Rogers, advising the Saints to move to Iowa. He said they would have better protection in a territory under the jurisdiction of the federal government, instead of a state "where murder, rapine and robbery are admirable traits in the character of a demagogue; and where the greatest villains often reach the highest offices." In Iowa, the Federal authorities could not have looked the other way because of "states' rights."

However, by the time of the exodus from Illinois seven years later, the situation had changed in Iowa. The population had increased, as had anti-Mormonism, and Iowa was about to become a state, removing any Federal protection.

Joseph Smith once made a prophecy concerning Stephen A. Douglas. What was it and did it ever come to pass?

In May 1843, while dining with Douglas in Carthage, Joseph detailed the Saints' persecutions in Missouri. Douglas agreed on the wrongful actions of Boggs and the Missourians, after which Joseph prophesied to Douglas: "Judge, you will aspire to the presidency of the United States, and if you ever turn your hand against the Latter-day Saints, you will feel the weight of the hand of the Almighty upon you; and you will live to see and know that I have testified the truth to you, for the conversation of this day will be with you through life."

Years later, Douglas did turn, for popular political reasons, against the Saints, voicing disparaging remarks about them as he aspired to the Presidency. Running against Lincoln in 1860, he went down to defeat, as Joseph had predicted. His friends eventually deserted him, and he died in the prime of his life, a disappointed man.

What are the earliest photographs of Nauvoo?

American photography was born in 1839, the year the Saints settled Nauvoo, when images on metal plates, called daguerreotypes, were made. One of those first daguerreotypists, Lucian Foster of New York, joined the Church and moved to Nauvoo in 1844. He established a gallery on Parley Street between Hyde and Partridge Streets and started making the first images of Nauvoo. Only a few of these images are known to exist today, but among them is believed to be the famous Temple on the Hill image.

The Prophet received the law of tithing (Doctrine and Covenants 119) at Far West on July 8, 1838, and yet Church histories say the law was instituted in Nauvoo in 1841. Which is true?

Both. Section 119 gives the reason for the law as for the "building of mine house," and so on. Although other purposes were mentioned, they all revolved around the prospect of the proposed temple at Far West, which had to be postponed. Between that date and the founding of Nauvoo was a time of intense turmoil, and Church leaders had no opportunity or sufficient reason to put the law into effect. The reason came with the commencement of the building of the next temple—the one in Nauvoo— and for this reason, the law of tithing was finally instituted in 1841 for the reason given in the original 1838 revelation.

Did William Smith, the surviving Smith brother, attempt to assert a claim to Church leadership?

Yes. However, he did not have much chance to make his challenge before the Saints approved the leadership of the Quorum of the Twelve and Brigham

* *

Young after the martyrdom in 1844. For the next several months, he was still a member of the Quorum of the Twelve but manifested a rebellious feeling toward the other members and Brigham's leadership. In spite of this fact, the Quorum ordained him as Church Patriarch in the summer of 1845. He then felt his new calling gave him precedence over the Twelve and tried to convince others of this authority and the need to make him a caretaker until Joseph III came of age. At the October Conference, because of his rebellious spirit, the people refused to sustain him as patriarch or apostle. A week later, he was excommunicated, and by the end of October, he was lecturing in St. Louis on the "corruption of the Twelve." Ironically, William, the most rebellious of the six brothers and the one who had given the Prophet the most grief, was the only one to survive into old age.

For a brief time, Zarahemla became the second most important stake and community of Saints in the United States. Where exactly was it located?

Because of the large number of Saints settling in the Iowa half-breed tract, the Church organized the Zarahemla stake as early as October 1839. Montrose was the center of the stake and more prominent because it was on the river and that was where the high council regularly met. In January 1842, however, the stake was discontinued, ostensibly, to build up Nauvoo. By that time, hostility had reached such a level in Iowa that Joseph was fearful of visiting due to a greater danger of capture and transport back to Missouri.

The community of Zarahemla, which no longer exists, was located about four miles west of Montrose.

When was a branch of The Church of Jesus Christ of Latter-day Saints reestablished in modern Nauvoo?

On March 17, 1956, the first branch of The Church of Jesus Christ of Latter-day Saints in modern Nauvoo was organized. Meetings were conducted in a visitors' center and missionary residence located on the northwest corner of the temple block. It then moved to the *Times and*

* *

*   *

Seasons building on the flats in 1960 and back to the temple site in the old Icarian school building in 1964. The branch moved into the present building on Durphy and Hubbard Streets in 1969, the first LDS chapel ever built in Nauvoo.

When did the Catholic Church establish its monastery in Nauvoo?

In October 1874, five sisters of the St. Benedict Convent in Chicago arrived in Nauvoo to open the St. Scholastica Academy. Later known as St. Mary Academy, it opened for seven "day students" in the old Mormon Arsenal on November 2 of that year. By September 1961, the school registered 228 girls and the sisters numbered 180. The school finally closed in 1997, and in 1999 the entire St. Mary Academy complex was purchased by the Mormon Church and renamed the Joseph Smith Academy.

Who were the Germans who came after the Icarians?

Even while the Icarians were here, German and Swiss immigrants learned of the abandoned Mormon city and started settling here. Word went back to their friends and relatives in Europe, and soon Nauvoo had the largest German-speaking population of any city in Illinois. The immigration started about the year the temple was burned. The Germans were the ones who established the wine culture in Nauvoo.

There appears to be much controversy over the question of whether Nauvoo ever became the largest city in Illinois. Did it?

The Illinois census takers of 1845 counted 11,057 residents in Nauvoo, while Chicago's figures for the same year were slightly higher. Remember, however, that in the last several months of 1845 and early 1846, Nauvoo was flooded with refugees from outlying settlements who were being burned out and driven from their homes by the mobs. On September 10, 1845, a mob attacked Morley's settlement south of Nauvoo and burned between seventy and eighty homes along with their crops and belongings. Some reports estimate that close to 400 residents fled to

*   *

Nauvoo from that one attack. During the fall and winter of 1845, mobs had found the answer to "reclaiming" Hancock County. It is therefore quite likely that during the last few months before the exodus in the spring of 1846, Nauvoo had a population larger than any city in Illinois, temporary though that status may have been.

After Joseph's death, Nauvoo was renamed the "City of Joseph." Why is it still called Nauvoo in journals and memoirs and even today?

President Brigham Young proposed the name change, and the Saints voted on it in the General Conference on April 6, 1845. As much as anything, the change seemed to be a direct response to the enemies of the Church, who had recently canceled the Nauvoo Charter. The Church wanted to give the martyred Prophet an even greater honor by making the city itself a memorial to him. Since no further legal attempt was made to change the name of the city, either with the proper state officials or through the postal service, the name change was more symbolic than literal and thus it was and is viewed by the Saints.

Note that eight years after the exodus, an attempt was made to settle a "city of Joseph" on the island of Lanai in the Hawaiian Islands. Mainly because of environmental reasons, that attempt failed.

How did the area of Commerce first come to the attention of the Latter-day Saints?

It happened because of a "lost refugee" from Missouri. An elder by the name of Israel Barlow, a refugee from Bogg's extermination order in Missouri, lost his way traveling eastward and ended up near the Des Moines River mouth in Iowa. Because of the destitute conditions of Barlow and his friends, the Iowans in that area befriended him and introduced him to gentlemen who might be of aid to the refugees. Among them was Isaac Galland, owner of much of the Half Breed Tract and the abandoned Fort Des Moines barracks near Monstrose, who was looking for buyers. Barlow reported back to the Church leaders in Quincy and the rest is history.

* *

Who was the last living person to have personally known the Prophet Joseph?

There probably is no definitive answer, but a name often mentioned in LDS history is Mary Field Garner. Mary lost a husband and two children as well as her father during the Mormon years in Nauvoo and recalled the resulting difficult time when her mother was left alone with six children. The Field family had to remain in Nauvoo until 1852 before going west. Mary, however, was in the Poor Camp on the Iowa shore after the Battle of Nauvoo and described the "miracle of the quails": "We did not have any bread and butter or any other food to eat, so we ate stewed quail and were very thankful to get that, for we were starving."

In Utah, Mary married William Garner, who had helped tend the Prophet's farm in Nauvoo, and settled in Hooper, Utah. Mary died in 1943, at the age of 107.

In the history of Nauvoo, we occasionally come across what is called *The Book of the Law of the Lord*. What exactly is that?

The Prophet Joseph kept a specially prepared book in which he recorded the names of those who ministered to him in kindness and where he recorded the names and special blessings upon friends who had helped in furthering the Gospel of the New Dispensation. He listed also the names of those who sacrificed in building the temple, revelations about the furthering of the Kingdom, and his feelings about the sisters and brethren around him. Today, *The Book of the Law of the Lord* is in the First Presidency's vault in Salt Lake City.

On Gustavus Hill's Map of the City of Nauvoo, two blocks are labeled Kimball's Garden and Park Place. What are they?

They were planned city parks, which, because of the forced exodus of the Saints, never materialized. Interestingly enough, the Park Place block has few buildings on it even today, and the Kimball's garden block is still farmland. The idea of a park in Nauvoo was indeed carried out with the setting aside of

* *

the 143-acre State Park east of Durphy Street, which opened in 1950.

Did Nauvoo have taverns?

In the nineteenth century, although some of them served liquors, the term tavern was synonymous with inn or hotel. Especially during the temperance movements of the 1840s, taverns that did not sell liquors were fairly common. Nauvoo had very strict controls and regulations, requiring fees from $10 to $100 for a liquor license and setting penalties for illegally dispensing liquor.

It is interesting to read the words of Josiah Quincy, mayor of Boston, who visited Nauvoo in 1844 and described his visit to Joseph's Mansion House: "On the right hand, as we entered the house, was a small and very comfortless-looking bar-room; all the more comfortless, perchance, from it being a dry bar-room, as no spirituous liquors were permitted at Nauvoo." Emma had forbidden Joseph to set up a liquor-bar for non-Mormon guests but later relented when her second husband, Lewis Bidamon, decided to equip the Mansion with the same—possibly as a convenience for himself.

Money and Mercantilism

One can find in Old Nauvoo store ledgers items marked for 6¼ cents. Were there coins for this amount?

Yes. Some historians claim it started with the widespread use in American commerce of the Spanish real (12½ cents) and the half-real (6¼ cents). With a similar value, however, and more common at this time was a York sixpence, an English silver coin with a value of six pennies or half a shilling. It served for items marked 6¼ cents, which was half a bit. Items were commonly priced in multiples of this amount: 12½ cents (a bit or an English shilling), 18¾, 25, and so forth.

Besides American coins, therefore, Nauvooans had to be familiar with English coins, brought in by immigrants, and Spanish coins, brought up the river from New Orleans. There was no federal currency at this time; the federal government minted only coins, such as the gold double eagle ($20.00), the eagle ($10.00), the half eagle ($5.00), the quarter eagle ($2.50), the silver dollar, half dollar, quarter dollar, dime, half dime, cent, and half cent.

Were there taxes in Nauvoo, and if so, what kind?

All Hancock County residents were required to pay a ½ percent tax on a number of items of personal property, including cattle, horses, wagons, clocks, watches, and so on. In addition, according to its charter, the city of

Nauvoo could also assess a ½ percent tax on real estate, which it did. An article describing the growth of Nauvoo in the *Times and Seasons* dated December 15, 1842, praised its citizens:

> They have converted a desolate waste into fields and gardens; they have enhanced the value of property, for many miles around Nauvoo, tenfold; they have created a market that takes in a great portion of the surplus produce, that is raised within thirty and forty miles of Nauvoo; and in the city of Nauvoo alone (which three years ago was a barren waste) their city and county tax amounts to upwards of four thousand dollars, (as per last assessment).

At the time, such taxes came to little more than a dollar per person per year or about an average workman's daily salary. The assessments were apparently quite low.

Did Nauvoo ever issue its own currency as other American communities did?

Cities during the Nauvoo era commonly issued their own scrip. Nauvoo did likewise in a denomination of one dollar. Both the Nauvoo Legion and the arsenal also issued scrip to raise funds for arms maintenance of buildings. Such scrip could only be redeemed or accepted in the immediate vicinity. The federal government did not issue any paper currency until the Civil War, and the country was flooded with state, city, and private bank currency that might not be accepted as money, depending on where it was being passed or how solvent the city, state, or bank was believed to be. This inconsistency of currency was a serious problem for travelers who were forced to carry hard money. Even the hard money caused problems because of the amount of counterfeiting, raising suspicion on any traveling strangers.

Did Nauvoo have banks for loans and savings?

Although larger cities had banks, Nauvoo had not yet established any. The city had little need for a place to deposit savings, since any surplus money, in a new city like Nauvoo, was normally invested in new homes, businesses, or real estate. Loans were either made with out-of-state banks for large sums, or like Isaac Galland, creditors were willing to make long-term loans. Small sums would be borrowed from friends or from local businessmen. Amos Davis, who had a store and hotel on Mulholland Street, lists in his daybook small loans he made to his customers in amounts ranging from 25 cents to $12.50.

The Church had ventured into the banking business in Kirtland and the results were disastrous. Such an experience, plus a popular distrust of such institutions, was certainly a factor in discouraging any thoughts of starting such an institution in Nauvoo.

Finally, Nauvoo was founded during the most severe financial panic the nation had ever experienced. It started in 1837 and lasted for about five years, which includes the banking crisis beginning in 1841 when a third of the nation's banking capital was lost. Bank closings and specie shortages throughout the country in 1841 and 1842 did little to encourage the idea of any banks in Nauvoo.

Were there any exports from Nauvoo? Imports only could economically destroy a community seeking self-sufficiency.

The best answer might be found in the records of cargos the *Maid of Iowa* carried while it was in the service of the Nauvoo Saints. In addition to carrying lumber from the northern Mississippi region and coal from Iowa, it carried wheat, corn, and pork from Illinois. Although these latter exports could have been loaded at Moline or Quincy, we also know farmers were starting to grow wheat, corn, and pork in abundance in western Hancock County by 1843. We can safely say some of the bumper farm yields were shipped from Nauvoo aboard the Mormon steamer as well as other docking steamships.

Exports of those few items did not suggest self-sufficiency for the Saints. Essential imports still far outstripped the cash-generating exports, but the Saints were making progress before 1845. Mob destruction of crops, orchards, barns, and livestock that year signaled the loss of any hope for self-sufficiency as long as the Saints remained in Illinois.

* *

There are no large streams near Nauvoo for waterpower. Was the Mississippi River harnessed for power, and if so, how?

Joseph Smith suggested establishing water-powered manufactories along the river. In response, Newell Knight petitioned and received permission to run a wing dam into the river and build a mill adjacent thereto, a gristmill that operated until the exodus in 1846. Similar privileges were granted to others, but we do not have a definitive answer on the number of actual mills constructed. A Hancock County history provides a list of ten mills in Mormon Nauvoo, all but one of them along the river. Some of these were steam mills and required no dams, only a water source.

For water-powered mills, a wing dam, constructed at an angle against the current, could create enough of a fall to run under-shot water wheels to power machinery of almost any kind.

Without banks, where did the people of Nauvoo keep surplus money or other valuables?

Most of the Saints had little surplus money, but when they did, they kept it in their homes. In her autobiography, Sarah Leavitt mentions an English immigrant by the name of Fox who claimed to have $50,000 in gold hidden in his home in the settlement of Big Mound, east of Nauvoo. Such amounts, if true, would demonstrate the need for banks in the community.

Were there any major industrial plans abandoned after the death of Joseph or after the decision to leave Nauvoo?

Near the end of 1843, Joseph suggested a petition to Congress for the building of a canal bypassing the Lower Des Moines Rapids. This canal would finally be built more than thirty years later. He also initiated the idea of erecting a huge wing dam out into the river to provide power for several mills and factories. Although the dam briefly started in 1845 as the Nauvoo Water Power Company, it was soon abandoned because of the planned exodus and the need to quickly finish the temple. Joseph's plans

* *

* *

had the potential for making Nauvoo one of the major manufacturing centers of the Midwest, if not the United States.

Did Nauvoo residents haggle over prices of goods in the local stores?

In any economy where bartering exists, there will obviously be price negotiations, and the same was true of Nauvoo. If the question concerns non-bartering situations, there might still be a variety of prices, depending on whether payment was by scrip, coin, or credit. Like today, pricing and payment could also depend on such nebulous things as building good will, friendships, and so on. These discrepancies are the reason many stores of that era advertised themselves as "One Price" stores, putting an end to the centuries-old habit of haggling and bargaining that caused so much ill-will in merchandising.

We have often heard the Prophet Joseph ran his Red Brick Store for such a short time because he had difficulty refusing credit and was thus not making a profit. An equally plausible reason would have been the seemingly unequal treatment and resulting resentment of the Saints over the results of such common practices. Joseph simply didn't have the temperament to be a hard-nosed businessman.

* *

Native Americans

Were any Native Americans living in this area when the Saints arrived in 1839?

None were living on the east side of the river. A treaty forced upon the Sac and Fox Indians of Illinois in 1804 ceded to the United States all of their lands east of the Mississippi. As long as any of this land remained public, however, the tribes understood their right to hunt, fish, or grow crops. Greedy settlers challenged this right, however, and troubles escalated and became one of the causes of the War of 1812. The war still did not solve all the problems between the races, and when the Americans attempted to remove the Sac Indians from a region north of the Rock River, the conflict escalated into the Black Hawk Indian War of 1832, after which there were no longer any Sac or Fox in Illinois. Thus the Saints had little contact with any Native Americans when they arrived at Nauvoo in 1839. Not until 1841 did the Fox and Sac Indians in Iowa start making contact with the Saints, and friendly feelings and visits continued until the Saints were forced west in 1846.

Did any Native Americans belong to the Church?

Yes. As early as 1840, according to Phoebe Woodruff writing to her husband Wilford, a Native American family was baptized into the Church. Three other members also gave Brigham counsel on the traits of the Native Americans before the exodus to the West. Those members were Joseph and George Herring, Mohawk brothers (although Heber C. Kimball called them Shawnees), and Lewis Dana of the Oneida nation.

On September 29, 1845, five Native Americans met in council with Brigham and others at Daniel Spencer's home. That evening, according to Heber C. Kimball's journal, Brigham "baptized three red men, and confirmed them at the water's edge." Heber does not mention any names for these three converts. They may, however, have been three of the Native Americans Hosea Stout had dinner with the day before: Edward Whiteseye, Peter Cooper, and Moses Otis.

The chief of police, Hosea Stout, was apparently a good friend to these Native American members and often dined and socialized with them. In his diary for the day of that dinner, he recorded: "Returned home about one o'clock took my dinner then went home with Captain [J. D.] Hunter in company with George L. M. Herring, Brother Herring, Edward Whiteseye—Peter Cooper and Moses [Otis], to partake of a dinner prepared for us by the kindness of Captain Hunter's Lady—& we had a complete jollification and then went with George Herring to see Cyrus Daniels, who is still very unwell." In 1846, while crossing Iowa, Hosea reported that he stayed one night with "George & Joseph Herring, my two Mohawk friends . . . had a joyful and entertaining evening together nor was I ever better received & entertained by my white brethren."

Did any Native Americans receive their endowments or sealings in the Nauvoo Temple?

On October 14, 1845, Mary Gont (a white woman) was sealed to Lewis Dana by Brigham Young. Brother Dana was the first Native American to have a wife sealed to him under the new and everlasting covenant. Panina S. Cotton, a Cherokee, and Brother Dana, who had moved to Nauvoo in 1840 and joined the Church, had earlier received their temple blessings.

Chief Keokuk once spoke to the Saints in the Grove. What did he talk about?

He spoke on August 1841, but not long. Joseph preached to Keokuk and approximately 100 chiefs and braves of the Sac and Fox Indian tribes about the Book of Mormon and its promises to them and advised them not to fight among themselves. Keokuk responded by saying: "I have a Book of Mormon at my wigwam that you gave me a number of moons ago. I believe you are a great and good man. Keokuk looks rough, but I am a son of the Great Spirit. I have heard your advice. We intend to quit fighting, and follow the good talk you have given us." After the talk in the grove, they all sat down to a feast together, and the Native Americans entertained the brethren with some of their dancing.

Did any of the Nauvooan Native Americans go west with the Saints?

We know the Herring brothers got as far as Winter Quarters. Records indicate the leaders had a problem with the Herring brothers and alcohol. They both expressed dissatisfaction with the Twelve, and in January 1847, Joseph Herring was excommunicated. Hosea Stout does not mention what became of the Herring brothers, but William Hickman, a bodyguard for Brigham, mentions in his notorious book, *Brigham's Destroying Angel*, the fate of Joseph Herring. After threatening to take Brigham's life and scalp, Hickman claims he caught up with Joseph, "used him up, and scalped him." Since much of Hickman's book was an exaggeration, his report of Joseph Herring's fate may be in the same category.

Lewis Dana was actually made a member of the Council of Fifty and was not dropped until 1848. He was the first Native American member of any quorum of the Church. Since the Church has a record of his death date in 1885, it is quite possible he reached Utah.

Nauvoo Legion

Did the Nauvoo Legion have uniforms?

When the Legion was organized, one of its ordinances provided "that the discipline, drill, rules, regulations, and uniforms of the United States' Army, so far as applicable, be and they hereby are adopted for the legion." However, nothing like that ever came to pass since the same ordinance also allowed each company to "adopt its own uniform for the non-commissioned officers and privates belonging to it." Some of the officers, to make their rank more obvious, had uniforms fashioned for themselves. These varied according to the taste of the officer. The rank and file members, however, made do with what they had, using only ribbons, lacings, scarves, and such to distinguish their particular company. It was a motley-looking militia, as were most state militias at that time, but better trained and more enthusiastic than most.

Did the Nauvoo Legion have cavalry?

Yes. The Legion had two cohorts, which is Roman military terminology for 1,000 men, although each of the Nauvoo Legion's cohorts had far more than that. The first cohort was a mounted unit that included cavalry, lancers, flying artillery lancers, and riflemen. The Legion made more use of this cohort than the second, which was infantry, especially during the final months of Nauvoo, when outlying settlements needed speedy rescue from the rampaging mobs.

* *

Was Joseph Smith's military rank of Lieutenant-General self-assumed?

The city charter granted by the Illinois State Legislature signed by Governor Carlin specified that the commander of the legion should hold that rank, making Joseph Smith the highest-ranking military officer in the country. He once joked that he could not be court-martialed because he could not have a jury of his peers. The only other military officer to have held that rank was George Washington. Brigham would hold it for a brief time after Joseph's death, and Ulysses S. Grant would be the next army officer to hold it.

Why didn't the Legion stay to defend the Saints remaining in Nauvoo? The Battle of Nauvoo might have ended differently.

They didn't stay for three main reasons:

1. The Saints who had started the exodus had reason to believe enemies would attempt to halt the migrating Saints as they were moving west, either by Missouri militia or, more likely, by federal forces who feared the Saints might join the British in the Northwest. The Legion would be needed against any such forces that tried to block their exodus.

2. The families of the Legion members were among the migrating Saints and needed their men in their march westward.

3. Brigham and the other leaders were fairly confident that when the anti-Mormons saw the exodus actually taking place, they would be satisfied and let the Saints depart in peace.

Since the Missouri mobs had confiscated the Saints' weapons, how was the Nauvoo Legion armed?

Once Illinois had issued a charter for a militia unit, the Saints were qualified to receive state arms, which they did. Unfortunately, John C. Bennett, who soon apostatized, was appointed quartermaster-general. He kept no

* *

records and disposed of the arms as he pleased. At the time of Governor Ford's disarming of the Nauvoo Legion just before the martyrdom, Ford was only able to determine that the Legion had been issued three cannons (six pounders) and about 250 stand of small arms, which was about the number they surrendered.

Outsiders' estimates of Mormon arms, however, ran as high as that mentioned in an October 1845 issue of the *St. Louis Reveille*, whose editors believed the Nauvoo Legion had twenty-four cannons (twelve pounders), 1,000 revolving rifles, and a large number of other arms. Such exaggerations fed the fears of anti-Mormons, who believed the Saints were planning an all-out war when they felt strong enough. Even the building of an arsenal by the Saints was evidence to the anti-Mormons of the Legion's need for a building to house such a large stock of weapons.

Several brethren worked at gunsmithing in Nauvoo, actively supplying the arms lost in Missouri. In 1844, Theodore Turley was made Armorer General of the Legion and quickly made purchases of arms in New Orleans to resupply the Legion with arms to replace those returned to the state authorities in June.

The Nauvoo Legion was formed with the intention of protecting the Saints from the type of mob action that had occurred in Missouri. When did violent mob activity begin in Illinois?

Some of the first cases of violence against outlying farms and communities began late in 1843. Three days before Christmas of that year, a mob burned David Holman's house, near Ramus. From this point on, depredations and violence increased until it culminated in the Battle of Nauvoo in September 1846.

Was any use ever made of the Legion against the Illinois mobs before the exodus?

Absolutely, especially the cavalry cohort. After the death of Joseph and when the mobs became most active in their attacks on outlying Mormon settlements, companies of twenty to forty Legionnaires rode throughout

* *

Hancock County, chasing mobbers, trying to protect Mormon farms and communities, and rescuing those who were burned out and escorting them back to Nauvoo. In one rescue mission in the fall of 1845, a company rode directly into Carthage, skirmishing with mobbers on the way, to occupy the city.

There appear to be differing accounts as to the number of men in the Nauvoo Legion. What was the maximum size?

Francis Bouquet, in *The Compilation of the Original Documents Concerning the Nauvoo, Illinois, Mormon Settlement with Pertinent Observations*, observed that at the time of the death of the Prophet Joseph, the Legion consisted of no fewer than 5,000 men and was considered the "largest trained soldiery in the United States excepting only the United States Army." This account seems somewhat exaggerated, but unlike other communities, a great deal of pressure to participate in the militia was put on the Saints, including a local requirement that all males between 18 and 45 participate. Exemptions were permitted, but because of peer pressure and past experience with hostile neighbors, we can be sure the percentage of residents in the Nauvoo area who actively trained was considerably larger than any other Illinois community. Four thousand Legionnaires would probably not be much of an exaggeration.

How would this number compare in size with the total Illinois militia at this time?

The abstract of the United States Militia from the Army Register for 1845 lists the totals for each state according to the most recent reporting at the time. The total given for the Illinois State Militia is 83,234, the sixth largest out of thirty states and territories. Representing no more than 5 percent of the state forces, the Legion obviously could never stand up to a combined state force that could potentially be sent against Nauvoo.

* *

* *

Was fear of the Legion, a legitimate component of the Illinois Militia, a contributing cause for the growing hostility against the Saints in Nauvoo?

Although it was legally a unit of the vastly larger Illinois State Militia and chartered by the Illinois State Legislature, there is little question that the very existence of this large and well-armed Mormon "army" was perceived as a threat to the surrounding Illinois communities. A U.S. Army officer viewed the Legion in 1842 and sent his impressions in the form of a letter to the *New York Herald*. He described the Legion in such words as there being "no troops in the states like them in point of enthusiasm and warlike aspect" and predicted that the time would come when "this gathering host of religious fanatics will make this country shake to its centre." Considering such reports, it is little wonder their Illinois neighbors feared them and wanted them removed.

Was the Nauvoo Legion abolished with the demise of Nauvoo?

Officially, it was abolished before the exodus with the withdrawing of the charter by the State of Illinois. Unofficially, it continued to function right through the exodus in 1846. Since it had been organized as part of the Illinois Militia, it could not exist after the State legislature suspended the charter and certainly not outside the state. Still, the Nauvoo Legion furnished most of the "Mormon Battalion" for the Mexican War and their march from Iowa to San Diego. The Legion was reorganized in Utah as the "Nauvoo Legion" in 1848 and finally rendered inactive by an 1870 proclamation by Acting Governor Shaffer, who forbade any gatherings of the militia without his permission. It was finally disbanded by the Congressional Edmunds-Tucker Act in 1887, but revived again in 1894 as the National Guard of Utah.

Did the Nauvoo Legion have its own flag?

In April 1841, on the occasion of the laying of the Nauvoo Temple cornerstones, the sisters of Nauvoo presented the Legion with a large

* *

silk national flag they had made. Evidence of a special Legion flag can be gleaned only from the Prophet's journal just before his fatal trip to Carthage:

"June 22, 1844: * * * At 7 p.m. I instructed General Dunham [of the Nauvoo Legion] to cause the regiments of the 2nd Cohort to turn out tomorrow and work by turns three or four hours each with entrenching tools, and to take the best measures in case of attack. I also gave orders that a standard be prepared for the nations."

Other than this obscure mention of a special standard, little evidence indicates they flew flags aside from the nation's flag in their musterings and parades, unless we count the Pitt Brass Band flag. The band, which often marched with the Legion, had its own flag with an all-seeing eye at the top, stripes of blue and white silk, and two scrolls with the words "Nauvoo Brass Band" on a square of pink silk. This flag dates from 1840, was carried across the Plains, and is currently in the possession of the Daughters of Utah Pioneers.

Joseph and Hyrum's incarceration in the Carthage jail on a charge of treason has been linked to the Nauvoo Legion. How?

Governor Ford explained this link in the *History of Illinois*: "The overt act of treason charged against them consisted in the alleged levying of war against the state by declaring martial law in Nauvoo, and in ordering out the legion to resist the posse comitatus." As Joseph tried to explain, the Legion was called out to protect the city of Nauvoo against the possibility of invasion by the mobs. Nevertheless, the use of the Legion without the governor's authorization was an excuse for the Carthage authorities to hold Joseph without bail while the mob organized for his assassination.

Nauvoo Restoration, Inc.

When did the Church start buying property in Illinois?

The Church purchased Carthage jail in 1903. It had served as a jail until 1866, when it became a private residence. Under the direction of Hyrum's son, Joseph F. Smith, the Church bought the site, including two acres, for $4,000. The Church then assigned a caretaker, who rented the building to individuals until 1938. Starting in that year, action was taken to restore the jail as a shrine to the memory of the Prophet Joseph and his brother Hyrum while at the same time opening it to visitors.

When did the Church start buying property in Nauvoo?

Wilford Wood, a wealthy furrier of Bountiful, Utah, who felt strongly about the preservation of historic Church sites and memorabilia, purchased the first sites. He started buying portions of the temple site in 1937, which was finally completed in 1961.

The restoration of what site prompted the creation of Nauvoo Restoration?

In 1954, after several years of negotiation, Dr. Kimball was able to purchase the Nauvoo home that had belonged to his great-grandfather, Heber C. Kimball. After being remodeled and dedicated in 1960 as a

* *

summer home for his family, Dr. Kimball's discovery of the interest the home created prompted him to approach the First Presidency with his ideas for a restored Nauvoo.

When was Nauvoo Restoration, Inc. (NRI) created?

On July 27, 1962, the official papers creating the corporation were signed, with Dr. LeRoy Kimball as the first president. Members of the first board of directors were Harold Fabian of the Citizens' Advisory Council to the National Park Service; A. Hamer Reiser, secretary to the First Presidency; David M. Kennedy, Secretary of the Treasury of the United States; and J. Willard Marriott, chairman of the Board of the Marriott Corporation.

How does a restoration like Nauvoo survive without charging admission?

All the missionary guides you see here, including the service missionaries, not only work without salary, but they also pay their own living expenses. Donations from Nauvoo pioneer descendants and family organizations often pay for the restorations. NRI, sponsored by The Church of Jesus Christ of Latter-day Saints, pays for the operating expenses.

Where does NRI obtain the artifacts we see on the sites?

Most of these are donated by members; many of them are of historical significance and owned by descendants of Nauvoo pioneers. Non-members who recognize the significance of the restoration and wish to further its objectives donated others.

Why are all the male missionary guides called elders? Aren't some of them high priests?

First of all, "elder" is the office of the Melchizedek Priesthood to which all worthy male members may be ordained at the age of eighteen. They are given the authority to perform all of the ordinances that will be required

* *

of them in the mission field. "Elder" is also the only general title that can be used for all bearers of that priesthood, regardless of the specific offices they hold. Also note that another term for the original twelve disciples was "elders."

The name Stephen Baird is mentioned in connection with NRI. Who was he?

Brother Baird worked for NRI as a paid architect in the late 1960s. His company in Utah designed and built, out of bronze, the large temple models seen here in Nauvoo.

What are examples of other crafts or occupations that existed in Old Nauvoo that are not represented in the restoration?

Broom making, book binding, cabinet making, photography (daguerreotyping), hat making, soap making, carriage manufacturing, grist milling, saw milling, dentistry, farming, fishing, basket weaving, comb making, match manufacturing, tanners, plasters, glaziers, architects, silver smiths, lawyers, physicians, surveyors, liverymen, iron mongering, and more. It is highly unlikely that most of these will ever be restored, since they represent a living city and would be most uneconomical for an historical restoration.

Outdoors
and Nature

What kinds of wild game lived in the vicinity of Old Nauvoo?

By the 1840s, game that was so abundant as to constitute a problem for crops twenty years earlier (bear, deer, wild turkeys, pigeons, opossums, ducks, geese, partridges, quail, prairie chickens, and squirrels) was still plentiful but was rapidly thinning out. David Cazier described his youth in Illinois in his autobiography: "Now Illinois furnished plenty of sports for boys in the way of wild fruit and game. The prairie chickens (hens) was so thick that they would darken the sun when they would fly and wild strawberries galore."

The *Millennial Star* informed its readers in 1842 of the availability of wild game when they emigrated to Nauvoo: "There are no game laws [as there were in England]; any person who pleases may hunt, shoot, or destroy rabbits, pigeons, wild ducks, geese, swan, turkeys, deer, antelopes, bears, elks."

Did Nauvoo residents fish the Mississippi, and what kinds of fish would they have found there?

All the rivers of the Northwest at this time had fish so plentiful that they were seldom mentioned in LDS journals, either because they were taken for granted or because the Saints had little experience in catching them. Some early reports, however, mention shoals of river fish covering half

* *

an acre and so plentiful that hook and line were considered too slow and seines were used. One memoir describes such fishing in 1830 in which "it was then quite common to catch 50 barrels of bass at one haul." Other varieties in equal abundance were wall-eyed pike, muskellunge, pan fish, carp, sturgeon, sauger, catfish, and perch. Channel catfish five to six feet long were not uncommon. The same source mentions 800 barrels of pike as the desired amount for a season's catch.

Some people have said the so-called tornado that blew down the walls of the temple in 1850 was really an unusually strong wind and that a tornado would have been an extremely rare occurrence in Nauvoo. Is this true?

There were obviously eyewitnesses, but most of them had never experienced a tornado, so they described it as a furious wind. Emile Vallet, son of one of the original French Icarians, described the storm in his book *Communism at Nauvoo*. He was on the site when the storm arose, and he left a description that fits the definition of a tornado. He said, "The wind was terrific, the rain blinding! The cloud touched the ground and we were almost paralyzed with fright."

Has Nauvoo ever been flooded—either before or after the construction of the Keokuk Dam?

A serious flood occurred in 1844 that destroyed a great deal of mill property along the river. Other floods periodically flooded the lower portions of Nauvoo until the dam at Keokuk was finished in 1913. The most recent flood was in 2008. Fortunately, the Keokuk Dam was able to control to a large extent the level of Lake Cooper in front of Nauvoo, and water damage in the restored village was minimal.

What is the "Mormon Fly" early travelers to Nauvoo mentioned?

The Mormon Fly is the mayfly (also called "shade fly" or "fish fly"). These obnoxious winged insects, found in great quantities along the river, live

* *

only long enough as adults, sometimes merely a day, to mate and lay eggs. During mating, adult males fly in huge swarms waiting for a female to enter the swarm and be fertilized. Elder Andrew Jenson, who visited Nauvoo in the 1920s, reported that "the people from the surrounding country do not like to visit Nauvoo for fear of being eaten up by flies, ravens, and other vicious birds." There is actually no reason to fear the flies: the adults never feed.

Pastimes and Youth

What is the correct position of hands for the stick pull?

One person should hold the stick with both hands inside and the other person with both outside. Otherwise there is an imbalance. Where to place both hands was not necessarily a problem for the Prophet Joseph: he often used just one.

What are quoits and how were they played?

Dictionaries of the time define quoits as "a kind of horse shoe to be pitched or thrown at a fixed object in play. In common practice, a plain flat stone is used for this purpose." The target was two pegs (megs) driven into the ground about twenty feet apart, and teams were chosen as in horse shoes. Quoit is an early English verb that means "to throw" and was a fairly common game in Nauvoo.

How old were the boys in the Whittling and Whistling Brigade?

Most of them were teenagers or young men. Samuel Woolley reported that during a conference meeting held in Nauvoo in the spring of 1843, an officer came to arrest Joseph. In order to prevent him from doing so, "a number of boys, including myself, commenced whittling sticks and whistling, and every time the officer neared the house where the Prophet was, we would stand in front of him and whittle and whistle. The result of this was that he did not arrest Joseph Smith that day." Samuel was eighteen.

Did the Nauvoo youth play any game similar to baseball or softball?

Yes. It was called "Old Cat." Depending on the number of players available, it might be One Old Cat, Two Old Cat, and so on, the number representing the number of bases used. Like baseball, the batter, using a trimmed stick, would hit the ball, usually made of rags wrapped with string, and run to the base. He was out if the ball was caught in the air or on one bounce. Variations of this game were called town ball or rounders. Whatever the case, modern observers would recognize the similarities to baseball or softball.

How common would it be to find "spoiled" children among the early Saints?

A large number of foreign visitors mentioned the lack of discipline in American childrearing. This observation, of course, might have been in comparison to what some scholars believe was overly severe discipline of European children. Whatever the case, journals and diaries suggest no more than the normal amount of delinquency or misbehavior among Mormon children for a number of reasons. Life was harsh, and the children had to learn work and responsibility at a very early age. Nauvoo was a religiously oriented community and moral training was more emphasized there than in most American cities. Joseph led the adults in demonstrating an interest in young people and became a role model for a large number of youth as later diaries suggest. Spoiled? Perhaps only in the sense of greater love and concern emanating from the trying times the families had been subjected to in the past and an attempt by the parents to compensate for what their children had suffered in their persecutions.

Were children's books available in the 1840s?

The nineteenth century saw the beginning of publishers putting out books

* *

for the amusement of children rather than just moral training, as was the practice in the previous century. We find such books as Clement Moore's *A Visit From St. Nicholas* in 1822 and Irving's *Rip Van Winkle* three years earlier. In 1827, when fairy tales and nursery rhymes were becoming especially popular, Peter Parley started a whole series of children's books. Publishers were also designing books in smaller sizes and with fewer pages. The number of such books in stores in Nauvoo was undoubtedly limited, but they were certainly available in the nation, and converts probably brought in many.

Were the games and toys we find at Pastimes available in such stores as the Amos Davis or Red Brick Store?

A perusal of the Amos Davis Store daybook shows only one item out of more than 250 that could be classified strictly as a toy: a tin horn for 25 cents. Parents or craftsmen friends made most of the games and toys of that period. Most Latter-day Saints are familiar with the story of the Prophet taking some boys to Brother Hancock's carpenter shop in Nauvoo to make some tippies and wooden paddles for playing a street game. Such incidents could be multiplied many times, especially during the long winter evenings when fathers and mothers enjoyed making for their children the same toys, dolls, and games they had played with as children.

Boys also commonly made their own play "things" such as bows and arrows, willow whistles, kites, and even corn-stalk fiddles. Girls wanting a jump rope, which might be difficult to acquire, could make do with small grape vines from the woods or fence rows, and for the popular game of "jack-stones," they could gather pretty pebbles along the river or streams.

Did the Saints have large numbers of children in the 1840s, and, if so, was it for religious reasons?

Procreation as a commandment was not an entrenched doctrine in the 1840s, so religion had relatively little to do with family size. Mormon women had a lot of children for the same reasons non-Mormons did in the 1840s: knowledge and use of birth control was not as prevalent; there

* *

was a need for large families for labor in a rural economy; and high child mortality was an inducement to have more children, guaranteeing help and security as the parents aged.

Note: Even though the birth rate in the United States was much greater than in Europe (one in twenty compared to one in twenty-seven), the death rate among the very young in Nauvoo was also high. The sexton's death list in Nauvoo indicates that 44 percent of all deaths were of children five years of age and younger. Families of eight or more children were not in the least uncommon in the rest of the country, but because of their previous persecutions, resulting impoverishment, poor health, and especially the high death rate in Nauvoo, family sizes among the Saints were much below that of comparable socio-economic groups in other parts of the nation.

What were the most popular competitive sports that did not require strength such as wrestling or stick pulling?

Bowling (either Ninepins or Tenpins) was so popular in the rest of the country that the City Council felt it must be regulated. Players rolled wooden balls down alleys (smoothed over ground) to knock down nine-inch-high wooden pins. This game became so popular that by the time the Saints left Nauvoo, the game had moved indoors and was being operated primarily by non-Mormons. The "alleys" were becoming disreputable places of amusement, and visitors spoke of them disdainfully.

Actually, there was fear of such "alleys" while the Saints were still in Nauvoo. Section 35 of the Legislative Powers of the Nauvoo City Charter mentions the power "to license, regulate, and suppress, and restrain, billiard tables, and from one to twenty pin alleys."

The younger boys played such games as "antony over," "prisoners base," "rounders," "corner ball," and "fox and hounds."

Was Sunday play restricted in any way for the youth of Nauvoo?

Definitely. Sunday was observed much as it was by any religious group of the early nineteenth century, which was not much different than by their

* *

Puritan forefathers. Sunday was a day of long religious public meetings and quiet activities at home, either reading scriptures or playing quietly with games or toys that had a religious significance. A toy ark and animals that would have been appropriate toys for Sabbath play are on display in the Brigham Young home. Sunday was also a time for family walks, especially to the cemetery to learn about those who had passed away and to contemplate the meanings of mortality and immortality.

* *

Education

How many schools existed in Nauvoo?

We must first understand that there were two kinds of schools, determined by the way teachers were paid—either by parents, in what were called subscription schools, or by the county, in what were called common schools. The latter were not "public" schools, since the county only paid a small set amount for each student and did not "support" the schools in any other manner. Between 1842 and 1845, Hancock County records list twenty-seven Nauvoo teachers who received county funds. We do not know how many received such funds for the entire period of Nauvoo's history nor do we know exactly how many private (subscription) schools existed, since most were for indefinite periods of time and might have met in any home or public building. One source states that at least eighty different men and women served as teachers in Nauvoo.

How were the teachers paid?

When the county paid the teachers, they paid up to four cents per day per student, depending often on the gender of the teacher, his or her qualifications, or the generosity of the government at the time. In subscription schools in which the parents paid, the amounts varied from perhaps $2 to $4 per subject for a twelve-week term as some teachers charged, or 17 to 25 cents per subject per week as others charged. Mary

* *

Wilsey taught thirty-five common school students for thirteen weeks over the Red Brick Store. Her total salary from the county at the end of the term was $43.75, which amounted to approximately 67 cents per day.

Were any buildings built specifically as schools?

No. Since there were no such things as "public" schools in Hancock County, education depended strictly on the initiative of men or women who saw education as merely a part-time profession. There were, therefore, no funds for the construction of schools. The teachers either held classes in their homes, as was the case in the Pendleton home, or the students were allowed to meet in such public buildings as the Cultural Hall or the Seventies Hall. School was held for a time over the Prophet's Red Brick Store. Some buildings were referred to as schoolhouses, as we note in the Prophet's journal for March 12, 1844: "A meeting of the inhabitants of the Tenth ward was held this evening at the schoolhouse on the hill, in Parley Street." These were most likely empty buildings used as schools without being specifically designed as such.

Did the teachers need any special qualifications?

They did if they were receiving any public funds. Although there was no need for professional training, teachers were examined and certified. "Examinations" were undoubtedly very cursory and informal, but for the most part, evidence suggests fairly competent teachers in Nauvoo. We do know they were interested in giving the students the best education possible. A notice appeared in the *Nauvoo Neighbor* on August 30, 1843, announcing a meeting of school teachers at the Nauvoo Seminary on September 2 to consider establishing a uniformity of class books and to promote greater "concert of action" among the teachers in promoting better education. This objective appears particularly admirable when one considers there was no directing authority for such a meeting other than a voluntary movement toward improving the qualification of the teachers.

* *

* *

How long was the school "year"?

There was no school "year." The teachers determined the terms, which varied usually from two to three months and were normally in the colder months when farm work was slack and families did not need the children at home. One amazing exception to this was an unusually long, warm weather school Eli Kelsy taught at the Seventies Hall from May 13 through December 20, 1844. We have no record of how successful he was in keeping the students in class during the summer months.

What kinds of subjects were taught in Nauvoo schools?

We have a pretty good idea of this answer thanks to the ads for the subscription schools that appeared in the *Nauvoo Neighbor*. Various teachers, depending upon their training and qualifications, taught such subjects as orthography, geography, grammar, composition, oratory, philosophy, Greek, Latin, chemistry, Spanish, French, mathematics, and music.

Especially of interest are the subjects the schools did not teach. The State of Illinois, during the Nauvoo years, provided by law "that no literary institution or school shall have a religion department." Despite the importance of religion in Nauvoo, no evidence suggests it was taught. Another subject, strangely enough, that was not yet firmly established in American or Nauvoo schools was history. Although a few American schools were starting to offer history, no evidence exists that it was taught in Nauvoo. Since LDS leaders seem to have been well-versed in their history, we can only speculate on reasons for its absence among the Saints.

One reason for its general absence in schools was its perception as an inexact subject, which it certainly is. History has been a popular subject for centuries but not as a teachable "science" until well into the nineteenth century.

What kinds of examinations were given students in Nauvoo schools?

There were no written exams. All exams were oral. The first written exams in American schools began in Boston in 1845. Students did not have any

* *

report cards either. Instead, they received rewards of merit that were blank certificates for excellence in academics or behavior. The teachers filled them in with the student's name and then gave them to the students to take home. Although these were undoubtedly treasured by the students, whose teachers bought them in quantity, few of them exist today.

Did the University of Nauvoo ever conduct any classes?

Yes. The University of the City of Nauvoo was further advanced and had greater impact on the Saints of Nauvoo and the Church than many scholars like to concede. The reason it has been down played may be that the University never had a central campus. It did, however, have a distinguished faculty including Orson and Parley Pratt, Orson Spencer, Sidney Rigdon, and Gustavus Hills. Evidence indicates classes were conducted over at least a three-year period on both an upper and lower "campus" in such buildings as the Concert Hall, the temple, Seventies Hall, and the Masonic Hall, as well as the private homes of the faculty.

Available courses included trigonometry, analytical geometry, differential calculus, astronomy, surveying, navigation, chemistry, philosophy, English literature, rhetoric, Church history, science of music, art of sacred singing, German, French, Latin, Greek, and Hebrew.

Pineries

How long did it take a lumber raft from the Pineries to reach Nauvoo?

Located in Wisconsin Territory, the Pineries were the forests where the Church established sawmills to provide the city of Nauvoo with needed lumber for building projects. Travel time from the Black River area where the camps were located would depend, of course, on the weather and such obstacles as sand bars, rapids, and so forth. George Miller, who arrived in Nauvoo on a raft in July 1843, reported that the lumber "was all sawed in two weeks and brought down in two more." This would have been normal with stops at night along the shore.

How large were these rafts and how much lumber could they contain?

The larger rafts might have been several hundred feet in length, a hundred or more in width, and covering an acre or more in area. Rafting from the Pineries began in the spring of 1842 and ended in the spring of 1845, with at least a dozen such rafts tying up at Nauvoo. They brought down an estimated 1.5 million feet of milled lumber, 200,000 shingles, and an unknown number of loose logs. Putting the logs into separate rafts, we can surmise that each lumber raft had no less than 150,000 feet of milled lumber plus several thousand shingles.

An average-sized raft that tied up at Lumber Street was probably like the one George Miller described, which he arrived on in July 1843. It contained 157,000 feet of lumber and 13,000 feet in shingles.

How were the raftmen able to steer and halt such large, unwieldy craft as the lumber rafts?

They were steered by several large steering oars or sweeps fastened to both ends of the raft. To stop the raft, the raftman took a heavy rope to the shore and secured it to a tree. He would then gradually play the rope out, bringing the raft in toward the shore where it was snubbed up for the night.

How were the lumber rafts fastened together?

There were different methods. The early, small rafts that traveled short distances could be fastened together by rope fastened to plugs driven into holes in the logs. For longer trips, the raft was fastened by poles laid across its width and wedged into holes in the logs. They could also be joined by short chains containing a sharp wedge on each end that could be driven into the logs.

Did the workers in the Pineries receive pay for their work or was it a Church calling?

Beginning in September 1841, with only thirty-two workers, the crews grew to as many as 200 during the 1843–44 season. The workers could draw provisions, supplies, and sometimes even cash, which was charged against their accounts. At the end of the year or when they left the Pineries, the workers were paid in tithing credit, temple credit, or Nauvoo House certificates. Occasionally, a worker might receive cash.

An unusually large number of Pinery workers seem to have apostatized after Joseph's death. Was his martyrdom the case, and if so, why?

A considerable number of the Pinery workers who actually lived in the Pineries over a two- or three-year period formed strong attachments to their leaders: George Miller, Alpheus Cutler, and Lyman Wight. When the Prophet was killed, they had not had that much contact with Brigham and questioned his authority. Following the leaders they were most attached to, they found it easier to sever their ties with the main body of the Church and settle in Wisconsin or Texas with their apostate leaders.

Were the Nauvoo Saints the first people to raft lumber or logs down the Mississippi River?

Ron Larson, in his book, *Upper Mississippi River History,* states that in 1844, Steven Hanks, a farmer near Albany, Illinois, was the first to take a long raft down the river. Lyndon Cook, in *The Revelations of the Prophet Joseph Smith,* noted that the first lumber rafts on the Mississippi reached Nauvoo from the Wisconsin Pineries on August 4, 1842, although Joseph does not mention this fact in his journal. On October 13 of that year, however, Joseph records a large raft arriving in Nauvoo. Unless research turns up an earlier raft by non-Mormons, we must give the Saints credit for the first lumber rafts on the Mississippi River.

Print Shop

What happened to the original presses after the exodus?

The equipment was left in the buildings to print the post-Mormon *Hancock Eagle* (April–Aug. 1846), the *Nauvoo New Citizen* (Dec. 1846), and the *Hancock Patriot* (1847–50). We know the Saints did not take the presses with them, since W. W. Phelps was sent east from Winter Quarters to purchase a press for the migrating Mormons.

Where did newsprint paper come from?

Most of it was shipped in from back east although some was purchased from a supplier in Cincinnati. Several times the editors felt compelled to apologize for late papers because the necessary newsprint was slow in arriving on the steamboats. Although some of the major presses used a type of cylinder press by this time, most presses were of the lever type you used in Nauvoo and the paper that was purchased was in sheet form for these types of presses.

Was the Book of Mormon ever printed in Nauvoo?

Although a total of five editions of the Book of Mormon were printed before the Saints went west in 1846, none were actually printed in Nauvoo. The first edition was printed in Palmyra, the second while the Saints lived in Kirtland. The third was printed in Cincinnati in 1840 where there were larger presses, but the finished books were returned to Nauvoo and distributed from the Print Shop. The fourth American edition was printed from these same plates in 1842. In the meantime, in 1841, the first European edition was printed in Liverpool under the direction of Brigham Young and the apostles who were then in England.

Were any books actually printed here at Nauvoo?

The first book known to have been printed on Nauvoo presses was Heber C. Kimball's journal in January 1841. Also printed in Nauvoo were some books on poetry by James Mulholland, Eliza Snow, and a young printer in the printing office who went by the pseudonym of Omer. Also printed here was Emma Smith's *Collection of Sacred Hymns*.

Were the presses located here on the first floor as they are now?

They were undoubtedly on the second floor. On the outside rear of the building, one might notice the construction of a pulley hoist that allowed the raising of newsprint and equipment to the second floor. The first floor was reserved for a store and post office.

Hadn't cylinder presses been invented by the time these presses were being used here in Nauvoo?

R. Hoe & Co., New York City, made the first cylinder press in 1831, and it was used to print a Temperance newspaper in Albany, New York. It was faster than the flat bed but was not a continuous feed. A successful continuous feed rotary type was not perfected until 1871. A cylinder press would have been too expensive and unnecessary for the limited number of papers printed in the Nauvoo Print Shop.

With no reporters on their staff, how did newspapers such as the *Nauvoo Neighbor* acquire their news?

Small-town weeklies were filled with editorials, notices, advertisements, and

* *

"fillers" the editors gleaned from other papers and books. The "news" consisted primarily of articles from newspapers all over the country, which by the time those bits were printed in the local paper were several weeks if not months old. Still, coming from other parts of the country or the world, it was news to most of the readers, who had perhaps no other sources of "news."

What other activities were conducted in this building besides the printing upstairs and the book and stationery shop and post office on the first floor?

The building also housed a book bindery and stereotype foundry. During this era, people would often purchase books without covers and then order the kind of cover they wanted. A stereotype foundry made fixed metallic plates of any pages they didn't want to have to repeatedly set the type for (books, pamphlets, or pages of advertising). A major problem was the cost of the metal and storage for the plates.

Where was the printing office located before 1845?

It was first located in 1839 in the basement of a 16-by-32-foot wooden building on the corner of Water and Bain Streets. Within a short time, a brick building was built on the same lot to house the printing complex, where it remained until 1845, when the presses were moved to the present Main Street site.

Do we know how many subscribers the *Times and Seasons* had?

Records don't indicate how many subscribers the paper had, but we know the *Hancock Eagle*, which took over after the exodus, printed 2,000 copies. The *Eagle* would have had a much larger "gentile" market and catered to an entire county, but the population of Nauvoo had dropped to less than one tenth the pre-exodus size. With the pre-exodus LDS population of Illinois at least 15,000, we can reasonably assume a publication run for the Mormon paper comparable to the later *Hancock Eagle* or perhaps a little less.

* *

Post Office

How long was unclaimed mail kept before it was returned to the Dead Letter Office in Washington to be destroyed?

On January 15, 1842, Postmaster Sidney Rigdon published in the *Times and Seasons* a "list of letters remaining in the post office at Nauvoo Hancock co. Ill, Jan. 1st 1842. Which if not taken out before the first of April next, will be sent to the Post Office Department as dead letters." The list contained more than 190 names, including Daniel Wells, Lyman Wight, Sheriff Backenstos, John Taylor, Brigham Young (who had two letters), Hyrum Smith (who had three letters), and Joseph Smith (who had twelve letters).

Why did so much mail go unclaimed?

Postage was not only expensive, but it was often sent with the postage to be paid by the recipient. The postmaster would place the words "paid" or "due" on the outside of the letter, indicating whether the postage still had to be paid. If it didn't appear important, the recipient often left it at the post office.

Was the cost of mailing newspapers comparable to that of letters?

No. In fact, in an effort to promote the publication and reading of newspapers, the federal government "franked" (free mailed) newspapers for a distance of up to thirty miles from the site of publication. If not carried over 100 miles, the price was only one cent, and over 100 miles, 1½ cents. Letters, on the other hand, cost 6 cents up to thirty miles and then in varying amounts up to 25 cents for over 400 miles. A "letter" was considered one sheet of paper. If two sheets were sent, the cost was doubled.

How could the postmaster or recipient tell where the letter originated or when it was sent?

Postmarks were first used in New York in 1772. By the 1800s, these hand-stamped postmarks, often made by the postmasters themselves, even started including the method of travel—by steamboat, train, and so on. The method of travel on postmarks was phased out by 1870.

Did the same postage cost philosophy apply to magazines?

It did to some extent. Magazines were cheaper than letters but still charged by the page. Periodicals were charged 1½ cents per sheet under 100 miles and 2½ for anything over. Because so many magazines went unclaimed, postmasters often became agents for publishers, using unclaimed copies as samples.

We know the 1845 post office was in what is now the Print Shop. Do we know what was in the current post office building?

James Ivins, who had considerable property in Nauvoo but became disaffected and decided to move, originally built and operated this complex. After deciding to move, he offered the property to John Taylor for a printing office for the Church for $3,200 in 1845. Taylor described the property as "a first rate large brick house, brick store, and large pine board barn, on a half acre of land on Main street, corner of Kimball." John Taylor described the store (current Print Shop) as the future location of the Printing Office but makes no mention of the store now shown as the post office.

However, A. Shoemaker is listed as a resident of this complex in 1845 and Dr. F. Merryweather as a resident in 1844. We lack the evidence necessary to confirm whether either of these individuals had a store here in 1844–46.

Where was the post office before 1845?

Most of the time, it was in the kitchen of the home of Sidney Rigdon, which home can still be found just north of the Mansion House. Sidney Rigdon was the postmaster for the longest period of Nauvoo's Mormon history: from February 1841 until May 1844.

The number of boxes in the present post office would not have been nearly enough for all the residents of Nauvoo. We are talking about as many as perhaps 2,000 heads of households. Where were all the boxes?

Although mail was picked up at the post office, most residents did not have boxes. The postmaster would have given them the mail since postage may have been due. Charlotte Haven, a non-Mormon living in Nauvoo, mentions in her journal going to the post office and having Brother Rigdon hand her mail to her. Such boxes as the ones you see now were for use by the postmaster for sorting the mail alphabetically. They could easily handle the volume since mail was not nearly as abundant as it is today.

What kind of drink was carried to the fields in the circular ceramic field canteen (seen in the post office building)?

The canteens would carry a fairly common drink, designed to quench the thirst, called "switchel," which was a mixture of molasses, water, vinegar, brown sugar, and ginger (and sometimes rum).

When were envelopes and stamps introduced?

The first postage stamps were issued in 1842 in 3 cent denominations but could be purchased for $2.50 for 100 stamps. Envelopes, of course, were

* *

often made by hand, but the first commercial envelopes had to await a practical envelope-folding machine. Jesse Park and Cornelius Watson received a patent for one in 1849, but Dr. Russell Hawes invented the first commercially practical machine in 1853.

How reliable was the mail service in the 1840s?

It was not unusual, at that time, to duplicate important mail and send the copies at different times to be confident of the mail getting through. During the Saints' last couple of years in Nauvoo, the mobs would search and often destroy both incoming and outgoing mail from the city. Even postmasters in other cities were destroying mail to and from Nauvoo. Beginning in 1844, Church leaders discovered the necessity of sending important correspondence under armed guard to a distant point before entrusting it to the postal authorities. The federal government was apparently as helpless in protecting the mail as they were in protecting the rights of the Latter-day Saints.

How was most mail carried at this time?

In Illinois in 1844, most mail was carried by stage and coach (1,024,384 miles), next was horse and sulky (377,986 miles), and the least by railroad and steamboat (35,776 miles). So you see, it was not difficult to interfere with mail service as the anti-Mormon mobs began to regularly do at this time.

Who was the last postmaster of Old Nauvoo?

In May of 1846, the Print Shop and Post Office complex was transferred to the trustees who remained in Nauvoo to dispose of all unsold property. Almon Babbitt, one of the trustees, apparently lived in the John Taylor home and made the complex his real-estate center. Mr. Babbitt was, at that time, appointed postmaster and remained as such until the fall of 1848, when he also left for the West. Brother Babbitt was later killed in the West by the Cheyenne.

* *

* *

The job of postmaster seems to have been a much sought after job. What was the salary for this job?

The 1843 American Almanac doesn't specifically mention Nauvoo, but it does give the salaries of postmasters in other Illinois towns, so the compensation would likely have been comparable. In Alton, the annual salary was $946, in Galena it was $970, and in Chicago it was $1,991. In Nauvoo, it was probably closer to the lower figures but still a handsome salary, considering the average worker's salary was around $300 per year.

* *

Relief Society

What was the relationship of Hiram Kimball, Sarah Granger's husband, to Heber C. Kimball?

Hiram was a fifth cousin once removed to Heber C. Kimball, a sixth cousin to the father of Spencer W. Kimball, and a sixth cousin to the grandfather of Dr. Leroy Kimball. Their common ancestor was Richard Kimball, who came to America in 1634. There is no evidence these cousins knew each other before Heber's move to Commerce.

Where was Hiram Kimball's store located and what did he sell?

Hiram operated his store for only a short time, from sometime in 1837, four years after he arrived in Commerce, to sometime in 1839, when he is listed as a customer in the daybook of Amos Davis, who operated a store on Mulholland Street. Kimball's store was located west of the present Sarah Granger Kimball (and Hiram's) home, close to the river. The store, traditionally identified as a barn-like structure, was still standing in the 1960s.

Some evidence exists that George Y. Cutler, the first postmaster of Hancock County, originally built and operated this store. He undoubtedly operated the first county post office here when the area was called Venus, later selling the property to Hiram. In this store, probably the first one in the Commerce area, Hiram sold traditional goods sold in any general mercantile store of the time, from foods to kitchen supplies to general home and farm items to textiles.

Hiram was supposedly quite well-to-do, and yet his home is not as fine as some of the brick homes of the less prosperous Saints. Why not?

This home was built before the arrival of the Saints and before their construction of brickyards. Therefore, at the time of this home's construction, the only materials available would have been logs, boards, or stone. This home, therefore, is more representative of the prestigious homes in New England where Hiram was from.

Did the Relief Society, the idea of which originated in this home, appoint "visiting teachers" in Nauvoo?

The Relief Society appointed a Necessity Committee of sixteen sisters "to search out the poor and suffering, to call upon the more affluent for aid, and thus, as far as possible relieve the wants of all." This was the origin of the Relief Society visiting teaching program.

Did Sarah ever marry again after the accidental death of Hiram?

No. She died in Utah in 1898, after being a widow for thirty-five years. Her husband died in a steamboat explosion en route to a mission in the Hawaiian Islands in 1863. Sarah's remaining years were devoted almost exclusively to the Relief Society and the suffrage movement for women, being president of the Utah Woman Suffrage Association as well as a ward Relief Society President for forty years.

How far from Kimball's home and store was the Kimball steamboat landing?

The landing was almost directly west of the store and home, which were built as close to the landing as possible without being endangered by the

* *

river's annual rise and fall. This was one of the four major steamboat landings in Nauvoo.

Why is the street the Sarah Granger Kimball home is on set at an angle and called Main Street? Were there two Main Streets?

This street was the original Main Street of the City of Commerce, which was not laid out north and south but rather parallel to the riverbank. In 1841, the Nauvoo city council passed an ordinance to vacate the town plats of Commerce and Commerce City because they were not laid out according to the cardinal points of the compass; thus most of those early platted streets were abandoned. However, since the Kimball home was one of the few standing homes on these plats, the council allowed the street running past that home to remain.

Does this small kitchen suggest a summer kitchen for hot-weather cooking?

Summer kitchens are normally associated with southern homes, where they were once deemed a necessity among the more affluent. Since Hiram was from New England (not noted for summer kitchens), however, and he built this home, he would not have been likely to construct such a building. In fact, a summer kitchen in Nauvoo would have been a rarity, since the Illinois climate would not necessitate such an additional cost. The Homestead has a small reconstructed log cabin on its northwest corner, which is referred to in Community of Christ literature as the "summer kitchen." It may or may not have served that purpose, but we know it did serve as the first home for Joseph Smith Sr. and Lucy when their son Joseph moved into the log Homestead.

How widespread was membership in the Relief Society when it was first organized?

One can easily imagine it became extremely popular with Joseph's blessings and Emma's Presidency. It was organized on March 17, 1842,

* *

and by June 2, two and a half months later, it had between 800 and 900 members. Before its final Nauvoo session in 1844, its membership reached nearly 1,300.

Did the Relief Society continue during the exodus from Nauvoo?

Although much was accomplished during this period, the Relief Society's final meeting in Nauvoo occurred in March 1844, only two years after its organization. A major factor in its Nauvoo demise was Emma's opposition to plural marriage and her attempted use of the Society to combat what she felt was a wrong doctrine. Brigham Young revived the Society permanently in Utah in 1867.

Specifically, what did the Relief Society accomplish in its brief two years in Nauvoo?

It helped unemployed women find jobs, donated to the poor, found homes for orphans, helped pay tuition for the children of widows, and saw to the daily needs of the elderly, such as the plowing of gardens and so on. Joseph deeded a city lot to the Society and at the time of its demise, it had plans for the erection of homes for the poor—an early "Habitat for Humanity."

Is the Church justified in characterizing the organization of the Relief Society as the beginning of the women's suffrage movement in the United States?

In view of later developments, yes. Most historians date the origin of the suffrage movement as 1848 in Seneca Falls. The Relief Society was organized six years earlier. Even without such statements as that by Sarah G. Kimball or Emmeline B. Wells, who frankly declared it initiated the national suffrage movement, we are still left with the fact that the women of Utah were the first in the nation to actually cast votes, the first in the nation to sit on juries, among the first to become medical doctors, among the first to own major businesses, and so on. All of these accomplishments

* *

were a legacy of Nauvoo, where women were forced by absent husbands to bond together and assume typically male roles and where their religion gave them partnership in the all-important priesthood. The Relief Society was the first organization in the nation to formalize such a role of equality.

As a typical example of the progress LDS women made in the nineteenth century, when the Deseret Hospital opened in Utah in 1882, a women's Board of Directors managed it and women doctors staffed it. These are astounding accomplishments when compared with the status of women in the rest of the nation in such areas as corporate management and the practice of medicine.

* *

Religious Practices

What was the "stand" so often mentioned by Joseph in his journal history?

Technically, it was the elevated platform on which the authorities sat and from which they presented their talks in the Groves in Nauvoo where meetings were held. In common practice, it was often merely a euphemism for the meeting place.

Where were sacrament meetings held and when?

There were no ward sacrament meetings, since there were no ward buildings or chapels and it was not the bishop's responsibility to hold such meetings. Sacrament meetings were generally citywide meetings held in the open, in groves, or at the temple site. On Sunday, May 4, 1845, for example, Bishop John Higbee helped administer the sacrament at the general Nauvoo Sunday meeting to between 600 and 700 people. Sacrament meetings could also be and often were held for particular quorums, for example, for the Seventies in the Seventies Hall.

In inclement weather, members would hold meetings in homes and receive the sacrament there as well. On February 23, 1845, the Prophet Joseph recorded in his journal, "I preached at Hiram Kimball's, Elders Heber C. Kimball and George A. Smith administered the sacrament: had a good meeting."

* *

Did the Church build any meetinghouses before the move to Utah?

Yes. What may have been the first meetinghouse in the Church, built exclusively for that purpose, was at Ramus (now Webster). At the time, this was a stake and the second largest Mormon community in Illinois after Nauvoo. Few people live there today, and a community church stands on the site of the former LDS meetinghouse.

Was everyone welcome at these sacrament meetings?

At the sacrament meetings, yes. At the Church business meetings, no. Sacrament meetings were often conducted in the morning. There would then be a noon break, and in the afternoon, there might be a business meeting and only those in good fellowship were allowed to attend. This probably posed a problem since so many of the meetings were outdoors. At one such meeting, however, Hosea Stout, the police chief, recorded in his diary that his police were forced to flog three men determined to attend. No explanation was given as to the seriousness of the flogging or why the three insisted on attending the meeting.

Was there singing at sacrament meetings—either by the congregation or a choir?

Nauvoo had a choir that was praised by visitors. The choir played a prominent role in the large general meetings. Composed of both men and women, it rehearsed every week, with the Prophet often in attendance. The large open-air meetings usually opened with a hymn by the choir, an opening prayer, and then often another hymn before business or the talks. A shortage of hymn books and the talents of the choir limited congregational singing more than they would have liked. That changed on April 6, 1841, when, as later reported in the *Times and Seasons*, during an open-air commemoration of the twelfth anniversary of the Church, "the religious services were commenced by singing from page 65 of the new hymn book."

* *

Were women ever invited to speak at the general meetings?

It was not customary, although there were exceptions, as when Brigham invited Lucy Smith to speak to the Saints at a general meeting before the exodus. Sisters did participate, however, in bearing testimonies, during which their words often expanded into "talks." Women also commonly spoke without invitation, as when they spoke and interpreted in tongues, and they were often encouraged to do so. They fully participated in smaller home gatherings and were even called upon to visit and bless the sick.

When we consider the role of Mormon sisters in the Relief Society and in temple ceremonies, they undoubtedly enjoyed greater participation in the religious life of their faith than the women of any other church at this time.

Were there Sunday schools for teaching the youth?

Before the exodus from Nauvoo, small groups were meeting regularly as Sunday schools in Nauvoo, Kirtland, and among a few LDS congregations in England. The Sunday school organization as it is recognized today began in Utah after the Saints had settled.

Were sacrament talks assigned to different members of the ward as they are today?

Certainly in the small outlying branches, members would take turns, but in Nauvoo, the larger general meetings were almost always addressed by members of the First Presidency or the Quorum of the Twelve. In the quorum meetings, the speaker would be one of the quorum leaders or a more popular speaker. Little concern was demonstrated in giving everyone an "opportunity."

Did young men hold the Aaronic Priesthood as they do today?

Aaronic Priesthood offices in Nauvoo were filled almost entirely by adults. Because of the duties assigned deacons, teachers, and priests in the revelations, leaders felt that maturity, not age, was the prerequisite for ordination. Nevertheless, there were exceptions when the leaders felt a young man was mature enough to be ordained. Daniel Tyler, not quite eighteen, filled a mission by himself when his older companion failed to show up. Joseph's younger brother, Don Carlos, received the priesthood at age fourteen, filled a mission that year, and at nineteen became the Nauvoo high priests quorum president. Erastus Snow, baptized at fourteen, preached extensively in Ohio, New York, and Pennsylvania before he was nineteen.

Was the sacrament administered much as it is today?

Yes and no. Yes, in the sense that the prayers and the purpose were the same. No, in the sense that the mechanics, as in many Church procedures, have changed. There were no small disposable cups, so regular-sized cups or goblets were used and passed from one to another, with each member taking a sip until the goblet was empty, at which point the priesthood holder passing the sacrament put in more. In the very earliest Church sacrament meetings, leaders also felt that the sacrament should be closer to the last supper in the sense of eating more than merely a small piece of bread.

Helen Mar Whitney recalls her father describing an early sacrament in the Kirtland Temple: "A sufficient quantity of bread having been provided to feed the whole assembly (approx. 400), it was broken by the First Presidency, and afterwards the Twelve took it and administered to the congregation until they were filled." When the Church authorities decided to administer only small pieces is not clear.

Modern Saints might also be disturbed at the seeming lack of reverence during the earliest administrations of the sacrament. The fault was not necessarily the children's, because they were not encouraged to attend sacrament meetings, but it was the adults who were not compelled to remain silent during the passing of the sacrament. At that time, speakers might even talk or music would be played.

Were other religious groups free to practice their faiths in Nauvoo?

An early ordinance the city of Nauvoo passed, at the urging of Joseph, provided "that the Catholics, Presbyterians, Methodists, Baptists, Latter-day Saints, Quakers, Episcopalians, Universalists, Unitarians, Mohammedans, and all other religious sects and denominations whatever, shall have free toleration and equal privileges in this city; and should any person be guilty of ridiculing or abusing or otherwise depreciating another in consequence of his religion, or of disturbing or interrupting any religious meeting within the limits of this city, he shall on conviction thereof before the Mayor or Municipal Court be fined or imprisoned at the discretion of the Mayor or Court."

Of interest is that various religious groups took advantage of this city ordinance to establish small congregations in Nauvoo, where they practiced their beliefs freely. Joseph often invited visiting ministers to preach to the people from the "stand," or permitted them to use public buildings, which they did, and their talks were respectfully received. In February 1844, Joseph recorded in his journal, "Wednesday 21.—The Rev. Mr. De Wolfe, Episcopalian, lectured in the assembly room in the evening. I attended and, after the sermon, at his request, spoke to the people."

How many wards were in Nauvoo?

This answer requires some explanation since the concept of ecclesiastical wards originated in Nauvoo. When the city was first settled, it was divided into political wards, like most cities of that time. It started out with three wards: the upper, middle, and lower. This early division led to the practice of dividing the Church membership along the same lines and adopting the term "ward." Eventually, as the population of Nauvoo increased, there were ten Church wards within the city.

Before this time, congregations were called either branches or churches, as in "the church at Fayette" or the "church at Colesville."

Why were so few revelations received during the Nauvoo years? Only eight appear in the Doctrine & Covenants.

There were many in addition to those in Sections 125 through 132. The entire Nauvoo period is filled with private and public revelations. The complex theology dealing with man's origin and destiny as outlined in the King Follett Discourse was revelation. Many revelations revolving around marriage and baptisms were revealed in different discourses during the Nauvoo years. It is a common misconception that the Prophet was not receiving revelation from the Lord unless it is canonized in the Doctrine and Covenants.

Canonization is merely one process of making doctrine official within a Church. When the Prophet Joseph gave the King Follett Discourse, the doctrines expressed therein became official or "canon." This practice is still true today in the form of conference talks, written pronouncements, and so forth from the Quorum of the Twelve or the First Presidency.

To include all revelations in the Doctrine and Covenants would have made the volume too unwieldy. Also remember that many revelations are merely clarifications of information already found in the scriptures but that have become obscured by time and tradition. An example would be the plurality of gods, which is indicated more than twenty times in the Bible.

Riser Boot Shop

* *

Why would a shop such as this be so small? Was adding a few more square feet to improve working conditions really that costly?

The lot this building is on has only a 16-foot frontage, so the answer may be as simple as that. But then why not make the building longer?

The term "ten-footers" was used in the early days of the craft, referring to the small front-yard workshops that so many cordwainers built in front of their homes and actually were around 10-by-12 or 10-by-14 in size. It was not unusual for shops this small to house five or six workers. Thus, this shop is not so unusual in its small size; it is apparent boot and shoemakers traditionally worked in small shops.

It was also a matter of making the building easier to heat in a cold climate. Craftsmen, such as cordwainers, cannot do their work well with numb fingers.

What was the major source of leather for boot and shoe shops in Nauvoo?

The *Nauvoo Neighbor* carried advertisements for two or three tanneries in Nauvoo. One tannery advertising in the *Wasp* newspaper in 1843 claimed to have thirteen vats—a very sizable operation. A year later, another tannery advertised for 5,000 cow hides and 5,000 calf skins. Unfortunately, many such hides were being shipped out of Nauvoo while

* *

* *

great quantities of shoes and boots were being shipped in. Appeals by the Church authorities to buy and sell locally were being made throughout the life of Nauvoo. Incidentally, one tanner's ad mentioned his tannery was "in the best part of town." Such a location would have been very unusual. Although America had few zoning laws at that time, most towns and cities put pressure on tanneries to locate their foul-smelling operations away from "the best part of town."

When did left and right become common in the making of shoes?

At one time, a single "last" (wooden mold for shoe or boot from Middle English *laste*, meaning "sole" or "footprint") sufficed for each customer. Strangely enough, in spite of the obvious difference in the shape of the left and right feet, not until after the Revolutionary War did shoemakers start making separate lasts for each foot. Then, rather than using the word "last," they starting using the terms "lefts" and "rights," and the word "last" became a forgotten word in shoemaking.

What were the prices of some of the types of shoes and boots made in this shop?

Nauvoo had at least fourteen shoe retail stores during its seven-year period, and many of them advertised in the *Nauvoo Neighbor*. Types of footwear the ads mentioned included men's kips, mocks, pumps, and women's gater boots, Jeffersons, and turn corners. Prices in general varied between $1 for a pair of slippers to more than $5 for a pair of well-made men's boots.

Explain the differences, if there are any, between cobblers, cordwainers, and shoemakers.

A cobbler is someone who merely mends shoes. In the early 1800s, the term was rather derisive, with contemporary dictionaries referring to cobblers as "menders" and "bunglers." This low opinion is how the word "cobble" came to mean "to put something together in a clumsy manner." A "cobbler" could be any kind of a clumsy workman. Thus, shoemakers

* *

* *

would have been offended to be called cobblers.

A cordwainer was a shoemaker or bootmaker. The word cordwainer is derived from a worker in cordwain or cordovan leather, a superior leather that came from Cordova, Spain.

Weren't some shoemakers, cobblers, and so forth itinerant?

There were itinerant shoemakers and cobblers in the country at large, but they likely could not have made a living in Nauvoo. When the population is scattered in remote homes and farms, itinerant shoemakers serve a purpose, but in Nauvoo, with a dense population and so many competing shoemakers and cobblers, they would have been totally unnecessary. In addition, shoe repair or cobbling was not a difficult skill to acquire then, and many men would have taken care of their families' footwear repair needs at home.

Within a decade after the exodus, machinery was being introduced into the shoemaking industry in New England, and by the end of the Civil War, shops such as this were becoming a thing of the past.

In shoemaking, there was a term called "whipping the cat." Where did that term come from?

In attaching the sole of a shoe, the shoemaker would pull the thread through the holes in the leather with a full-arm motion—"whipping the cat."

Were wooden pegs the earliest means of fastening soles to shoes?

No. Strangely enough, sewn shoes were common throughout history, and on occasion, ancient shoemakers used iron and copper nails and even screws. Actually, wooden pegs for general use was a fairly recent innovation at the time of Nauvoo. At first, such pegs were split by hand from a piece of maple, cut across the grain and the thickness of the peg length. By the 1840s, shoemakers purchased them in bulk from factories in New England that specialized in making the pegs.

* *

* *

How long could shoes be expected to last before wearing out?

How long they lasted varied, of course, depending on their use, but people walked more in those days and under much worse road conditions (mud, water, stones, and so on), so the life of a shoe could be much shorter without proper care. "Care" meant constant oiling or greasing. A skillet filled with tallow was kept handy in the home for constant rubbing into boots and shoes. They looked better with such care, but more importantly, tallow made them more impervious to water. And then constant repair by owners would allow shoes to last much longer than they do today.

It was not uncommon for children to go barefoot during the warmer months, thus adding to the life of shoes. In addition, the average Nauvooan felt no need to have different pairs of shoes for different outfits. They not only could not afford such luxuries, but frontier conditions made shoes more of an indispensable element to locomotion than a fashion statement.

How much did shoemakers earn in Nauvoo?

A central New York shoemaker's shop in 1850 had thirty-five workers, whose total wages averaged $600 per month. This meant a daily wage of approximately 75 cents. The owner, of course, would have made much more. Such wages would have been comparable in the 1840s in Nauvoo.

* *

The River

How many steamboat landings did Nauvoo have?

Almost any part of the riverfront could be and was used for landing river craft, depending on the height of the river and the size of the boats. There were, however, four major landings. One was near the Nauvoo House at the southern end of Main Street, a second was the Dundey or Parley Street Landing, the third was the Kimball Landing near his store and home in Commerce, and the fourth was the upper landing at the northern end of Granger Street. Because of the popularity of the upper landing, Granger Street became such a much-traveled street that its residents petitioned in 1843 to have it widened. The City Council approved adding eight feet to both sides of the street.

Was Nauvoo a very active commercial center for riverboat traffic compared with other Mississippi River towns?

From 1823 to 1848, approximately 365 steamboats worked the Upper Mississippi above Keokuk. Two hundred of these steamers carried lead from the mines at Galena, 170 miles north of Nauvoo. During the boating season, spring through fall, about ten of these would pass Nauvoo each day. Adding to these the other steamers carrying furs, lumber, military supplies, and so on, Nauvooans would probably have seen at least fifteen steamers per day in the city's final years. Many of these might have had no passengers or supplies for Nauvoo, but the ones that did dock at one of the Nauvoo landings certainly made the city an active commercial center on the Upper Mississippi. During the mid-1843 season, four or five steamers per day docked at Nauvoo.

Were all the landings used for ferry crossings to Iowa?

They could have been used but normally were not. The closest one to Montrose, the Iowa destination of the ferry, was the Parley Street Ferry. This was also the major ferry crossing during the exodus.

Obviously passage on the ferries was not free. What were the charges?

Rates were established by city ordinance in 1843. Some of the charges were:

Two horse wagon with contents & river	$1
Two wheel carriage for one horse	50¢
Foot passenger	12½¢
Horse with rider	37½¢
Oxen per yoke	25¢
Under one year old sheep, hogs, &c.	6¼¢

The ferrymaster, appointed by the city, collected the tolls and turned them over to the treasurer of the City Council every week. These proceeds, although records fail to reveal their amounts, were a steady source of income for the city.

At this time, the average laborer's wage ranged from only 75 cents to one dollar per day. Because of such relatively high toll charges, residents who lived near the river or made numerous trips to Montrose owned their own small boats, which they kept tied up along the river bank.

How were the ferries propelled?

Various types of river craft were used as ferries, each propelled in a different manner. The first ferries were merely skiffs, or rowboats, propelled by oars. Other river craft used as ferries were flatboats, also propelled by oars and normally larger than skiffs, although people commonly interchanged these names. Depending on the river current, these larger craft would often land below Montrose and have to be hauled back along the shore by horses. Shortly after the Church purchased the *Maid of Iowa* steamboat, renamed the *Iowa Twins*, it was put into brief service as a ferry. One of the city's main ferries was a horseboat, propelled by paddle wheels and operated by two horses on treadmills on each side of the craft.

In addition to horseboats and steamboats, what other kinds of river craft would Nauvooans be familiar with?

One of the most common river craft, and already mentioned, was the skiff, defined as a small boat that was normally propelled with from two to four oars, and was often used as a ferry. Wilford Woodruff mentions the transporting of his stock across the river during the exodus in July 1846. He had twenty cows and oxen and said that skiff he used could ferry only five or six animals at one time, so the word "small" is obviously a relative term. It's also possible that Woodruff was using the term "skiff" for what was actually a "flatboat." The average skiff would not be able to carry that large a load.

Brigham Young's manuscript history mentions that the crossing of the river during the exodus was under the direction of Hosea Stout and the police who "gathered several flatboats, some old lighters, and a number of skiffs, forming altogether quite a fleet, and were at work night and day, crossing the saints."

How much was passage on a steamboat, for example, from New Orleans or St. Louis to Nauvoo?

Prices varied somewhat, depending on the particular steamer. There was also a difference between deck passage and cabin accommodations, deck passage being only one-third the cost. Because of the cheaper price and the fact that most of the Mormon immigrants had limited funds, they normally

* *

took deck passage. Between New Orleans and St. Louis, about 1,200 miles, the cost was about $3.00. A passenger then transferred at St. Louis to a smaller steamer to navigate the rapids farther north. Passage from St. Louis to Nauvoo, less than 200 miles, would be another $2.50. Time for the entire trip up river would be between two and three weeks, and unless the Saints could have afforded a cabin, they had to provide their own meals.

A connection between Robert E. Lee and the Saints is mentioned at times. Was there?

Yes. In 1837, Lee, then a member of the Army Corps of Engineers, was ordered west to improve the St. Louis harbor and navigation on the upper Mississippi, specifically the Des Moines rapids between Keokuk and Nauvoo. For this purpose, Lee used a small steamboat and several smaller craft for blasting limestone outcrops and removing snags. Lee was forced to discontinue his operations in the summer of 1840 due to a federal shortage of appropriations. He then sold his boats at a public auction in Quincy in September, at which time the Mormons, then settled in Nauvoo, bought the steamboat *Des Moines* (which they renamed the *Nauvoo*), two keel-boats, and eight large deck stows (storage receptacles). Robert E. Lee signed as agent for the United States, and Peter Haws signed as agent for the Saints. The Saints put the *Nauvoo* into immediate business hauling lead from Galena to St. Louis, but the steamer was wrecked that very fall.

Some believe the hotel where Lee stayed while doing his work on the river and while the Saints were moving into Nauvoo still stands on the River Road between Keokuk and Nauvoo, approximately two miles north of Hamilton. Others believe it was a similar chalet nearby, now gone.

Some scholars also believe that while working near Nauvoo, Lee would stay on occasion in the Stone House at the Parley Street landing.

What was a "lighter" and how was it used?

A lighter was a large, open, flat-bottomed boat, normally used to load and unload ships that had too much draft to approach the dock. On

* *

the upper Mississippi, however, lighters were normally tied alongside the steamboats. By unloading the cargo onto the lighters, captains could "lighten" the weight of the steamer, allowing it to pass over the rapids. Lighters varied in size from as small as 50 feet long and 10 feet wide to 130 feet long and 20 feet wide. When not attached to the steamers, they were handled by two sweeps or oars on each side with a steering oar in front in charge of the rapids pilot.

Is it true that Joseph once proposed a dam at Keokuk? What are the details?

This story appears to have originated with Melvin J. Ballard, who in a Conference talk in April 1921 related his attendance some years before at a meeting of the Military Tract Press Association in Nauvoo. There he heard an editor read a paper, recalling hearing the Prophet Joseph sending a petition to Congress, asking Congress to erect a dam at Keokuk to provide power as well as containing locks to overcome the Des Moines rapids. The editor even mentioned Joseph's estimate of the cost, which was close to the actual cost when the dam finally was built early in the twentieth century.

Were any streets in Nauvoo lost when the Keokuk Dam was completed in 1913, raising the water level near Nauvoo approximately 25 feet?

The most vital was a portion of Lumber Street that extended east and west parallel to Water Street and one block south of it. The dam inundated a portion of that unimproved street, which connected mills and wharves along that part of the city shoreline. Actually, the dam also inundated a continuation of that street northward, most of it even less improved but laid out to give the city control of the riverfront and running almost the entire length of the shore.

Was the freezing of the Mississippi during the exodus a rare event?

No. Mormon history mentions it because of its appropriate timing. The wagons waiting to cross the river during the February exodus were piling up awaiting the slow crossing of the ferries. When the river froze shortly after the exodus began, hundreds of wagons were able to cross on the ice toward their temporary destinations in Iowa. The exodus began February 4, and by the last week of that month, wagons were crossing on the ice.

During the winter of 1842–43, according to Wilford Woodruff, the river froze over for four months, and as late as April 2, teams were still crossing on the ice.

There are always questions about the width of the original river, since the Keokuk Dam forming Lake Cooper has obviously increased the width. How much wider is it now?

There is not as much difference between Nauvoo and Montrose now as one might think. One reason is because the river frontage in the southwest section dropped off rapidly to the river, at the foot of which was Lumber Street. This street, of course, is now inundated, but that did not widen the river a great deal. We find one bit of evidence in an article in the *Times and Seasons* for January 1, 1844, announcing the proposed erection of a power "dam upwards of a mile long." That dam was to "intersect with an Island" opposite the village of Montrose. The reference here is to Dundey Island, which was about two-thirds of the way across the river. If the estimated distances were fairly accurate, the river would have been approximately one and one-half miles wide in 1843, not much less than it is now.

Gayle Hammond and Don Enders, who created the relief map of Nauvoo in the visitors' center, discovered after extensive research that the building of the Keokuk Dam took relatively little of Old Nauvoo. They found that the water encroached on about 100 feet of land. Other than the 100 feet, they believed the size of the river is pretty much the same as it was in the 1840s.

We hear stories of the shallowness of the Mississippi before the dam was built. Just how shallow was it near Nauvoo?

Wandle Mace describes his crossing of the Mississippi in the latter days of

* *

the exodus: "The river was very low at this time and I waded most of the way across guiding the boat to keep it from going too far down stream. Where the water was too deep for me to wade I jumped into the boat until we came to shallow water, when I again got out and waded to guide the boat. We started from the Nauvoo House and landed a mile and a half below Montrose."

On September 4, 1845, the *Rochester Democrat* mentioned the level of the river near Nauvoo: "The navigation of the upper Mississippi, in consequence of low water is extremely hazardous. At this time there is not over 28 inches of water on the lower rapids, and all rock bottom at that. These rapids lie between the famous city of Nauvoo and the village of Keokuk."

Why wasn't a canal ever constructed to bypass the Des Moines Rapids?

The Prophet Joseph suggested such a canal, but the federal government did not build it until 1877. It ran along the west bank of the river, was 7.5 miles long, and had three locks. This canal system was extensively used until it was submerged when the Keokuk Dam was completed in 1913, creating Lake Cooper.

Church history mentions islands between Nauvoo and Montrose. What happened to them?

There was one major island about two-thirds of the distance across the river near the Iowa shore. It was approximately three-fourths of a mile to one mile in length and varied from 50 to 200 yards in width. The island, called Dundey Island, is mentioned in Church history as a place where wood was cut, where Joseph hid from his enemies at times, and as the western terminus of a proposed power dam to be erected according to an ordinance Joseph passed and signed in December 1843. It was never built. The island was inundated when the Keokuk Dam was completed in 1913.

There is only one known mention of anyone actually living on this

* *

island. In the winter of 1840–41, William Holmes Walker, who lived near Quincy, heard his mother living in Nauvoo was very sick. He saddled up and rode seventy-five miles to Nauvoo where he went "to Joseph Smith's, and was made welcome. I learned that mother was living on the island in the Mississippi River, and that it was dangerous to cross because of so much ice running." She was likely not living there alone, so at that early stage of Nauvoo's development, some homes were probably established on the island. When the Saints learned how susceptible this island was to flooding, such homes were abandoned.

A lot of river traffic passes Nauvoo even today, especially barges. What are the boats called that push the barges?

Even though they push them, they are called "tow" boats because the barges are called "tows." Such "tows" or barges are a standard size: 35 feet wide and 200 feet long. One can see at times a "tow" of sixteen or even seventeen barges, fastened three abreast, passing Nauvoo. In entering the locks, these three-wide tows have a clearance of 2.5 feet on each side.

The Red Brick Store and Others

When did the Community of Christ start its restoration project?

In 1909, the Community of Christ purchased the Nauvoo House and the block where it is located from Charles Bidamon. Then, in 1915, it acquired the Homestead across the street. Two years later, it acquired the Mansion House from Alexander H. Smith's family. These purchases began what is known today as the Joseph Smith Historic Center. This center consists of the Homestead, Mansion House, Nauvoo House, Red Brick Store, and Visitors' Center as well as the homes of Sidney Rigdon, William Marks, Aaron Johnson, Hiram Clark, and the remaining south wing of the Masonic Hotel.

The log portion of the Homestead was already here when Joseph moved into it in 1839. Do we know who built it and when?

Some evidence suggests it was built more than thirty years before the Saints arrived in Commerce in 1839. In Deed Book 5 in the Hancock County Courthouse is the record of an 1819 deed transferring a piece of property from Dennis Julien to Rufus Eastin. The property encompassed 640 acres on which Julien settled in 1805 and contained "a log house, hen house, stable, and about ten acres in cultivation and a garden fenced." It was described as at the head of the rapids (Des Moines) in the county of Madison (from which Hancock was later carved), "about twenty

* *

miles above the River Des Moins." It was described as "just below an Establishment made by William Ewing Indian Agent to teach the Sacs and Fox Indians agriculture," which was quite possibly the later site of the White Stone House near the exodus site.

The description of this property fits well with the site of the Nauvoo House Landing area, with the "log house" being the log portion of the Joseph Smith Homestead. If this is the case then the Homestead would have been one of the first homes in the Nauvoo area and built by Dennis Julien thirty-four years before the arrival of the Saints.

Would the Homestead have been the first home in the Nauvoo area then?

Not necessarily. Zebulon Pike, who set out in 1805 to discover the headwaters of the Mississippi River, reported visiting the home of William Ewing, agent to the Sac Indians, at the head of the Des Moines rapids. Some scholars believe the agency was on the same site where James White later built his stone house near the end of Parley Street. Pike describes the agency as opposite the Indian village that was located on the Iowa side at the present site of Montrose. Ewing would have built his log home around 1803, and although not a permanent settler, as James White later was, he would have been the first American to build a house in what later became Nauvoo.

How large was Joseph Smith's original Mansion House?

The original, built in 1842, was about the same size it is now. After briefly moving in, Joseph was overrun with guests, so friends suggested he make the Mansion House a hotel and take in paying guests. He moved back to the Homestead briefly while he added an east wing in the summer of 1843. On August 31, 1843, Joseph moved his family into the 22-room mansion where he would live for the last ten months of his life. By 1890, the newer addition was deteriorating, and when a tree fell on it that year, that wing was dismantled. Ten hotel rooms were upstairs in that portion of the house.

* *

* *

Is the Red Brick Store a restoration or a reconstruction?

It is a reconstruction. After years of neglect, the Hudson Brothers, Nauvoo butchers, purchased it in 1883 and converted it into a pork-packing plant. In 1890, they tore it down for its bricks, which they used to build a large meat market on Mulholland Street, now a part of the Nauvoo Hotel. The Community of Christ rebuilt the Red Brick Store in 1978–79 with donated funds, dedicating it in 1980.

Why was it called the "Red Brick Store"? Aren't most bricks red?

It was known as the Red Brick Store because the inside of the first-floor merchandise room was painted a rich red color.

The Sarah Granger Kimball home is mentioned as the birthplace of the Relief Society and yet we are told the Relief Society was organized in the Red Brick Store. What is the story?

The idea for such an organization was worked out at a gathering of some sisters in the front room of the Sarah Granger Kimball home early in 1842. Sarah and her seamstress had decided to make shirts for the temple workmen, prompting the meeting in Sarah's home where a discussion took place as to what else the sisters of Nauvoo could do to further the building of the temple. The purposes of the proposed organization were extended at the official organization shortly thereafter. With Joseph Smith presiding, that organizational meeting took place on March 17 in the upper room of the Red Brick Store.

Do we know where Hyrum Smith lived in Nauvoo? And did he give his patriarchal blessings there?

Hyrum Smith had a home on the northeast corner of Water and Bain Streets. The office of the *Times and Seasons* was on that same corner next to the street in 1839. After Hyrum became Patriarch, he had an office constructed across the street (probably Water Street) where he gave his patriarchal blessings. Hyrum also had a farm about a mile east of the

* *

temple on what is now Winchester Street. It was here that part of the Battle of Nauvoo was fought in September 1846.

Did Sidney Rigdon's small home serve as both residence and post office?

Yes. As a matter-of-fact, the post office was in the kitchen. Charlotte Haven, a visitor to Nauvoo in 1843, described a visit to the post office in Rigdon's home: "We enter a side door leading into the kitchen, and in a corner near the door is a wide shelf or table, on which against the wall is a sort of cupboard with pigeon-holes or boxes this is the post office."

How far was the river from the Nauvoo House previous to the building of the Keokuk Dam?

The river was quite close, but the dock was at the foot of a steep incline. In an early photograph, taken apparently before the construction of the Keokuk Dam, a small boat can be seen at the dock, which was located at the bottom of the descent, about where the embankment has been built.

Why are Community of Christ sites not open to "drop-ins" like the LDS sites?

One reason is a shortage of guides. Another reason is that the church feels the present system of a film followed by guided tours is the best way the Community of Christ can present its story.

How long did the Joseph Smith family live in the Homestead and in the Mansion House?

Joseph and Emma moved into the log portion of the homestead on May 10, 1839. The wooden frame portion was added to the home in 1840. Joseph's family continued living in the Homestead until the Mansion House was completed on August 31, 1843. Early in 1844, pressed by debt, the Prophet rented the Mansion House to Ebenezer Robinson, reserving three rooms for his own family. Joseph was able to live in the Mansion House for less than ten months, but his family remained there until Emma's second husband built the Riverside Mansion on the foundation of the Nauvoo House, where they lived together from 1871 until Emma's death in 1879 at the age of seventy-four. Lewis continued living there with his new wife and former mistress, Nancy Abercrombie, until his death in 1891.

Who "reorganized" or "founded" the Community of Christ?

A revelatory experience of Jason Briggs, in 1851, five years after Brigham Young led the main body out of Nauvoo, brought the "New Organization," as it was first called, into being. Briggs became the first President of the Quorum of Apostles in 1853, seven years before Joseph Smith III accepted the office of President.

There is a small stone building north of the Nauvoo House, incorporating part of the original Nauvoo House wall. When and why was this constructed?

Lewis Bidamon built it after the exodus for use as his office. When the Community of Christ restored the Nauvoo House, leaders decided this small office had enough historic interest to allow it to remain and be restored.

What happened to the original Book of Mormon manuscript, which was in the cornerstone of the Nauvoo House?

In 1882, while tearing down the walls of the east wing of the Nauvoo House, Lewis Bidamon came across the cornerstone in which the Prophet had placed several items in 1841. One of those items was the original manuscript of the Book of Mormon, which was in very bad condition, much of it destroyed by dampness and mold. On at least five occasions we know of, Lewis gave away portions of the manuscript. What happened to most of them we don't know, but 124 pages ended up in the Church Historian's Office in Salt Lake City.

The cornerstone itself is on display in the Joseph Smith Historic Visitors' Center.

Seventies Hall

George Watt is known as the first person baptized in Great Britain. He labored at record keeping for the Church in Nauvoo because of his shorthand knowledge. What kind of shorthand did George Watt teach? Was it the same as Gregg?

No. It was much earlier, invented by Sir Isaac Pitman in 1837 and called phonography. It was phonetic shorthand similar to Gregg that enabled a scribe to write every word as fast as a person could speak. Shorthand was a popular subject in the 1840s in both England and the United States. Not only did Watt teach classes on the subject in Nauvoo, but a Phonographic Society of Nauvoo was organized with Watt as its president. Because of the work Watt did for the Church in recording Conference talks and such, he was given a house and a lot south of the Seventies Hall toward the river.

George Watt was later involved in developing the unsuccessful Deseret Language in Utah.

Are the books in the upstairs Seventies Hall Library original?

If you mean are they from the original library, the answer is no. The original library was taken west with the Saints and became the nucleus of the first library in Utah and reportedly the first one west of the Missouri River.

If you mean are these books original to the Mormon era, the answer is yes. These books, donated in 1998 by George and Sylvia Givens of

＊ ＊

Lynchburg, Virginia, all date from 1846 or earlier. Many of these books are the same title and edition as the books in the original Seventies Library.

Was the library in the Seventies Hall the first library in Nauvoo?

No. In January 1844, several interested citizens, including Joseph Smith, met over Joseph's store to form the Nauvoo Library and Literary Institute. Joseph mentioned in his journal that the meeting was to found "another library institution in Nauvoo," so apparently there were others previous to this one. However, the one organized in January lasted less than a year, probably because it did not have official Church backing as the Seventies Library later did, and also because some of its founding members became some of the leading apostates within a short time.

How many books were in the original library and how were they checked out?

A list from the Seventies Library account book, compiled between the time the library opened in January 1845 and the exodus, indicates a total of 675 volumes. Of these, approximately 16 percent were religious books, 13 percent history, 13 percent belles-lettres, and 12 percent reference and learning. The rest ranged from self-improvement to philosophy to medicine.

Membership in the Seventies Library and Institute Association was opened by purchasing stock with cash or books. Although this last library was organized primarily for the use and training of missionaries, books were allowed to circulate for a small fee among non-members of the association.

Did the missionaries receive any special training before they were sent out?

Certainly not to the extent they do today. Although the Seventies Hall was designed with missionary training in mind, the design was not always carried out in practice. Men were often sent on missions soon after baptism, with the expectation that a senior companion would offer the training in

＊ ＊

* *

the field. The Hall was used for instruction by Church or Quorum leaders on a periodic basis and it had a library for use by members, but much of the training came from Nauvoo Lyceums, debating societies, Nauvoo University classes, and, of course, personal study.

Why was there a hall for the Seventies but not one for the Elders or High Priests?

After the death of Joseph, the Twelve developed a plan to rapidly expand the missionary force, which they felt should consist of Seventies. High Priests would only be needed to preside over the areas where the converts lived. There was, in practice, little need for elders at this time, since converts could be called to go on missions and be trained by more experienced companions. In the last couple of years of Nauvoo's existence, because of a decision that all elders under the age of thirty-five become Seventies, the city quickly had more Seventies than any other Melchizedek Priesthood office. By the end of 1845, most of the men in Nauvoo who held the Priesthood were either Seventies or High Priests. The Seventies Hall was the home of fifteen Quorums of Seventies, each of them with their own president.

Actually, the High Priests planned a Hall, but postponed building it because of the pressure for completing the temple. In January 1845, Brigham attended a meeting at the Masonic Hall where the subject of a High Priests Hall was discussed. In stead of undertaking another expensive building, he proposed the quorum instead finish off the upper story of the temple where they could all receive their endowments. The suggestion was carried unanimously.

Who was the first Seventy ordained in this dispensation?

Hiram Winters, born in Westfield, New York, in 1805, joined the Church in 1833. In that same year, he moved to Kirtland, where the Prophet Joseph ordained him a Seventy on February 28, 1835, making Hiram the first Seventy ordained in this dispensation. He was a member of the Seventies in Nauvoo and later went west with the Saints, dying in Utah in 1889.

* *

Streets and Roads

Who paid for the building of roads, bridges, and so on, in and around Nauvoo, and how was it accomplished?

The Saints constructed approximately seventy-five miles of streets in Nauvoo. The city government, which, according to the City Charter, required male citizens to perform the work, assumed responsibility for the initial surveying, grading (with horse-drawn scrapers and levelers), and bridge building. Section 26 reads:

> The inhabitants of the city of Nauvoo are hereby exempted from working on any road beyond the limits of the city, and for the purpose of keeping the streets, lanes, avenues, and alleys in repair, to require of the male inhabitants of said city, over the age of twenty-one, and under fifty years, to labor on said streets, lanes, avenues, and alleys, not exceeding three days in each year; any person failing to perform such labor, when duly notified by the Supervisor, shall forfeit and pay the sum of one dollar per day for each day so neglected or refused.

Such a "road tax" was common in towns and villages throughout the United States during the nineteenth century.

Were all the streets the early Nauvoo maps show actually open and used?

* *

City Council minutes often addressed the question of opening streets that were on the original plat but never opened. As new areas were annexed to the east, the Council received petitions for opening new streets or extending existing ones, requests it could never fully keep up with. With the influx of new residents in the final months before the exodus, due to mob pressure on outlying settlements, the problem became even more acute. Thus, when the Saints left in the spring and summer of 1846, several miles of platted streets had never been opened.

What feature of Nauvoo was once mentioned in *Ripley's Believe It Or Not?*

Nauvoo was described as the only city in America having a Main Street with both ends on the same river.

Is the present River Road where the original river road ran?

Not entirely. Much of it ran along the ridge east of the present road. Part of that route today is the present Warsaw Street, which enters Nauvoo past Camp Nauvoo and was a main road into the upper town during the Nauvoo era.

The state did not complete the present twelve-mile scenic river road drive between Hamilton and Nauvoo until 1939.

What kinds of vehicles would be found on the streets of Nauvoo besides wagons?

Part of the answer to this question may be found in Section 18 of the Legislative Powers of the Nauvoo City Charter, which reads, in regard to commercial vehicles, "To license, tax and regulate hackney carriages, wagons, carts and drays." In addition, numerous private vehicles such as buggies, carriages, shays, and coaches, as well as winter vehicles such as sleighs and bob-sleds could be seen on the roads. Since men did the most travel, riding a horse was much easier, which is why Nauvoo had so many stables for horses as opposed to carriage houses.

* *

* *

The most common summer vehicles, (and preferred by those who traveled extensively were carriages—light, four-wheeled, two-horse wagons mounted on springs and often with canopy tops. The demand for such vehicles was great enough that Nauvoo supported its own carriage manufactory. When the Saints made their exodus, many of their vehicles were carriages. One of Brigham's wives, Margaret Pierce Young, wrote of her journey west: "We had a comfortable carriage and consequently did not suffer as much as others did during our wanderings through the wilderness."

When did paving of streets and roads begin? Did they have it here?

"Paving" is merely making a road smoother and more resistant to wear by covering it with broken bits of stone or brick. People have paved roads since ancient history. If you mean asphalt, that did not begin until 1870 in Newark, New Jersey. In Nauvoo, there was an attempt at "paving." The worst places were filled with stone, gravel, or broken brick. Thomas Kane, in his account of a visit to the deserted city in September 1846, tells of walking along a "solitary street, no grass growing up in the paved ways." This was possibly literary license, since too many accounts mention the extremely muddy conditions of the streets after a rain. At times, Parley Street was almost impassable even by foot. There is little question that given time, the streets would have been vastly improved, but the city had other priorities.

Did Nauvoo have sidewalks and how were they made?

By city ordinance, sidewalks were required, varying from eight to ten feet wide, depending on the width of the street. Although we like to think of wooden sidewalks for frontier cities like Nauvoo, we have no evidence that such walkways existed. Excavations reveal the sidewalks were constructed of broken stone, pieces of brick, and gravel. Original limestone edging, separating the sidewalks from the streets, can still be seen along several of the streets in Nauvoo today.

* *

* *

How responsible were homeowners for the streets or sidewalks in front of their homes?

Although the city officially assumed responsibility for the construction and maintenance of streets and walkways, financial problems prevented Nauvoo from carrying out an adequate street-improvement program. For practical purposes, therefore, property owners found it necessary to keep their streets and walkways in repair as much as possible, especially in front of their homes and businesses.

Water Street seems quite close to the river and ends at Parley Street. Was it like that originally?

No. South of Water Street was Lumber Street, which was actually on the beach and is now inundated. Originally, Water Street did not end at Parley Street either. It continued on north along the beach to the northern limits of the city, although the most northern part was not as well traveled. Officials decided in 1844 to extend the street northward because of a dispute over wharfage rights. Property owners along the river felt they controlled all wharfage in front of their property. The city disputed this claim and extended Water Street along the river to give it complete control of the riverfront. The southern portion connected the steam and water mills along the beach and provided an access to the lumber rafts and other boats that tied up along this city-owned property.

* *

Taylor Home

The story of the little rocking horse doesn't sound logical. Wasn't the little boy eight years old? Would he have cried for two days for something he was too old to play with anyway? And would his father have tolerated this behavior from an eight-year-old?

The youngest son, Joseph James, was eight years old and seemingly too old to cry for a toy he had outgrown. There may have been a slight exaggeration in the story about the two days of crying, but it is nevertheless possible that the young boy's distress over the loss of a favorite possession prompted his father to return for the little horse. And those who might question such indulgence from a father must remember that parents were subjecting their families to great difficulty in the name of religious convictions that young children might not comprehend. It is not unreasonable to believe John Taylor's feelings for his child would lead him to do what sounds illogical to a modern parent. With child mortality as high as it was in the early nineteenth century, especially among the Latter-day Saints, it would be a rather uncaring parent who did not feel it essential to "indulge" children whose lives were often so short.

James Ivins, who built this home, was apparently fairly prosperous. Why didn't he have larger closets for what could have been a larger wardrobe?

The closets were small for perhaps several reasons. First of all, the home is not necessarily indicative of the money an owner might be inclined to spend on clothes. Second, even if the means were available, owning several dresses or suits would be considered poor taste among neighbors who could not afford such luxuries. People also believed large closets took up valuable floor space when there was little reason not to hang clothing on wall pegs. And finally, like many other aspects of home construction, tradition plays a major role. It took some time to overcome the tradition of no closets at all.

The belief that larger closets would be taxed as rooms is commonly mentioned, but there is no evidence for this practice in Illinois.

Why did Ivins sell this complex to the Church? Did he stay in Nauvoo?

The best answer seems to come from John Taylor's Nauvoo Journal:

> A man of the name of James Ivins had considerable property, and wished to part with it, for the purpose (as he said) of placing his sons at some business, not having an opportunity in this place; the conclusion I came to, from his actions, was, that he was disaffected. He leaned towards Law (one of the dissidents) when he was cut off; when Rigdon went the same way he had such another leaning. In consequence of these the people lost all confidence in him, and he knowing it, was desirous of leaving.

He therefore sold the printing complex to Taylor for $3,200 and moved to St. Louis.

* *

The Temple

* *

There is the persistent story that the Salem Evangelical and Reformed Church in Cincinnati in 1867 somehow acquired the Moroni weather vane on the temple. A replacement was made after lightning knocked it from the steeple in 1966, and the original was sent to Nauvoo Restoration, Inc. Is this story true?

The Cincinnati church apparently did send a weather vane, but all evidence is against that being the original temple vane. The Cincinnati vane shows a colonial-style winged angel with no book in her hands. Perrigrine Sessions, who lived in Nauvoo at the time the vane was placed on the temple, describes in his journal the original as being Moroni (never with wings) and having a Book of Mormon in his hand. The Sessions description matches the originally planned vane, not the one from the Cincinnati church. It is somewhat illogical to believe that the original vane, made of tin, could have escaped the burning of the temple in 1848.

What happened to the temple bell?

The bell was still on the temple after the final exodus in September 1846. Several contemporary journals mention the mob desecrating the temple and ringing a bell after the final exodus. Some reports indicate this may have been a ship's bell put there by the mob to replace the missing temple bell. According to some family records, Andrew and David Lamoreaux

* *

heard that a minister had removed the temple bell for his own church after the exodus. Since the 1,500-pound bell still belonged to the Latter-day Saints, the brothers, along with Daniel Wells and some others, returned to Nauvoo and removed it from its new tower one night and took it across the river. We do know that the Nauvoo temple bell was erected at the Stand on Main Street in Winter Quarters.

The Lamoreaux records say the brothers took the bell across the plains to Utah, arriving in Salt Lake City on September 10, 1850. The load was so heavy that the family had to walk most of the way. This story conflicts with Church records, which state Charles C. Rich brought the temple bell from Winter Quarters to Salt Lake City in the summer of 1847. The Lamoreaux records most likely deal with another bell, often referred to as the Hummer bell, which was designed for a Presbyterian church in Iowa City. This bell appears to have disappeared from history, whereas the bell the Rich company carried across the plains and that hung for years on Temple Square in Utah has been returned to the newly reconstructed temple in Nauvoo.

Were there quarries in Nauvoo other than the temple Quarry?

Limestone was excavated from four main quarries, but only the one west of Main Street in the northern part of the city was known as the Temple Quarry. The other three quarries were the Hiram Kimball Quarry, the Robert D. Foster Quarry located at Robison and Ripley, and the Loomis Quarry, located along the river southeast of the city. In addition to these major quarries, there were small, privately operated quarries for the use of the landowners, since limestone is abundant throughout the area.

What gave the temple dome its gold appearance? Was it real gold leaf?

The dome itself was made of wood covered with tin. Phillip B. Lewis, a tinner by trade and one of the trusted brethren who helped rebury the remains of Joseph and Hyrum when they were removed from the Nauvoo House cellar, did the tin work on the tower. Thomas Kane,

* *

who visited the almost deserted city after the exodus, described how the temple, with its spire of white and gold, shone in the sunlight. Gold leaf for such a large surface as the dome was rather expensive and difficult to apply; evidence suggests the tin was covered with an amalgam. Such amalgams could contain gold powder, but because even this process was expensive, bronze powders were often substituted. Since the temple was still relatively new when Kane and other visitors saw it, it would still have the burnished gold appearance, especially in the light of the setting sun.

One other possibility exists, which is less likely because of the difficulty in obtaining it. A tin-and-copper-coated dome (12 percent tin) would have the appearance of 24-karat gold. Whether knowledge of such an alloy or its availability was known to the Saints is doubtful, however. And again, the copper would have been prohibitively expensive.

What happened to the carved wooden oxen the stone font oxen replaced?

Since we find no record of any of those oxen showing up in the century and a half since the temple fire, we can safely assume they were destroyed-perhaps while in temple storage or later as firewood.

There are two types of stars adorning the temple. Normal-looking stars are under the cornices, but those at the tops of the columns are unusual with an elongated bottom ray. Is that significant?

The stone stars at the tops of the columns with the longer bottom rays are significant. They represent the Morning Star (the planet Venus), which is drawing its light from the sun, which is still below the horizon and is thus heralding the morning. The Morning Star also, of course, represents Christ, who receives His glory (light) from His father (the greater light). Nativity paintings often use the same long-rayed star to represent the birth of Christ.

* *

* *

Do we know who the temple arsonist was?

A number of sources list Joseph Agnew as the main culprit. Lewis Bidamon, who married Emma Smith, widow of the Prophet, was one such source. He told Elders George A. Smith and Erastus Snow in 1856 that the inhabitants of surrounding communities contributed a purse of $500 to Joseph Agnew for the burning of the temple. When B. H. Roberts visited Nauvoo in 1885, by M. M. Morrill, the mayor of Nauvoo, informed him that Agnew was the confessed arsonist. In 1872, after Agnew's death, *The Peoria Transcript* reported his confession as did the *Keokuk Gate City*. The latter paper included details as reported by George Rudsill, who claimed to know the men involved but agreed not to divulge the facts until Agnew and two accomplices had died. The two companions were allegedly Thomas Sharp, former editor of the *Warsaw Signal*, and Squire McCauley of Hancock County.

In spite of these sources, there is much evidence against the story, and the Agnew family vehemently denied Joseph's role. Here is a story still waiting to be revealed.

Do we know why the temple was burned?

The normally presumed reason is the fear by the anti-Mormons that its presence might influence the Saints to return and put the temple to use. However, there might be more to it than that. It was burned at the time the Saints had been negotiating to sell the temple to the Catholics. There was almost as much anti-Catholic feelings in the country at that time as there was anti-Mormon. One non-Mormon Illinois letter writer wrote to her fiancé in Minnesota: "Now methinks . . . I would much rather the Mormons have possession than the Catholics. Doubtless they have deep designing well laid plans and when once they get a foothold, there is no telling what they may do connected as they are with a foreign power." We can logically assume such thoughts had not escaped the minds of the arsonists.

* *

* *

How does limestone (Nauvoo temple material) compare with granite for strength and permanence?

Limestone is a sedimentary rock, much less resistant to weathering and water than granite, which is an igneous rock. Most large caverns have been carved out of limestone, indicating its lack of resistance to water. Unfortunately, no available granite formations were close to Nauvoo, whereas limestone was quite abundant. Limestone for the temple did have the advantages of its whiteness for beauty and the property of becoming harder after exposure to air. With the original walls five feet thick, the strength of granite was not so essential. The facing on the reconstructed temple is of the same type of stone, but since it is merely a veneer, strength is again not a major consideration.

How was the temple heated?

The temple was heated with stoves. On November 24, 1845, Heber C. Kimball recorded in his journal, "The painters are putting on the last coat of paint in the upper rooms of the temple. Two stoves were put up in the largest room."

And then, on February 9, 1846, as the first contingent of Saints was evacuating Nauvoo, an overheated stovepipe being used to dry some clothes in the upper room caused a fire on the temple roof. The fire was soon extinguished, but not before burning a 10-by-15-foot hole in the roof. It was repaired before the final exodus.

Some temple stones looked polished. How was that accomplished?

Sand was poured on the limestone then another large flat stone was placed on top and ground back and forth. Nahum Curtis and his son Lyman had the job of polishing stones for the Nauvoo Temple.

Were temple recommends necessary for entering the Nauvoo Temple?

After endowments began in the temple in December 1845, so many

* *

people were engaged in receiving their endowments (5,500 in the final eight weeks before the exodus) that Brigham and other officiators were staying in the temple around the clock. To maintain order, Heber C. Kimball had to limit endowments to only those with official invitations. Such invitations were apparently based on such criteria of worthiness as we would expect today. During a discourse in Salt Lake City, Franklin D. Richards said he had in his possession a receipt signed by the Prophet Joseph and the tithing clerk that stated that "Franklin D. Richards, having paid his tithing in full to date, is entitled to the benefits of the baptismal font in the Nauvoo Temple." These invitations perhaps marked the beginning of the temple recommend policy.

Cranes were used to lift the huge limestone blocks onto the temple walls, but how were stones lifted onto the wagons at the quarry?

Few contemporary descriptions exist of work in the Nauvoo quarries, so we can only assume that methods were the same as those used in other quarries in that era. If the stones were not too large, several men could lift them or move them up inclined planes into the wagons. One common method for the exceedingly large stone blocks was to use wagons with the beds removed and leather slings attached in such a manner that they would be pried up just enough for the straps to go around them and then hoisted only a short distance above the ground and transported in that manner between the wheels.

Sidney Rigdon prophesied the temple would never have a roof and others predicted the temple would never be completed. Was it?

The 1828 Webster's Dictionary has two generalized definitions for the word "complete." The first is "having no deficiency; perfect." This, of course, can apply only to our Heavenly Father and Jesus Christ, so we must go to the second more temporal meaning, which is "finished; ended; concluded; as, the edifice is complete." By this definition, there is little question: the temple was "finished, ended, concluded" and acceptable to the Lord. Any job or construction work is "ended" or "concluded" if nothing more is added. To debate this issue is to split hairs and apply a modern, popular concept to nineteenth-century understanding and knowledge.

Would more "finishing" work have been done if the Saints had not left?

The Saints obviously would have worked on many details. The upper Assembly Hall certainly required work, but for the needs of the Saints in performing their endowments, the temple was complete. Carpeting had been installed in the celestial room in the attic, and the basement floor was being bricked over even as the exodus was taking place.

In April 1845, work also commenced, but was never completed, on a temple wall that was planned to enclose not only the temple block but the block west of the temple also.

Does it matter whether the temple was "completed"?

Some critics have charged that the Lord said the Church would be rejected unless the temple was completed. That claim is not true. What the Lord said through revelation to Joseph was "if you do not these things [referring to temple ordinances] at the end of the appointment ye shall be rejected as a church, with your dead" (D&C 124:32). The ordinances were done in the temple, about which there is no question. The "completion" or "incompletion" of the temple is irrelevant.

How far along was construction on the temple when Joseph and Hyrum were martyred?

The walls were approximately 12-feet high above the basement, and meetings had already been held on the first floor. Brigham Young, in a discourse in 1871, said the temple walls were complete only halfway up the first-floor windows. Andrew Jenson, in a 1923 conference talk, said they were only up to the first windows. Whatever the case, paintings showing Joseph looking at much higher walls are merely cases of artistic license and not historically accurate.

* *

The speed with which the Saints completed the temple is amazing. Only seventeen months after Joseph's and Hyrum's deaths, the attic story was dedicated.

The Saints estimated the cost of the temple at various times from $500,000 to $1 million dollars. Since so much labor and material was donated, how can such a cost be determined?

Records were kept of the labor and materials donated or tithed. In fact, before the temple's completion, the Church warned that if some of the members did not put forth greater efforts, they would be denied the privilege of receiving their endowments. However, we find no evidence that the records were actually tallied up to determine the final construction cost. The leaders more likely merely estimated the costs of construction if a similar building had been constructed in a commercial manner. Do such estimates sound logical? On the basis of today's dollars, the $500,000 figure would be over $30 million—an astounding sacrifice for a people as impoverished as those early Saints.

Such an edifice could not have been constructed by tithed labor or clothing and food alone. Cash was needed and not just pennies. How was it raised?

Goods in kind were sold for cash, but the small items so commonly donated were not sufficient for that. Much of the cash came from consecrations of cash by wealthier converts and donations of larger items such as livestock and land. There was a tithing lot across from Brigham Young's home where tithed or donated livestock was penned and then periodically driven for cash to places like Quincy. Land also was donated. Between May 1843 and July 1844, more than 2,500 acres of farmland and several city lots were donated. Such donations added considerably to the cash needed.

* *

* *

Were the excavations for such buildings as the Nauvoo temple done by hand?

No. Workmen used horse-drawn or ox-drawn, heavy, two-handled scoops called earth-scrapers or team-shovels as well as plows to loosen the soil. Benjamin Johnson, in his autobiography, recorded on September 25, 1833, in reference to the Kirtland Temple that the members were so poor "there was not a scraper or hardly a plow that could be found among the Saints." One of these scrapers is on display at the brickyard.

When was the first meeting held in the Nauvoo Temple?

The first General Conference was held in the temple on October 5, 6, and 7, 1845. However, the unfinished temple had been used for meetings since 1842 when a general assembly was convened therein on October 30. In his journal, Joseph noted for that day, "The Saints met to worship on a temporary floor, in the temple, the walls of which were about four feet high above the basement; and notwithstanding its size, it was well filled." John Taylor addressed the Saints at that meeting.

Do we know who was the first child born in this dispensation under the New and Everlasting Covenant as a result of the ordinances instituted in Nauvoo?

Elizabeth Ann Whitney, having been sealed to her husband by the Prophet Joseph shortly before the birth of a daughter, always treasured the knowledge that one of her daughters was the first child to receive this cherished birth right in this dispensation. Elizabeth recalled the birth month as January, although family genealogy puts the date as February 17, 1844.

Who was the first woman to receive the temple ordinances in Nauvoo?

Emma Smith, who, in turn, administered the initiatory rites to other women, including Emmeline Wells, who noted that when the Nauvoo Temple was completed, "woman was called upon to take her part in

* *

administering therein, officiating in the character of priestess."

So did Emma remain a faithful Saint after the death of Joseph?

No. The temple ordinances she received were not in the completed temple. She received them and administered them to other women before the death of her husband, when the rites were being done in the Mansion House, Red Brick Store, and so on. When the temple was ready for endowments, she was estranged from the Church leaders and not willing to participate in the actual endowments within the temple.

Is it true that dances were held in the Nauvoo Temple?

There was dancing. According to *The History of the Church,* Brigham Young and the Quorum of the Twelve "danced before the Lord" to the music of a small orchestra in the Nauvoo Temple after long days of joyous participation in temple ordinances.

William Weeks, the architect of the Nauvoo Temple, was not the architect of any other temples. Was Brigham unhappy with his work?

Actually, Brigham was very pleased with his work and intended to have William build the next temple in Utah. William and his family were among the 1847 pioneers, but the following year he returned to Iowa after becoming disaffected with the Church. When he spurned Brigham's counsel to return to Utah, he and his wife were excommunicated. The causes for his disaffection are not known, but by 1852, he was back in Utah and, according to T. Edgar Lyon, was rebaptized. By then, however, Truman Angell had been named Church Architect and supervised the Salt Lake Temple.

Who designed the faces on the sunstones?

When William Weeks questioned the prophet on a certain architectural aspect of the temple, Joseph replied, "I wish you to carry out my designs. I . . . will have it built according to the pattern shown me." In the spring of 1844, a visitor to Nauvoo observed a stonecutter asking Joseph if the face of the sunstone was like the face he saw in vision. Joseph replied, "Very near it" and then made a minor correction.

How many sunstones still exist out of the original thirty?

Only two complete sunstones still exist. One is in Nauvoo on the grounds of the Visitor Center, on loan to the Church by the State of Illinois. The other is in the Smithsonian in Washington, D. C. A few others do exist, but they are either badly defaced or are incomplete.

Since the temple was not complete enough for endowments when Joseph was killed, did he or Hyrum ever receive theirs?

If this is a question of the brothers receiving their endowments after death, it should be noted that that practice did not begin until the St. George Temple was completed. However, it was not necessary in this case since Joseph had introduced the endowment ceremony to a select group on the second floor of his brick store in Nauvoo in May 1842. He and Hyrum had received their endowments there. By the time of his death, Joseph had officiated the endowment to more than sixty men and women, in a variety of other places, including the Homestead (his first home in Nauvoo) and the southeast corner of the second floor of the Mansion House. Several were also given in Brigham Young's home.

The temple bell has been referred to as a "recast" bell. Does this mean it was recast in the foundry or after the Church acquired it? And what cracked it?

Before the bell could be installed on Temple Square in Salt Lake City, the severe winter of 1849–50 cracked the bell. Melted down and recast, it was enlarged to 782 pounds. Recasting simply consists of making a sand mold of the original bell, melting the cracked bell, and pouring it back into the mold, thus duplicating the original.

Some discrepancy arises over the number of endowments performed in the Nauvoo Temple. What is the most accurate figure available?

From December 10, 1845, when the first endowments were given, until February 7, 1846, when the temple was closed for ordinance work, 5,669 ordinances had been performed. However, since daily totals were often given in round numbers, we can only safely say the number exceeded 5,500.

What important architectural features are missing from the temple model displayed at the Visitors' Center?

The original temple had a double row of skylights on the roof and a 23½ foot semi-circular window at the east end of the attic story. These provided light for the Council Chamber where the endowments took place. Canvas partitions divided this chamber for the endowments, with the Celestial Room on the east end where the large Gothic window was located. Other minor exterior differences can be noted when comparing the model with the reconstructed temple. The handicap entrance is the only major change on the exterior of the new temple.

LDS temples today do not have bells. Why did the Nauvoo Temple have one?

The Nauvoo Temple had dual functions. Since there were no meeting houses or chapels in Nauvoo, the assembly hall of the temple was to serve that function and the Saints felt a bell would serve to call the people to worship as in churches the Saints were familiar with. It apparently was also rung to signal the noon hour. Heber Kimball, in his journal for December 5, 1845, mentions some sisters commencing work in the temple "at twelve o'clock, at the ringing of the temple bell." Leaders also used the bell in the final months to assemble the Saints on special occasions, especially when Legion members had to be warned about threatening mob action.

What was the reaction of the Saints in Winter Quarters and Salt Lake City when they heard of the burning of the Nauvoo Temple?

Brigham Young summed the reaction up best: "I hoped to see it burned before I left, but I did not. I was glad when I heard of its being destroyed by fire, and of the walls having fallen in, and said, 'Hell, you cannot now occupy it.'"

Why didn't the Nauvoo Temple face east like most LDS temples?

It's true that most of the earlier temples were oriented eastward for symbolic reasons. The "wind of God" originates from this direction. Jesus Christ enters his temples from the east (Ezekiel 43:1–2 and 10:19), and at the Second Coming, the Lord will come from the east (Joseph Smith—Matthew 1:26; Matthew 24:27). However, the location of a front door or any door would be of little consequence to the Lord, and once the Lord accepts a temple, its orientation is irrelevant. We do not know if there might have been an entrance in the east end. There was a large gable window on that end, which is little known because no illustrations and pictures show that end. Also, with the river and valley to the west, the temple had to face west for aesthetic purposes.

What kind of music was provided for meetings in the temple?

A description of the October 1845 Conference held in the temple answers this question best. Helen Mar Whitney Kimball mentions being present with the choir on that occasion. She describes the choir and orchestra occupying a gallery at the west end of the temple, opposite the stand. This undoubtedly was the same orchestra Thomas Kane witnessed the following year at a party held in honor of the Mormon Battalion just prior to its leaving on its trek. He said on that occasion, "Well as I knew the peculiar fondness of the Mormons for music, their orchestra in service on the occasion astonished me by its numbers and fine drill."

There have been some questions about the two objects held by hands directly over the face of the Sunstone. They are trumpets, are they not?

Yes. Brigham Young and contemporary journalists identified them as "Trumpet Stones." The Lord commanded Moses to make two silver trumpets for the priests to blow to summon the Israelites to assemble in the tabernacle. And when the Lord comes a second time, a heavenly trump "shall sound both long and loud." These stone trumpets have a rich symbolic meaning.

Did Church members wear temple garments in Nauvoo?

Charles Shook, who later apostatized, stated that in the year 1843–44, at Macedonia, Illinois, John Smith showed him both the endowment garment and robe and that they were identical to the garments and robes with which he became familiar in Utah. On January 15, 1846, Hosea Stout recorded in his diary, "I stopped at home & put on an undergarment for the first time to wear it." In 1846, as the Mormon Battalion was preparing for its overland march, Brigham Young admonished the officers to wear their garments.

Are temples ever "undedicated"?

It is never necessary. Whenever temporal activities such as remodeling or unworthy persons invade a temple, it becomes desecrated ("undedicated") and must then be rededicated. The Nauvoo Temple served a dual purpose, so unworthy persons might enter the less sacred portions without desecrating it. On occasion, law enforcement officers were permitted to search the temple looking for Church leaders. Not until December 1845 were the attic ordinance rooms put in place, and these dedicated rooms were closed to even members without invitation.

* *

Why was it so important that the Nauvoo Temple be finished before the exodus?

The Lord had told Joseph by revelation (D&C 124) that unless the temple was available for endowments before the Saints left, the Church would be rejected. By December 1845, it was ready for such ordinances and more than 5,500 (the majority of adult members) received their endowments. Many of those who did later testified that they felt it would have been near impossible to face the hardships ahead without such spiritual strengthening. This was essential, as it would be more than thirty years before the next temple would be dedicated in St. George, Utah, in 1877.

What was the seating capacity of the Nauvoo Temple?

The first general conference of the Church to be held in the temple was on October 5, 1845. Helen Mar Whitney reports, "There were five thousand persons seated comfortably." This total, of course, would have been on the main floor. The second floor, identical to the first, could have held a similar number.

Did the temple tower have all four clocks installed and how were they operated?

A daguerreotype of the temple and architectural drawings suggest four clocks in the tower, one facing each direction. We know that a congregation in England collected money for one of the clocks, which was probably the clock facing the front of the temple or west. With available funds needed for the construction itself, it is highly unlikely that funds were diverted for works for the other three clocks. Since the daguerreotypes show more than one clock, the other three clocks probably had only painted faces, waiting for the day when works could be provided for them.

* *

* *

The star stone in the Joseph Smith Academy appears to be disproportionately small compared with the temple models and to how it might be seen from such a height. In its original condition, it would have been approximately 15 inches across, whereas the stones on the models would suggest a star at least twice that size. Are we sure it is an original star stone?

As the story goes, that small star stone was found on the temple site many years ago, and it possibly was. However, it was obviously for another purpose since the original star stones measured 30 inches from the bottom of the descending point and a line drawn between the top two points.

The famous "Temple on the Hill" daguerreotype suggests a rather "trashy" looking city. How is this impression explained in view of such positive descriptions by residents of Nauvoo and visitors?

Most scholars believe the date of this picture to be sometime in 1846—quite possibly after the exodus was well under way and the city already deteriorating. There are also two conceptual explanations. We are tempted to compare the park-like restoration of present-day Nauvoo with the more realistic picture of a frontier city in nineteenth-century America. The second conceptual explanation lies in the very obvious image of an outhouse in the foreground. Although real and not bothersome in 1840, it projects an unappealing picture today. It is difficult, but again we must not be so tempted to judge the past by contemporary standards. By nineteenth-century standards and in comparison with other frontier cities, Nauvoo was undoubtedly quite pristine.

Records indicate the temple was approximately 35 feet higher than the water tower east of it. Is that about right?

First, we must agree on the height of the temple tower. Various sources describe the height from 110 feet to 200 feet. The most often quoted and

* *

* *

normally accepted figure gives the height as 165 feet. Archaeological reports from the 1960s give a more specific height of 158½ feet to the top of the spire. The architect of the reconstructed temple describes an exact height from grade level to the top of the tower as 144 feet plus another 12½ feet for the vane, making a total overall of 156½ feet. The water tower has been measured at approximately 119 feet. This measurement would mean the temple tower would have been between 35 and 40 feet higher than the tower.

Is it true that admission was charged for the dedication of the Nauvoo Temple?

Issuing tickets for admission to temple dedications is not unique, but today there is no charge for them and they are distributed because of limited seating. In Nauvoo, however, a $1 fee was charged for the public dedications in May 1846, with the funds going to help the temple workmen move their families to join the main body of Saints already crossing Iowa westward.

Why was the Nauvoo Temple, like the Kirtland Temple, designed with multiple pulpits at each end of the assembly halls?

An explanation lies in the understanding that the conducting of many of the Sunday Services was the responsibility not of the ward leadership but of the Priesthood Quorums. Each end of the assembly hall contained four tiers of pulpits for the various offices of the Aaronic and Melchizedek Priesthoods. The two Priesthoods were at opposite ends and the public seats designed so they could face either way, depending on which Priesthood was conducting the services.

What were the opinions of non-LDS Illinois residents of the Nauvoo Temple?

Opinions varied widely *The Burlington (Iowa) Gazette*, which wrote: "The Temple, which is destined to be the most magnificent structure in the

* *

* *

West, is progressing rapidly. . . . Its style of architecture is . . . unlike anything in the world . . . but is at the same time chaste and elegant" The *Warsaw Signal* wrote, "The Temple, in reality, is designed, in our opinion for fortification. It has regular port-holes, in the shape of round windows, in the second story, and is in every respect well situated for a fortification."

Were baptisms in the Nauvoo Temple for the dead only? And how many were performed?

To the first question, the answer is no. In November 1841, the Prophet Joseph was giving instructions on baptisms for health. Samuel Rolfe was present with a painful felon (swelling in one hand). Joseph advised him to wash his hands in the font, which he did, and one week later he was completely cured. After word circulated of this, it became a not uncommon practice to be baptized for health in the temple font.

The number of baptisms for the dead performed in Nauvoo, according to existing records (some were not recorded), either in the temple or nearby streams or the river, was 15,626.

What was the original cost of the temple lot?

It cost almost the same as it was sold for along with its ruined temple. It was purchased from Daniel Wells, a non-Mormon who had moved to the Commerce area in 1827 and became a land speculator. He owned much of the land on the Bluff and sold the temple site to the Church for only $1,100, but the prospect of building the temple on that land immediately raised the value of his surrounding land from which he profited very nicely. Wells joined the Church during the exodus and died in the faith in Utah.

Did the temple have a Holy of Holies?

Yes, although it was not as restricted as in modern temples or as in the temple of Solomon. Located in the southeast corner of the attic, it also

* *

served as a clerk's office and a sealing room for marriages.

On January 19, 1846, Jacob Norton recorded in his journal, "In the evening I went into the Holy of Holies with Emily my wife where by President Brigham Young we were, according to the holy order of the priesthood, sealed together for time and all eternity, and sealed up into eternal life." Today, sealings are performed in rooms set aside for that purpose. This is another example of a religious practice or ritual evolving as it becomes better understood by Church authorities.

Was there a door in the east wall of the temple?

We do not know for sure. On December 26, 1845, Heber C. Kimball wrote in his diary, "Sheriff Backenstos came to the temple, was admitted to the office No. 3 (in attic near southeast corner) by the back stairs." We might logically assume that if there were "back stairs," there might also have been a "back door." However, it is more probable that there were stairs merely connecting the east end of the top assembly hall with the offices in the east end of the attic, which would have enabled visitors to reach the offices in the east end of the attic without going through the endowment rooms.

Has the original sunstone, on loan to the Church by the State of Illinois, been here since the temple was burned?

No. One of only two complete sunstones known to exist of the original thirty, this stone was removed from Nauvoo to Springfield about 1870. The State Capitol Building was being constructed of Nauvoo-type limestone, and the sunstone was displayed next to the Capitol steps as an example of that type of stone. Sometime after 1891, it was presented to the Illinois State Historical Society and moved to the state fairgrounds where it remained until the mid-1950s when it was returned to Nauvoo and placed in the State Park. In June 1994, the state gave permission to move it and place it on display at the temple site. When construction began on the new temple, it was relocated immediately north of the Visitors' Center.

* *

Was a time capsule ever placed in a cornerstone of the Nauvoo Temple?

Nancy N. Tracy, a sister who lived near the temple site at the time, mentioned such a "time-capsule" in her autobiography. She claimed to have been present when it was placed there and related the following: "In the huge chief corner stone was cut out a square about a foot around and about as deep lined with zinc, and in it Brother Joseph had placed a Bible, a Book of Mormon, hymn book, and other church works along with silver money that had been coined in that year. Then a lid was cemented down, and the temple was reared on the top of this." It is of interest that more diarists did not make note of this event and that no public record was made of the discovery of such a box.

Q. Were non-members permitted to enter the temple?

As previously stated, the temple served a dual purpose. Since it served as a meeting place for conferences, Sabbath meetings, and so forth, it allowed non-members access. In fact, the Church even allowed the small Catholic congregation in Nauvoo to celebrate mass in a portion of the temple.

However, since the holiest portion, the endowment rooms, were in the attic, restricting entrance to that section was much easier. Even so, authorities from Carthage insisted at times on searching for Church leaders and were allowed access to the entire temple. Once the endowment sessions began in December of 1845, access to the attic area was restricted, but temple access in general was not as severely restricted as in today's temples.

* *

Tin Shop

Is tin a metal like iron, steel, and so on?

Tin is not what it seems to be. First of all, it is a metal extracted from ore but seldom used in its solid block state since it cannot withstand even moderately high temperatures without going into a molten state. Tin is therefore most extensively applied as a coating to other metals stronger than itself. The sheets, usually called "tin" (as under the bench in the tin shop), are thin plates of iron that have been dipped into liquefied tin. The tin actually penetrates the iron, and forms an alloy. The number of times it is dipped gives it greater wearability and a variation of color. In the 1840s, tin was mined in many countries, but the most productive mines were in Cornwall and Devonshire in England.

Do we know what happened to the Stoddard family?

Sylvester Stoddard was baptized into the Church in 1936 and later served in a bishopric in Nauvoo and as a missionary to Maine in 1844. However, he later became embittered, left the Church, and returned to Kirtland. By October 1845, he had joined the Kirtland apostates who were doing everything they could to injure the Saints. He joined with Jacob Bump, Hiram Kellogg, Leonard Rich, and Jewel Raney as leaders of a group of apostate rioters who broke into the Kirtland Temple and took possession of it. They also attempted to take possession of the Church farm.

* *

Explain the difference between "tole" ware and "Japanned" ware.

"Tole" is a more modern term for tinware that craftsmen in the 1840s called "japanned," which meant ware finished with an application of glossy, usually black, varnish and decorated in a Japanese style. The word "tole," referring to the decorating of tin or metal, is not found in dictionaries of that period. The word was more recently imported from French, meaning sheet metal.

The Tinners Association donated the temple weather vane, which was gold-leafed. Wasn't this very expensive? How was it done?

A small amount of gold, when hammered into leaf form as thin as 1/280,000 of an inch, can cover an amazing amount of surface. The gold was undoubtedly acquired from gold watches, rings, jewelry, and so forth that members had donated and would therefore not require any outlay in cash.

The surface (tin, in this case) must first be sized and coated with rust-resistant red lead or iron oxide paint. An adhesive coat of lacquer or sealing glue is then applied, and while still sticky, the small beaten leaves of gold are applied and burnished to a high luster. It requires skilled craftsmanship, but the results may last almost indefinitely. Unfortunately, the temple weather vane never got a chance to be tested for longevity. When the temple was burned in 1848, the vane was undoubtedly destroyed.

How far back in history does tinsmithing go?

Tin, as an alloy with such metals as bronze or copper, was used hundreds of years before the birth of Christ. Tinned-iron vessels appeared in Bohemia by the fourteenth century. But the tinplate used in shops such as this was not commercially successful until the Allgood brothers at Pontypool in England developed a process of rolling sheets of iron and dipping them into molten tin. In the United States, tinware manufacturing, as in this shop, was said to have begun with Edward and William Pattison, brothers in Berlin, Connecticut, who in 1740 started turning out household articles made of sheet tin and peddling their wares from house to house.

* *

* *

What were the prices of some typical tin items, for example, lanterns, cups, and so on?

The Amos Davis store on Mulholland Street was selling skimmers for 50 cents, a set of six tin cups for 37½ cents, a tin pan for 43 cents, a tin bucket for 50 cents, and a tin horn for 25 cents.

The tin shop was apparently profitable. The Stoddards were among the economically elite in Nauvoo.

With tinware being such a common item, were there other tin shops in Nauvoo to supply the demand?

There was a Tinners Association in Nauvoo that took the responsibility for tinning the dome of the temple and making the weather vane, so there must have been several tinsmiths. We know of the well-known tinner, Phillip Bessore Lewis, who lived with the Prophet Joseph when he first settled in Nauvoo, was a member of the Association. Two other members we know of were Dustin Amy, who had been through the Missouri persecutions, and John Mills.

* *

Visitor's Center

How many Church members actually lived in Nauvoo? We know there were 11,000 to 12,000 people in Nauvoo, but were they all members of the Church?

The only census we have that would be close to the maximum population was taken in 1845 and listed over 11,000. Remember, however, that between that census in 1845 and the exodus in 1846, hundreds of Saints were being burned and driven from their homes in outlying LDS settlements throughout Illinois, most of them seeking sanctuary in Nauvoo. We have no population figures for Nauvoo immediately prior to the February 1846 exodus, but there is good reason to believe that at that time, no fewer than 13,000 or 14,000 people would have been in the metropolitan area. Of that number, no fewer than 10 percent were non-members.

In discussing population figures, note that all of the Illinois Saints did not exit the state from the Nauvoo landings. A large number left Illinois to establish congregations in and around St. Louis, 190 miles to the south of Nauvoo. In February 1847, when we think of the vast majority of Saints being in and around Winter Quarters, the St. Louis Conference numbered between 7,000 and 10,000 Latter-day Saints.

* *

How many Saints stayed in Nauvoo? Did the members who stayed apostatize?

The majority (perhaps 3,000 people) of those who did not go west lived outside of Nauvoo. The ones who did stay in Nauvoo, or even Illinois, either left the Church or became inactive. Even the faithful aged, such as Lucy Mack Smith, felt compelled to leave Nauvoo for a short time because of the fear of the mobs. Some of the faithful did stay for awhile in nearby Iowa towns such as Keokuk or Iowa City, but by 1850, most of them had migrated westward. Latter-day Saints such as Emma Smith were permitted to return and live in Illinois because they, like those who apostatized, did not practice their religion. Emma actually associated with the Methodist Church before finally joining the Community of Christ under her son's leadership.

How accurate is the relief map of Nauvoo in relation to buildings shown, elevation, and so forth?

First of all, the elevation has been exaggerated three times. Otherwise, the map would look almost flat. There are about 6,000 buildings depicted on the model, and of these, approximately 2,500 are residences and shops. Of these 2,500, the creators of this map, Don Enders and Gayle Hammond, were able to identify about 250 homes based on land records, tax records, and so on. Thus, about 90 percent of the model's buildings are not identifiable. The streets are accurate, however, as are the timber and prairie areas that were derived from survey records. The Illinois Agriculture Census for 1850 showed vital data on sizes of cultivated fields and their crop content as well as orchards. All in all, a resident of the 1840s would probably have been able to recognize much of this map immediately.

* *

Woodruff Home

Were homes such as the Woodruff home ever used for Sunday services?

No meeting houses were ever built in Nauvoo. Sunday services normally began at 10 a.m., and the place of meeting would depend largely on the weather. Saints from across the river often mentioned arriving in Nauvoo on Sunday mornings, never knowing where they would be meeting. Members were quite free to attend any meeting they wished when they were not conducted in one of the Groves, where they normally were held in mild weather. During inclement weather, they would be conducted in any of the numerous public buildings or in homes such as the Woodruff home. Joseph Smith's mansion house was a favorite meeting place, and the crowds were often so large that the windows had to be opened so those outside could hear. When the first floor of the temple had been laid, meetings were also held there.

The membership did not meet as wards, although wards existed. Bishops of wards were primarily responsible for their members' welfare and not with conducting meetings.

Why didn't Wilford have stoves in his home?

Stoves were quite expensive and still inefficient, and Wilford and his wife, like many people of that era, were not convinced iron stoves were as effective as the fireplaces and brick ovens with which they were familiar.

The larger fireplace in the southwest room was the kitchen fireplace with a brick oven next to it.

The inferior coarseness of bricks on the outside almost looks deliberate. Why didn't he replace them?

We can only speculate on the reason. The brick masons might have progressed too far before Brother Woodruff noticed them and he perhaps did not want to tear down the walls. This batch might also have been of inferior brick that took on their weathered inferior looks only after a period of exposure to the elements. Whatever the case, incorporating such inferior-looking bricks into this nice home would not likely have been a deliberate act.

How authentic a restoration is the Woodruff home?

It was the first Old Nauvoo building to receive an authentic architectural restoration, completed in 1969. Wilford did much of the actual original construction himself between his missions for the Church.

Conclusion

The Unasked Question: Why Nauvoo?

One of the most significant questions visitors to Nauvoo could ask but never do is "Why did the Saints settle and build Nauvoo in the first place?"

In retrospect, Nauvoo seems not only to have been unnecessary and impractical but detrimental to the Church's cause. Other religious groups of that era were interested only in making converts and setting up congregations where the people lived. The exceptions would have been those who were interested in establishing such religious communes as the Shaker communities, Oneida, New Harmony, and so forth. After the persecutions in Ohio and Missouri, some Church leaders realized that gathering into predominantly Mormon communities was a cause of many of their persecutions.

After their expulsion from Missouri, Sidney Rigdon urged Joseph to refrain from again gathering the Saints into such enclaves, which appeared so threatening to non-Mormon neighbors. Was he right? In almost every sense—politically, economically, militarily and socially—he probably was. So, why didn't Joseph follow the advice of his practical-minded counselor? Why did he go to the trouble of building another entirely new city that would inevitably become the perceived threat Sidney visualized?

The answer, of course, lies in a revelation Joseph had received. He,

* *

as well as some members of the Twelve, realized from the very beginning that Nauvoo was not supposed to be a permanent headquarters for the Saints. It was to be a preparatory base for a move to their Rocky Mountain sanctuary. Therefore, potential hostility as a result of assembling together again didn't matter. For a successful removal and planting in the west, the Church had to be strong, which meant the Saints needed to gather in preparation for such a feat. Knowing he would not be participating in the removal, Joseph realized a temple must be constructed in the meantime where the ordinances could be introduced and taught to the general membership. Only a gathering of members could give the Church the workers necessary to build such a temple and to be available for the ordinances once it was ready. The apparent long-range features of the city were seemingly carried out in the ardent hope that the Lord might somehow change his mind about his people leaving Illinois.

Joseph was inspired to gather his people into such a city because the Prophet still had much doctrine and instruction to impart to the members, and to be most effective, he had to do this by mouth. In the five years Joseph lived in Nauvoo, he gave an average of forty discourses per year, constantly lamenting the difficulty of making his people understand the doctrines the Lord imparted to him. Such teachings could not have been so effective without the advantages of a close-knit population for his personal instruction, as was found in Nauvoo and communities conveniently nearby.

To mourn the short, tragic life of Nauvoo is to overlook its reason for being. It served the Lord's purpose well. It was a necessary school for those who had to carry on what Joseph began and has continued to be an inspiration for those who continue the Lord's work today.

* *

Appendices

A Nauvoo Chronology

***

1839

May 1, 1839: The Church buys the first land in Commerce–a farm from Isaac Galland for $9,000 and a 135-acre farm from Hugh White for $5,000.

May 10, 1839: Joseph moves his family into what is now referred to as the Homestead, a log home on the Hugh White property in Commerce.

July 22, 1839: "Day of Healing" in Commerce and Montrose when hundreds lie prostrate with malaria along the river. Joseph walks among them, healing almost all he touches.

August 8, 1839: Wilford Woodruff and John Taylor are the first to leave from Commerce for their missions in England, both still ill with the ague and fever.

August 30, 1839: The name Nauvoo is used officially for the first time on city plat. The name, Joseph said, was Hebrew, connoting "beautiful place."

Sept. 14, 1839: Brigham Young and Heber C. Kimball leave for their missions in England, both of them also very ill, as are the families they leave behind.

***

* *

Mid-Oct. 1839: King Follett, last of the Missouri prisoners, is finally freed.

Oct. 29, 1839: Joseph Smith, O. Porter Rockwell, Sidney Rigdon, and Elias Higbee leave in a carriage for Washington to petition Congress for a redress of grievances for their persecutions in Missouri-all to no avail.

Nov. 15, 1839: First issue of *The Times and Seasons* comes from the press in Nauvoo.

Dec. 29, 1839: The Nauvoo High Council votes to print a new edition of The Book of Mormon as well as 10,000 copies of a new hymnbook.

1840

Feb. 5, 1840: Joseph preaches in Washington, D. C., before a large congregation that includes several Congressmen. Shortly thereafter, he heads for Nauvoo, leaving Elias Higbee to continue the rather hopeless task of seeking redress from Congress.

April 15-16, 1840: General Conference of Church held in Preston, England. English members now total 1,686. Brigham Young chosen President of the Quorum of the Twelve.

April 21, 1840: Postmaster General in Washington officially changes name of post office from Commerce to Nauvoo.

June 1, 1840: Number of homes in and around Nauvoo total approximately 250.

June 6, 1840: First emigrant Saints from foreign nation (England) leave for America. Before the exodus, nearly 5,000 Saints will emigrate from the British Isles.

July 22, 1840: Joseph welcomes W. W. Phelps back into the Church after his apostasy in Missouri.

Aug. 10, 1840: Joseph preaches publicly for the first time on doctrine of baptism for the dead at the funeral of Seymour Brunson. He had,

* *

* *

however, referred to "preaching" to the dead as early as February 1832 (D&C 76:73).

Aug. 15, 1840: Baptisms for the dead begin in Mississippi River, the first one being Jane Neyman for her deceased son Cyrus. Before the Saints leave Nauvoo, over 15,000 such baptisms will be performed in the river, streams or the temple.

Sept. 14, 1840: Joseph Smith Sr., Patriarch of the Church, dies in Nauvoo.

Oct. 3-5, 1840: Nauvoo General Conference takes place in which the building of the temple is authorized and building committees are appointed.

Oct. 1840: Joseph's first vision is put into print for first time in a pamphlet published by Orson Pratt in Scotland. It was entitled *An Interesting Account of Several Remarkable Visions, and of the Late Discovery of Ancient American Records.*

Dec. 17, 1840: Illinois State Legislature passes the Nauvoo Charter, which also includes charters for the Legion and University. Will take effect Feb. 1, 1841.

1841

Jan. 15, 1841: The *Times and Seasons* reports that the temple "is in progress of erection."

Jan. 19, 1841: Joseph receives D&C 124, giving reasons why a temple must be built in Nauvoo. This section also requires the building of the Nauvoo House and Hyrum Smith to replace his father as Patriarch.

Jan. 1841: First edition of the Book of Mormon published in England.

Feb. 1, 1841: Nauvoo city charter goes into effect, making the city government not subject to any legislative act of Illinois but only to the Illinois and U. S. Constitutions.

Feb. 4, 1841: Nauvoo Legion organized with Joseph as Lieutenant General.

* *

* *

Mar. 1, 1841: Nauvoo divided into four wards by action of the City Council. It also passes a city ordinance granting total religious freedom to all denominations in Nauvoo.

April 6, 1841: Nauvoo General Conference. Cornerstones of Temple laid. Thomas Sharp, editor of the *Warsaw Signal* and later primary leader of anti-Mormon forces, invited to attend.

June 5, 1841: Joseph arrested on requisition from state of Missouri. Freed on writ of habeas corpus at Monmouth, Warren Co., Ill. Stephen A. Douglas was presiding.

July 1, 1841: Brigham Young, Heber C. Kimball, and John Taylor arrive back in Nauvoo from their mission to England.

July 1841: Heber Kimball writes back to Parley Pratt in England that although there were only thirty buildings in Nauvoo when they left two years earlier, there are now 1,200 completed and hundreds more under construction.

Aug. 7, 1841: Don Carlos, Joseph's youngest brother, dies in Nauvoo.

Sept. 22, 1841: A company of brethren leaves for the Pineries in Wisconsin to procure lumber for the Nauvoo Temple.

Oct. 15, 1841: Lodge of Masonry is established in Nauvoo.

Oct. 24, 1841: Orson Hyde dedicates Palestine for the gathering of the Jews.

Nov. 8, 1841: Temporary baptismal font is dedicated in Nauvoo Temple.

1842

Jan. 5, 1842: Joseph opens his Red Brick Store for business but by March, because of pressing Church business, he ceases active involvement in the store itself. Original store was razed in 1890 and rebuilt by Community of Christ in 1979.

* *

Feb. 6, 1842: A son is stillborn to Emma and Joseph.

Mar. 17, 1842: Female Relief Society organization is begun and completed on the 24th, with Joseph's wife, Emma, as President.

April 16, 1842: The *Wasp*, Nauvoo's secular newspaper, begins publication with William Smith as editor. Subscription price is $1.50 per year.

May 4, 1842: First endowments are given in Red Brick Store. Joseph had planned to begin these in the temple, but feeling he might not live that long, he started them now.

May 6, 1842: Ex-Governor Boggs of Missouri is shot but not killed. Suspicion falls on Porter Rockwell who denies it by saying he would not have missed.

May 11, 1842: John C. Bennett is disfellowshipped from the Church for immorality in addition to other charges.

May 17, 1842: John C. Bennett resigns office of mayor and by the following month is traveling the country speaking against Joseph and the Saints.

Aug. 6, 1842: Joseph issues famous Rocky Mountain prophesy at the installation of the Rising Sun Masonic Lodge in Montrose.

Oct. 30, 1842: First official meeting in temple. Walls were only four feet above the basement on which a temporary floor had been laid.

Nov. 15, 1842: John Taylor succeeded Joseph Smith as editor of the *Times and Seasons*.

Dec. 27, 1842: Joseph, along with forty companions, leaves for Springfield to give himself up for a trial on legitimacy of Missouri charges, thus ending several months of eluding law officers attempting to take him back to Missouri for ordering death of ex-Governor Boggs.

1843

Jan. 4, 1843: Joseph stands trial in Springfield on charge of being

* *

accessory in shooting of Boggs. Judge Pope rules the Prophet cannot be taken from Illinois to another state for a crime allegedly committed in Illinois. Joseph is freed.

Mar. 4, 1843: Porter Rockwell is captured and imprisoned in Missouri on charge of attempted killing of Boggs.

Mar. 15, 1843: Name of newspaper *Wasp* changed to *Nauvoo Neighbor.*

May 12, 1843: Joseph purchases half interest in steamboat Maid of Iowa.

May 18, 1843: Joseph dines with Stephen A. Douglas and prophesies that he will aspire to the presidency but will fail if he ever turns against the Saints. The prophecy proves true.

May 31, 1843: Brigham completes his brick home nearly two years after returning from his mission in England.

June 23, 1843: Joseph is arrested by a Missouri sheriff and Carthage constable while visiting Emma's relatives in Dixon, Illinois. He is freed on writ in Nauvoo court (nearest court having jurisdiction) where officers are forced to take Joseph according to a court in Dixon.

Aug. 26, 1843: Jonathan Dunham returns from 800-mile trip westward to explore possible migration route for the Saints when they move to the Rocky Mountains.

Aug. 31, 1843: Joseph moves his family into the Mansion House where he will live until his death ten months later.

Sept. 15, 1843: The Mansion House is opened as a hotel.

Oct. 3, 1843: Gala dinner party is held for opening of Mansion House hotel in which toasts are made to the 15,000 citizens of Nauvoo, the Nauvoo Legion, the Nauvoo charter, and Governor Thomas Ford.

Oct. 7-9, 1843: General Conference is held in Nauvoo. Joseph, distrustful of Sidney Rigdon, attempts to remove him as his counselor but conference votes to retain him.

* *

* *

Dec. 12, 1843: Nauvoo police force increased by forty men due to increased anti-Mormonism.

Dec. 13, 1843: Porter Rockwell freed in Missouri after all charges against him fail for lack of evidence.

1844

Jan. 23, 1844: Joseph leases Mansion House to Ebenezer Robinson for $1,000 a year, reserving three rooms for his family. John Taylor assumes ownership of printing office.

Feb. 17, 1844: As a result of increasing anti-Mormonism, Joseph instructs the Twelve to send out scouting parties to California and Oregon that he anticipates will be part of the Mormon colonization in the West.

Mar. 24, 1844: Joseph publicly reveals the names of the apostates who are conspiring to take his life: Dr. Robert D. Foster, Joseph H. Jackson, William and Wilson Law, and Chauncey Higbee.

April 5, 1844: Masonic Temple (Cultural Hall) is dedicated with 550 Masons from around the country attending. Hyrum Smith performs the dedication.

April 7, 1844: Joseph delivers the King Follett funeral sermon, describing the nature of God, how He came to be God, and the eternal progression and potential destiny of all of God's children.

April 18, 1844: Robert D. Foster, Wilson Law, William Law, and other apostates excommunicated for "un-Christianlike conduct."

May 15, 1844: Josiah Quincy (soon-to-be Boston mayor) and Charles Francis Adams (to be Lincoln's minister to England) visit Joseph Smith in Nauvoo. Quincy leaves the oft-quoted statement about the possibility of the nineteenth-century American who may exert the most powerful influence on his countrymen being "Joseph Smith, the Mormon Prophet."

May 25, 1844: Sidney Rigdon resigns as postmaster under pressure from

* *

* *

Joseph who suspects him of reading and not delivering Joseph's mail.

June 7, 1844: First and only issue of the *Nauvoo Expositor* is published.

June 10, 1844: City Council orders destruction of the apostate newspaper. Order is carried out by City Marshal John P. Greene using Nauvoo Legion troops. The destruction of controversial presses was not that unusual during this era and many believed such action was justified under the laws of England, Blackstone specifically. Usually overlooked, however, is the fact that such presses were usually destroyed by mobs, not by government bodies.

June 18, 1844: Joseph proclaims martial law in Nauvoo and gives his last public discourse to the Nauvoo Legion near the Mansion House.

June 24, 1844: Joseph, along with seventeen others, travels to Carthage to surrender on charges of riot in the destruction of the *Nauvoo Expositor*.

June 27, 1844: Joseph and Hyrum are martyred in the Carthage jail while incarcerated there on charges of treason. John Taylor is badly wounded.

July 30, 1844: Samuel Smith dies as a result of exertions on the day his brothers were killed.

Aug. 3, 1844: Sidney Rigdon arrives from Pittsburgh to claim Church guardianship.

Aug. 8, 1844: A special meeting of the Church is held in which the people unanimously sustain Brigham Young and the Twelve as the rightful heirs to Church leadership.

Sept. 8, 1844: Sidney Rigdon is excommunicated from the Church.

Dec. 6, 1844: Last capital stone (sunstone) is set above the thirty pilasters.

Dec. 26, 1844: Dedication of the Seventies Hall, a building designed

* *

* *

specifically for the Seventies and their missionary activities.

1845

Jan. 29, 1845: Illinois State legislature repeals the Nauvoo Charter.

April 6, 1845: Church issues "Proclamation to the World" announcing the presence of the Kingdom of God. In pamphlet form, it describes what will be the ideal government and society that will be achieved by the Church and will prevail when Christ returns.

April 6, 1845: At this same conference, the people vote to change the name of Nauvoo to the "City of Joseph." This decision is honored more in the spirit than practice.

May 10, 1845: John Taylor moves into his house and printing office on Main Street, property purchased from James Ivins for $3,200.

May 24, 1845: Capstone is put in place and ceremony held.

May 30, 1845: Murderers of Joseph and Hyrum are acquitted by a jury in Carthage.

Aug. 23, 1845: Dome of the Nauvoo Temple is raised.

Sept. 10, 1845: Mobs burn Morley's Settlement and Green Plains, driving over 400 Saints from their homes. Teams are sent from Nauvoo to take them there for safety.

Sept. 16, 1845: Porter Rockwell kills Frank Worrell while defending the life of Sheriff Backenstos.

Sept. 24, 1845: Church promises Hancock citizens it will move from Illinois in the spring.

Oct. 6, 1845: Only conference held in Nauvoo Temple. Completed portion is dedicated.

Oct. 12, 1845: William Smith is excommunicated from the Church at Nauvoo.

Nov. 30, 1845: Attic story of the temple is dedicated.

* *

* *

Dec. 10, 1845: First endowments are given in the Nauvoo Temple.

Dec. 23, 1845: Famous Bogus Brigham incident occurs, in which Carthage officers arrest William Miller and take him to Carthage, believing they had arrested Brigham Young.

Dec. 29, 1845: Noah Rogers returns to Nauvoo, becoming the first LDS missionary to circumnavigate the globe as a missionary. He had served in Tahiti.

1846 to Present

Jan. 7, 1846: First sealings of couples in Nauvoo Temple occur.

Jan. 25, 1846: First sealings of children to parents occur.

Feb. 4, 1846: The first wagons (belonging to Charles Shumway) head west.

Feb. 7, 1846: Last endowments given in the temple. Between December 10 and this date, more than 5,500 Saints received their endowments.

Feb. 9, 1846: Temple roof partly destroyed by fire from overheated stove pipe. Roof is repaired before evacuation.

Feb. 15, 1846: Last issue of *Times and Seasons* printed.

Feb. 25, 1846: Some of the departing Saints are able to cross the river on the ice. Temperature is six degrees at 7 a.m.

May 1, 1846: Public dedication of temple (by Orson Hyde and Wilford Woodruff) is held.

Sept. 10-12, 1846: Battle of Nauvoo takes place in which a few remaining Saints and some "new citizens," vastly outnumbered by the encircling mobs, gallantly defends the city for a few days until overcome and forced to surrender unconditionally. Most of the Saints are given only a few hours to abandon their homes, several of the sisters far advanced in pregnancy.

Sept. (4th week), 1846: Thomas L. Kane visits and later describes

* *

* *

this desolate and abandoned city in his famous Discourse Delivered Before the Historical Society of Pennsylvania.

Oct. 9, 1846: Visitation of the quail in the Poor Camp on the Iowa shore occurs, saving many of the destitute and starving Saints.

Oct. 9, 1848: Arsonists burn the Nauvoo Temple.

May 27, 1850: Tornado topples large portion of Temple Walls, leaving the West wall to be removed by order of the City Council in 1865.

1865–1936: Except for the well (raised to ground level), there was nothing to mark the site of the temple. Numerous structures are built on temple block during this time.

1937: Wilford Woodruff starts buying portions of the temple block for preservation by the Church.

July 27, 1962: Nauvoo Restoration, Inc. organized.

1962–1969: Archaeological work reveals exact emplacement of original Temple.

Oct. 24, 1999: Ground broken for reconstruction of Nauvoo Temple.

June 27-30, 2002: Dedication of Nauvoo Temple.

* *

Recommended Sources

Alexander, Thomas G. *Things in Heaven and Earth: The Life and Times of Wilford Woodruff, a Mormon Prophet.* Salt Lake City: Signature Books, 1991.

The American Almanac and Repository of Useful Knowledge for the Year 1843. Boston: James Munroe and Co., 1842.

The American Almanac and Repository of Useful Knowledge for the Year 1846. Boston: James Munroe and Co., 1846.

Andrew, Laurel B. *The Early Temples of the Mormons.* Albany: State Univ. of N.Y. Press, 1978.

Arrington, Leonard J. *Brigham Young: American Moses.* New York: Alfred A. Knopf, 1985.

Backman, Milton V., Jr. & Richard O. Cowen. *Joseph Smith and the Doctrine and Covenants.* Salt Lake City: Deseret Book, 1992.

Backman, Milton V., Jr. and Ronald K. Esplin. "History of the Church: 1831–1834, Ohio, Missouri, and Nauvoo Periods." *Encyclopedia of Mormonism.* 4 vols. Ed. Daniel Ludlow. New York: Macmillan Publishing, 1992. 2:604–13.

Barrett, Ivan J. *Joseph Smith and the Restoration, A History of the Church to 1846.* Provo, Utah: BYU Press, 1970.

Bartlett, Irving H. *The New Country: A Social History of the American Frontier, 1776–1890.* New York: Oxford Univ. Press, 1974.

Bateman, Newton, et al., eds. *Historical Encyclopedia of Illinois.* 2 vols. Chicago: Munsell Publishing, 1921.

Beecher, Maureen Ursenbach. "Eliza Snow's Nauvoo Journal." *BYU Studies* 15 (Sum 1975): 387–91.

Berge, Dale L. "The Jonathan Browning Site: An Example of Archaeology for Restoration in Nauvoo, Illinois." *BYU Studies* 19 (Win 1979): 201–29.

Berrett, William E. & Burton, Alma P. *Readings in Church History* (3 vols.). Salt Lake City: Deseret Book, 1953.

Bitton, Davis. *The Martyrdom Remembered*. Salt Lake City: Aspen Books, 1994.

Blum, Ida. *Nauvoo: Gateway to the West*. Nauvoo, Illinois: Ida Blum, 1974.

Bouquet, Frances Lester. *A Compilation of the Original Documents Concerning the Nauvoo, Illinois Mormon Settlement*. Dr. of Sacred Theology dissertation, Temple Univ., 1938.

Bray, Robert T. *Archaeological Investigations at the Joseph Smith Red Brick Store, Nauvoo, Illinois*. Columbia: University of Missouri, 1973.

Brooks, Juanita (ed.). *On the Mormon Frontier: The Diary of Hosea Stout* (2 vols). Salt Lake City: Univ. of Utah Press, 1964.

Brown, Lisle G. "The Sacred Departments for Temple Work in Nauvoo: The Assembly Room and the Council Chamber." *BYU Studies* 19 (Spr 1979): 361–74.

Brown, S. Kent, Cannon, Donald Q. & Jackson, Richard H. (eds.). *Historical Atlas of Mormonism*. New York: Simon & Schuster, 1994.

Browning, John & Gentry, Curt. *John M. Browning: American Gunmaker*. Garden City: Doubleday & Co., 1964.

Buley, R. Carlyle. *The Old Northwest: Pioneer Period, 1815–1840*. 2 vols. Bloomington: Indiana Univ. Press, 1951.

Burgess, Samuel A. *The Early History of Nauvoo*. Independence, Missouri: Reorganized Church of Jesus Christ of Latter Day Saints, 1925.

Burgess-Olson, Vicky, *Sister Saints*. (Ed. by James B. Allen.) Provo, Utah: BYU Press, 1978.

Bushman, C. L. (ed). *Mormon Sisters*. Salt Lake City, 1976.

BYU Studies 32 (Win and Spr 1991). Entire volume is dedicated to Nauvoo era. Some of the better articles are listed separately in this bibliography under the author's name.

Cannon, George Q. *Life of Joseph Smith, the Prophet*. Salt Lake City: Deseret Book, 1986.

Cannon, Janath R. *Nauvoo Panorama*. Nauvoo Restoration, Inc., 1991.

* *

Church Educational System. *Church History in the Fulness of Times*. Salt Lake City: Church of Jesus Christ of Latter-day Saints, 1989.

Cochran, Robert M., et al. *History of Hancock County, Illinois*. Carthage, Illinois: Board of Supervisors of Hancock County, 1968.

Compton, Todd. *In Sacred Loneliness*. Salt Lake City: Signature Books, 1997.

Conkling, J. Christopher. *A Joseph Smith Chronology*. Salt Lake City: Deseret Book, 1979.

Cook, Lyndon W. *The Revelations of the Prophet Joseph Smith*. Salt Lake City: Deseret Book, 1985.

Cottle, T. Jeffrey and Richard Nietzel Holzapfel. "The City of Joseph in Focus: The Use and Abuse of Historic Photographs." *BYU Studies* 32 (Win and Spr 1991): 249–68.

Cowley, Matthias F. (ed), *Wilford Woodruff: History of His Life and Labors*. Salt Lake City: Bookcraft, 1964.

Cox, Dorothy. *Mormonism in Illinois* (Master's thesis). Southern Illinois Univ., 1951.

Daybook from the Red Brick Store. Burlington: Masonic Library of Iowa.

Dickerson, Theodore Earl. *Conflicts between the Mormons and Non-Mormons, Nauvoo, Illinois, 1839–1846* (Master's thesis). University of Illinois, 1956.

Divett, Robert T. *Medicine and the Mormons*. Bountiful, Utah: Horizon, 1981.

Dunn, Loren C. "Introduction to Historic Nauvoo." *BYU Studies* 32 (Win and Spr 1991): 23–32.

Durham, Reed C., Jr. "Nauvoo Expositor." *Encyclopedia of Mormonism*. 4 vols. Ed. Daniel H. Ludlow. New York: Macmillan Publishing, 1992.

Ellsworth, Paul D. "Mobocracy and the Rule of Law: American Press Reactions to the Murder of Joseph Smith." *BYU Studies*, Vol. 20, No. 1 (Fall, 1979).

Enders, Donald L. "A Dam for Nauvoo: An Attempt to Industrialize

* *

the City." *BYU Studies* 18 (Win 1978): 246–54.

———. "The Steamboat *Maid of Iowa*: Mormon Mistress of the Mississippi." *BYU Studies* 19 (Spr 1979): 321–35.

———. "Platting the City Beautiful: A Historical and Archaeological Glimpse of Nauvoo Streets." *BYU Studies* 19 (Spr 1979): 409–15.

Flanders, Robert Bruce. *Nauvoo: Kingdom on the Mississippi*. Urbana, Illinois: Univ. of Illinois Press, 1965.

Foote, Warren. *Autobiography of Warren Foote*. Privately printed, n.d.

Ford, Thomas. *A History of Illinois from its Commencement as a State in 1818 to 1847*. Chicago: S. C. Griggs & Co., 1854.

French, James R. *Nauvoo: The Saga of a City of Exiles*. Orem, Utah: Raymont Publishers, 1982.

Gardner, Hamilton. "The Nauvoo Legion 1840–1845: A Unique Military Organization." *Journal of the Illinois State Historical Society*. Summer, 1961.

Gayler, George R. "The Mormons and Politics in Illinois, 1839–1844." *Journal of the Illinois State Historical Society*. 49 (Spr 1956): 48–66.

Gibbons, Ted. *Like a Lamb to the Slaughter: The Nauvoo Expositor: Traitors & Treachery*. Orem, Utah: Keepsake Paperbacks, 1990.

Gilchrist, Charles A. *An Illustrated Historical Atlas of Hancock County*. Chicago: A. T. Andreas, 1874.

Givens, George W. *In Old Nauvoo*. Salt Lake City: Deseret Book, 1990.

Godfrey, Kenneth W., Godfrey, Audrey M. & Derr, Jill Mulvay. *Women's Voices: An Untold History of the Latter-day Saints 1830–1900*. Salt Lake City: Deseret Book, 1982.

———. "Crime and Punishment in Mormon Nauvoo, 1839–1846." *BYU Studies* 32 (Win and Spring 1991): 195–227.

———. "Causes of Mormon Non-Mormon Conflict in Hancock County, Illinois, 1839–1846." (PhD dissert.), Brigham Young University, 1967.

Gould, Mary Earle. *The Early American House*. Rutland, Vermont:

* *

Charles Tuttle Co., 1965.

Gregg, Thomas. *The History of Hancock County, Illinois*. Chicago: Charles E. Chapman, 1880.

Halford, Reta Latimer. *Nauvoo—The City Beautiful*. M.S. thesis, Salt Lake City: Univ. of Utah, 1945.

Hamilton, Marshall. "From Assassination to Expulsion: Two Years of Distrust, Hostility, and Violence." *BYU Studies* 32 (Win and Spr 1991): 228–48.

Hampshire, Annette Pauline. *Mormonism in Conflict: The Nauvoo Years*. New York: Edwin Mellen Press, 1985.

———. "Nauvoo Temple." *Encyclopedia of Mormonism*. 4 vols. Ed. Daniel H. Ludlow. New York: Macmillan Publishing, 1992.

Hancock County Historical Society. *Historic Sites and Structures of Hancock County, Illinois*. Carthage, Illinois: Hancock County Historical Society, 1979.

Hancock County School Records, 1842–1845. Salt Lake City: Historical Department, The Church of Jesus Christ of Latter-day Saints.

Harrington, Virginia S. & Harrington, J. C. *Rediscovery of the Nauvoo Temple*. Salt Lake City: Nauvoo Restoration, Inc., 1971.

Hartley, William G., "Joseph Smith and Nauvoo's Youth." *Ensign*, Sept. 1979, 27–29.

Haven, Charlotte. "A Girl's Letters from Nauvoo," *The Overland Monthly* [San Francisco]. December 1890.

Hicks, Michael. *Mormonism and Music*. Urbana, Illinois: Univ. of Illinois, 1989.

Hill, Donna. *Joseph Smith, The First Mormon*. Garden City: Doubleday & Co., 1977.

Hill, Marvin S. "Mormon Religion in Nauvoo: Some Reflections." *Utah Historical Quarterly* 44 (Spr 1976): 170–80.

Hirshson, Stanley. *The Lion of the Lord*. New York: Alfred Knoph, 1969.

Historic Nauvoo: A Descriptive Story of Nauvoo, Illinois . . . Its History, People, and Beauty. Peoria, Illinois: Quest, 1941.

Hollan, W. Eugene. *Frontier Violence: Another Look*. New York: Oxford Univ. Press, 1974.

* *

Holt, Helene. "Nauvoo House." *Encyclopedia of Mormonism*. 4 vols. Ed. Daniel H. Ludlow. New York: Macmillan Publishing, 1992, 3: 997.

Holzapfel, Richard N. & Cottle, T. Jeffery. *Old Mormon Nauvoo, 1839–1846*. Provo: Grandin Book Co., 1990.

Holzapfel, Richard Neitzel & Holzapfel, Jeni Broberg. *Women of Nauvoo*. Salt Lake City: Bookcraft, 1992.

Jeffress, Melinda. "Mapping Historic Nauvoo." *BYU Studies* 32 (Win and Spr 1991): 269–75.

Jenson, Andrew, *Church Chronology*. Salt Lake City: Deseret News Publishing, 1899.

———. *Encyclopedic History of The Church of Jesus Christ of Latter-day Saints*. Salt Lake City: Deseret News Publishing, 1941.

Jensen, Richard L. "Transplanted to Zion: The Impact of British Latter-day Saints Immigration upon Nauvoo." *BYU Studies* 31 (Win 1991): 77–87.

Jessee, Dean C. (ed). *John Taylor, Nauvoo Journal*. Provo: Grandin Book Co., 1996.

———. *The Papers of Joseph Smith: Journal*, 1832–1842. (Vol. 2) Salt Lake City: Deseret Book, 1992.

———. *The Personal Writings of Joseph Smith*. Salt Lake City: Deseret Book, 1984.

———. *The Papers of Joseph Smith*. (Vol. 1) Salt Lake City: Deseret Book, 1989.

Johansen, Jerald R. *After the Martyrdom*. Bountiful, Utah: Horizon Pub., 1997.

Jolley, Jerry C. "The Sting of the *Wasp*: Early Nauvoo Newspaper-April 1842 to April 1843." *BYU Studies* 22 (1982): 487–96.

Jones, Arthur Rulon. "Historical Survey of Representative Recreation Activities among the Mormons of Nauvoo, Illinois, 1839–1846." (Master's thesis). Southern Illinois University, 1970.

Kane, Joseph Nathan. *Famous First Facts*. New York: H. W. Wilson Co., 1964.

Kane, Thomas Leiper. *The Mormons: A Discourse* Delivered before the Historical Society of Pennsylvania, March 26, 1850. Philadelphia,

Pennsylvania: King & Baird Printers, 1850.

Kimball, James L., Jr. "The Nauvoo Charter: A Reinterpretation." *Journal of the Illinois State Historical Society* 64 (Spr 1971): 66–78.

Kimball, Stanley B. "Heber C. Kimball and Family, The Nauvoo Years." *BYU Studies* 15 (Sum 1975): 447–79.

———. "The Mormons in Early Illinois." Dialogue 5 (Spr 1970): 9–12. Regional Studies, Illinois, Sperry—Bibliography, p.295

———. "Nauvoo West: The Mormons of the Iowa Shore." *BYU Studies* 18 (Win 1978): 132–42.

Larson, Captain Ron. *Upper Mississippi River History.* Winona, Minnesota: Steamboat Press, 1998.

Launius, Roger D., and F. Mark McKiernan. *Joseph Smith Jr.'s Red Brick Store.* Macomb, Illinois: Western Illinois University, 1985.

Launius, Roger D. & Hallwas, John E. (eds). *Kingdom on the Mississippi Revisited.* Urbana, Illinois: Univ. of Illinois Press, 1996.

Leonard, Glen M., "The City of Joseph." *BYU Studies* 15 (Aug. 1974): 125–27.

———. "Letters Home: The Immigrant View from Nauvoo." *BYU Studies* 31 (Win 1991): 89–100.

———. "Nauvoo." *Encyclopedia of Mormonism.* 4 vols. Ed. Daniel H. Ludlow, New York: Macmillan Publishing, 1992. 3: 987–93.

Luce, W. Ray. "Building the Kingdom of God: Mormon Architecture before 1847." *BYU Studies* 30 (Spr 1990): 33–45.

Lundwall, N. B. (ed). *Temples of the Most High.* Salt Lake City: Bookcraft, 1969.

Lyon, T. Edgar. "Recollections of 'Old Nauvooers': Memories from Oral History," *BYU Studies,* Winter 1978 (Vol. 18, No. 2).

Mace, Wandle. WandleMace Autobiography (Spec. Coll.) Provo: BYU Library.

Madsen, Carol Cornwall. *In Their Own Words: Women and the Story of Nauvoo.* Salt Lake City: Deseret Book, 1994.

McGavin, Cecil E. *Nauvoo the Beautiful.* Salt Lake City: Bookcraft Inc., 1972.

———. *The Nauvoo Temple.* Salt Lake City: Deseret Book, 1962.

Miller, David E. & Della S. *Nauvoo: The City of Joseph*. Peregrine Smith, Inc., Santa Barbara, 1974.

Moody, Thurman Dean. "Nauvoo's Whistling and Whittling Brigade." *BYU Studies* 15 (Sum 1975): 480–90.

"Mormons in Illinois." In Collections of the Illinois State Historical Library (1911) vol. 7.

Nauvoo Deaths and Burials: Old Nauvoo Burial Ground. Nauvoo, IL: Nauvoo Restoration, 1990.

The Nauvoo Expositor. Nauvoo, IL: William Law., v. 1, no. 1, June 7, 1844.

Nauvoo Journal (Semi-annual), Hyrum, Utah, 1989–1999.

Nauvoo Neighbor, May 1843–October 1845, Historical Department, The Church of Jesus Christ of Latter-day Saints,

Neumann, George C. *Early American Antique Country Furnishings*. Gas City, Indiana: L-W Book Sales, 1984.

Oaks, Dallin H., & Bentley, Joseph I. "Joseph Smith and Legal Process: In the Wake of the Steamboat Nauvoo." *BYU Studies* 19 (Win 1979): 167–99.

Oaks, Dallin H., and Marvin S. Hill. *Carthage Conspiracy*. Urbana: Univ. of Illinois Press, 1975.

Pease, Theodore Calvin. *The Frontier State, 1818–1848*. Chicago: A. C. McClurg, 1919.

Piercy, Frederick Hawkins. *Route from Liverpool to Great Salt Lake Valley*. (Fawn M. Brodie, ed.) Cambridge, Massachusetts: Harvard Univ. Press, 1962.

Poll, Richard Douglas. "Nauvoo and the New Mormon History: A Bibliographical Survey." *Journal of Mormon History* 5 (1978): 105–23.

Porter, Larry C. & Black, Susan Easton (eds). *The Prophet Joseph: Essays on the Life and Mission of Joseph Smith*. Salt Lake City: Deseret Book, 1988.

Proctor, Scot Facer & Proctor, Maurine Jensen (eds). *The Revised and Enhanced History of Joseph Smith by His Mother*. Salt Lake City: Bookcraft, 1996.

Purdy, William E. "They Marched Their Way West: The Nauvoo

Brass Band." *Ensign* July 1980, 20–23.

Quincy, Josiah. *Figures of the Past from the Leaves of Old Journals.* Boston: Little, Brown, and Co., 1926.

Quinn, D. Michael. "The Practice of Rebaptism at Nauvoo." *BYU Studies* 18 (Win 1978): 26–32.

Rawson, Marion Nicholl. *Handwrought Ancestors.* New York: E. P. Dutton, 1936.

Regional Studies. Illinois, Sperry, (Bibliography), 305.

Roberts, B. H. *A Comprehensive History of the Church of Jesus Christ of Latter-day Saints* (6 vols.) Provo: BYU Press, 1965.

———. *The Life Of John Taylor.* Salt Lake City: Bookcraft, 1963.

———. *The Rise and Fall of Nauvoo.* 1900. Reprint. Salt Lake City: Bookcraft, 1965.

Robison, Elwin C. *The First Mormon Temple.* Provo, Utah: BYU Press, 1997.

Rowley, Dennis. "Nauvoo: A River Town." *BYU Studies* 18 (Win 1978): 255–72.

———. "The Mormon Experience in the Wisconsin Pineries, 1841–1845." *BYU Studies* 32 (Win and Spr 1991): 119–48.

Scofield, Charles J. History of Hancock County. Chicago, Illinois: n.p., 1921.

Seymour, John. *The Forgotten Crafts.* New York: Alfred A. Knopf, 1984.

Smith, Henry A. *The Day They Martyred The Prophet.* Salt Lake City,: Bookcraft, 1963.

Smith, Joseph, Jr. *History of The Church of Jesus Christ of Latter-day Saints* (7 vols.). Salt Lake City: Deseret Book, 1976

Smith, Paul Thomas. "A Historical Study of the Nauvoo, Illinois, Public School System, 1841–1845." Master's thesis, Brigham Young University, 1969.

Sorensen, Parry D. "Nauvoo Times and Seasons." *Journal of the Illinois State Historical Society* 55 (Sum 1962): 117–35.

Stobaugh, Kenneth E. "The Development of the Joseph Smith Historic Center in Nauvoo." *BYU Studies* 32 (Win and Spr 1991): 33–40.

Sweeney, John. "A History of the Nauvoo Legion in Illinois." Master's thesis, Brigham Young University, 1974.

Taylor, Samuel W. *The Kingdom or Nothing: The Life of John Taylor, Militant Mormon.* New York: Macmillan Co., 1976.

————. *Nightfall at Nauvoo.* New York: Macmillan Co., 1971.

Times and Seasons, 1839–1846. Historical Department, The Church of Jesus Christ of Latter-day Saints.

Tracy, Shannon M. *In Search of Joseph.* Orem, Utah: Kenning House, 1995.

Tullidge, Edward W. *The Women of Mormondom.* New York: 1877.

Ursenbach, Maureen. "Eliza R. Snow's Nauvoo Journal." *BYU Studies* 15 (Sum 1975): 391–416.

Vogel, Dan (ed). *Early Mormon Documents, Vol. 1.* Salt Lake City: Signature Books, 1996.

Wasp, April 1842–April 1843. Historical Department, The Church of Jesus Christ of Latter-day Saints.

Whitney, Orson F. *Life of Heber C. Kimball.* Salt Lake City: Stevens & Wallis, Inc., 1945.

Winkler, Phillip Blair. "Mormon Nauvoo in Jacksonian America." PhD diss., Middle Tennessee State University, 1991.

Wright, Louis B. *Culture on the Moving Frontier.* New York: Harper & Row, 1955.

Yorgason, Laurence M. "Preview on a Study of the Social and Geographical Origins of Early Mormon Converts, 1830–1845." *BYU Studies*, Spring 1970, Vol. 10, No. 3.

Youngreen, Buddy, *Reflections of Emma.* Orem, Utah: Grandin Book Co., 1982.

————. "Sons of the Martyrs' Nauvoo Reunion 1860." *BYU Studies* 20 (Sum 1980): 351–70.

Index of Names

Abercrombie, Nancy 42, 202

Agnew, Joseph 214–15

Aldrich, Mark 23

Allgood Brothers 233

Amy, Dustin 234

Anderson, George 117

Angel, Truman 2, 221

Avard, Sampson 95

Babbitt, Almon 83, 173

Backenstos, Jacob 16, 21, 27, 29, 56–57, 170, 229, 250

Baird, Stephen 150

Ballard, Melvin J. 194

Barlow, Israel 132

Barnes, Dr. Thomas 27, 119

Bellemay Jennie, 17

Bennett, John C. 145, 245

Bessemer, Henry 5

Bidamon Lewis 14, 41, 43, 97, 121, 122, 134, 202

Bidamon Charles 198

Blair, Elizabeth Fife 113

Blum, Ida 121

Boggs, Governor 129, 245, 247

Braley, Dr. Jessee 110

Brannan, Samuel 48

Briggs, Jason 202

Brodie, Fawn 83

Browning Jonathan 6, 13–17, 96, 105

Bullock, Thomas 88

Bump, Jacob 232

Bushman, Elizabeth Degen 113

* *

Cabet, Etienne 123

Cahoon, William 36

Call, Anson 49

Cannon, M. Hamlin 25

Carling, Ann Green Duston 113

Clark, Hiram 78, 80, 199

Clayton, William 37, 45, 49, 80, 88, 121

Cobb, Augusta 122

Cooper, Peter 141

Cotton, Panina 141

Cutler, Alpheus 166

Cutler, George Y. 177

Dana, Lewis 141–142

Daniels, Cyrus 141

Davis, Amos 30, 34–35, 74, 125, 137, 157, 175

Davis, Jacob 23

Douglas, Stephen A. 53, 95, 128–129, 244, 246

Doyle, Arthur Conan 95

Duncan, Jo 125

Dunham, Jonathan 27, 140, 246

Eagle, John 28–29

Eastin, Rufus 198

Egan, Howard 53

Emmons, Sylvester 28

Enders, Don 195, 236

Fabian, Harold 150

Farr, Lorin 79

Fell, Dr. John 42

Finch, John M. 29

Follett, King 18–19, 68–69, 87–90

Foote, Warren 63

Ford, Governor Thomas 25–26, 29, 48, 55, 117–118, 125, 145, 148, 246

Foster, Charles 29, 90

Foster, Lucian 90, 129

* *

Foster, Robert D. 29, 59, 90, 92, 213, 247

Galland, Isaac 126, 128, 132, 137, 241

Gardner, Robert 1

Garner, Mary Field 133

Garner, William 133

Givens, George & Sylvia 203

Gont, Mary 141

Grant, Ulysses, S. 144

Greene, John P. 12, 248

Grey, Zane 95

Grover, Warren 23

Hale, Stephen 36

Hamilton, Artois 21

Hammond, Gayle 195, 236

Haven, Charlotte 75, 118, 172, 201

Helm, M. 38

Hendrix, James 124

Herring Brothers 141–142

Hickman, William 142

Hickox, George 12

Higbee, Dr. Charles 110

Higbee, Chauncey L. 28, 92, 247

Higbee, Francis 28

Higbee, John 180

Hill, Gustavus 133, 163

Hoelting, Capt. Peter, 103

Hofmann, Mark 27

Holman, David 145

Hotchkiss, Horace 126

Hudson Brothers 200

Hutchinson, Jacob 36

Hyde, Orson 84, 244, 257

Ivins, James 171, 210–211, 249

Jackson, Joseph H. 26, 247

Jenson, Andrew 154, 218

* *

Jessee, Dean 27

Johnson, Aaron 198

Johnson, Harriet 112–113

Jones, Daniel 103

Jones, K. 86

Julien, Dennis 198–199

Kane, Thomas 10, 52, 114, 208, 213–214, 224, 251

Kaufman, George 33

Kellogg, Hiram 232

Kelly, William 5

Keokuk, Chief 150

Kimball, Heber C. 28, 36, 78, 81, 84–85, 91, 111, 124, 141, 149 168, 175, 180, 26–217, 229, 241, 244

Kimball, Helen Mar 9, 36

Kimball, Hiram 51, 73, 92, 126, 175, 180, 213

Kimball, Leroy 17, 85–86, 150, 175

Kimball, Sarah M. 51

Kimball, Stanley 84–85

Kimball, Vilate 12

Knight, Joseph 124

Knight, Newell 138

Knight, Vinson 124

Knox, Gen. Douglas 95

Lamoreaux Brothers 212–213

Larson, Ron 166

Law, William 28, 247

Law, Wilson 28, 247

Layton, Christopher 81

Leavitt, Sarah 138

Lee, John, D. 14, 54, 114

Lee, Robert E. 193

Lewis, Phillip, B. 213

Lincoln, Abraham 116, 129, 247

Lott, Cornelius 64

Lovejoy, Elijah 58

* *

Lucas, Governor 124, 128

Lyman, Pauline Phelps 113

Lyon, Windsor 99

Lytle Brothers 5

Mace, Wandle 196

Marks, William 9, 198

Marr, S. M. 28

Marr, William, H. J. 28

Marriott, John 81

Marriott, J. Willard, 150

Maughan, Mary Ann 119

Merryweather, Dr. R. 172

Miller, George 47, 164–166

Milliken, Arthur 59, 97

Milliken, Lucy 59, 97

Monroe, James 108

Mulholland, James 43, 168

Murdock, John 64

Needham, John 64

Neibaur, Alexander 109, 123

Newberry, Lane 17

Norton, Jacob 229

Norton, Henry O. 29

Otis, Moses 141

Pack, John 36

Peck, Martin 5

Phelps, W. W. 59, 167, 242

Pickett, William 96, 122,

Pierce, Isaac 96

Piercy, Frederick 83

Pike, Zebulon 199

Pitt, William 36–37, 148

Pomeroy, Irene 55–56

Pratt, Louisa Barnes 119

Pratt Parley 6, 12, 22, 53, 72, 73 84, 162, 244

* *

Pratt, Orson 12, 97, 162, 243

Quincy, Josiah 135, 247

Ralston, James H 116

Raney, Jewel 232

Ransay, Elizabeth 113

Ransay, Mary Ann 113

Reader, George 95

Reiser, A. Hamer 157

Richard, Charles C. 213

Rich, Leonard 233

Richards, Levi 106

Richards, Franklin D. 217

Richards, Jenetta 16, 105

Richards, Willard 16, 21, 23–24, 26, 28, 88, 95, 106

Richards, Wm. P. 28

Rigdon, Sidney 29, 37, 163, 170, 173, 198, 201, 239, 242, 247, 249

Robinson, Ebenezer 201, 247

Robinson, Mary Elizabeth 113

Rockwell, Porter 16, 26, 242, 245, 246, 247, 249

Rogers, David 28

Rolfe Samuel 228

Roundy, Shadrack 49

Rudsill, George 215

Scovil, Lucius 1–2

Scovil, Lucy 1–2

Sessions, Patty 113

Sessions, Perrigrine 212

Sharp, Thomas 21, 23, 29, 117, 215, 244

Shaw, Joshua 15

Shoemaker, A. 171

Shoemaker Jacob 5

Skinner, O. C. 92

Smith, Agnes Coolbrith 122–123

* *

* *

Smith, Alexander 42

Smith, Bathsheba 119

Smith, Caroline 108

Smith, David 42–45, 109

Smith, Don Carlos 105, 108, 111–112, 121–122, 123, 244

Smith, Elias 94

Smith, Emma 28, 41–42, 45–46, 136, 168, 215, 220, 237

Smith, Frederick 42–43

Smith, Hyrum
16, 21, 23, 24, 25, 26, 27, 29–30, 62, 81, 83, 95, 109, 148, 170, 200, 213, 243, 247, 248, 249

Smith, Joseph
Carthage: 20–30, 221, 246, 248, 249; Follett Discourse: 68–69, 87–90; Masons: 39–40; Relief Society: 91, 177, 200, 245; revelations: 133, 182, 183, 184, 185; temple: 108, 124, 138, 180, 182, 212; wives: 10

Smith, Joseph Sr. 96, 117, 243

Smith Joseph, III 42, 202

Smith Joseph F. 86, 115, 149

Smith Julia Murdock 42

Smith, Robert F. 22

Smith, Samuel 24, 26, 122, 156, 248

Smith Warren 5

Smith William 108, 117, 129, 245, 250

Snow, Eliza 10, 48, 112, 168

Snow Erastus 51, 183, 215

Snow, Lorenzo 1

Spencer, Augustine 29

Spencer, Orson 163

Standing, James 36

Stevenson, Edward 68, 88

Stevenson, Robert Louis 95

* *

Stoddard, Sylvester 14, 232

Stout, Hosea 16, 92, 110, 141–142, 181, 192, 225

Syrupson, Alexander 28

Taylor, John 47, 55, 59, 64, 84, 117, 120, 170–171, 173, 210–211, 220, 244–245, 247–249

Taylor, Joseph James 210

Terrill, Therin 94

Thompson, Dr. Samuel 107

Tracy, Nancy N. 230

Turley, Theodore 78, 145

Twigg, Joseph 3

Van Tuyl, Mr. 45

Walker, William Holmes 74, 197

Warren, Calvin 55

Washington, George 145

Webb Brothers 5

Weeks, William 221

Weld, Dr. John F. 107

Wells, Daniel 93, 170, 213, 229

Wells, Emmeline B. 179

White David Nye 82

Whiteseye, Edward 141

Whitney, Alderman 93

Whitney, Elizabeth Ann 220

Whitney Helen Mar, *see Helen Mar Kimball*

Widtsoe, John 11,

Wight, Lyman 166, 170

Williams, Levi 23

Wilsey, Mary 160–161

Winters, Hiram 205

Woodruff, Wilford 36, 84, 85, 113, 192, 195, 241, 251,

Woodruff, Phoebe 118, 140

Woolley, Samuel 155

Worrell, Frank 16, 249

Yokum, William 107
Young, Brigham
    And Emma: 41, 45, 179; Exodus: 48,
    50–55; illness: 11; transfigured: 11;
    wives: 9–10, 122, 208
Young, Fanny 12
Young, Lorenzo 12
Young Margaret Pierce 208
Young, Mary Ann 9, 11, 59
Young, Phineas 12
Young, Rhoda 12

About the Author

George W. Givens spent twenty years teaching American history in schools in upstate New York, Arizona, and Virginia before opening what became the largest family-owned bookstore in Virginia. George joined the LDS Church while living in Tucson, Arizona, in 1964. He and his wife, Sylvia, have spent several summers in Nauvoo, Illinois, as in-house historians. They are the parents of eight children.

George developed an avid interest in LDS Church history upon learning of ancestors who joined the Church in upstate New York in 1830. His published titles include *In Old Nauvoo*, *The Nauvoo Fact Book*, *Out of Palmyra*, and *The Hired Man's Christmas*. He is also the author of *500 Little-Known Facts in Mormon History* and *500 More Little-Known Facts in Mormon History*, both published by Cedar Fort.

Brother Givens passed away in 2004.